Religion and Ritual in Ancient Egypt

This book is a vivid reconstruction of the practical aspects of ancient Egyptian religion. Through an examination of artifacts and inscriptions, the text explores a variety of issues. For example, who was allowed to enter the temples, and what rituals were performed therein? Who served as priests? How were they organized and trained, and what did they do? What was the Egyptians' attitude toward death, and what happened at funerals? How did the living and the dead communicate? In what ways could people communicate with the gods? What impact did religion have on the economy and longevity of the society? This book demystifies Egyptian religion, exploring what it meant to the people and society. The text is richly illustrated with images of rituals and religious objects.

Emily Teeter, PhD, is a Research Associate and Coordinator of Special Exhibits at the Oriental Institute of the University of Chicago. She has curated temporary and permanent exhibits of Egyptian art at the Oriental Institute Museum, the Seattle Art Museum, and the Art Institute of Chicago. The author and co-author of a wide range of popular and scholarly publications, her most recent books include *Ancient Egypt: Treasures from the Collection of the Oriental Institute*, *Egypt and the Egyptians*, and *The Life of Meresamun: A Temple Singer in Ancient Egypt*.

Religion and Ritual in Ancient Egypt

Emily Teeter

University of Chicago

CAMBRIDGE
UNIVERSITY PRESS

CAMBRIDGE
UNIVERSITY PRESS

University Printing House, Cambridge CB2 8BS, United Kingdom

One Liberty Plaza, 20th Floor, New York, NY 10006, USA

477 Williamstown Road, Port Melbourne, VIC 3207, Australia

314–321, 3rd Floor, Plot 3, Splendor Forum, Jasola District Centre, New Delhi – 110025, India

79 Anson Road, #06–04/06, Singapore 079906

Cambridge University Press is part of the University of Cambridge.

It furthers the University's mission by disseminating knowledge in the pursuit of education, learning and research at the highest international levels of excellence.

www.cambridge.org
Information on this title: www.cambridge.org/9780521613002

First published 2011
4th printing 2019

Printed in the United Kingdom by Print on Demand, World Wide

A catalog record for this publication is available from the British Library.

Library of Congress Cataloging in Publication data
Teeter, Emily.
  Religion and ritual in ancient Egypt / Emily Teeter.
    p.   cm.
  Includes bibliographical references and index.
  ISBN 978-0-521-84855-8 (hardback) – ISBN 978-0-521-61300-2 (paperback)
  1. Egypt – Religion.   2. Rites and ceremonies – Egypt.   3. Egypt – Antiquities.   I. Title.
  BL2441.3.T44   2011
  299′.31–dc22   2010040539

ISBN 978-0-521-84855-8 Hardback
ISBN 978-0-521-61300-2 Paperback

Contents

Contents

List of Maps, Plans, and Figures

Maps

Plans

Figures

List of Maps, Plans, and Figures

List of Maps, Plans, and Figures

List of Color Plates

Acknowledgments

I extend my thanks to a great number of people who assisted me in many ways with the preparation of this book. I thank Thomas James, Curator of Digital Images at the Oriental Institute, for his tremendous help with images, and I also thank Oriental Institute Museum Chief Curator Geoff Emberling and Archivist John Larson for their permission to reproduce so many images from the collection. The reconstruction of the votive bed was a labor of love by artist Angela Altenhofen. I thank my colleagues here at the Oriental Institute for sharing their forthcoming publications: Foy Scalf for his research on magic bricks, Hratch Papazian for his research on hieratic oracle texts, and François Gaudard and Janet Johnson for their translations of mummy labels. Tom Urban, our Director of Publications, assisted with general advice about the manuscript and images, and Leslie Schramer prepared the new maps and plans.

Among those outside the Oriental Institute, I thank Terry Wilfong for encouraging me to take on the project. Sofia Fenner's preliminary edit of the text improved it immensely, and I profited from early comments on the content from Joe Cain, William Peck, and the late Mary Grimshaw. I also thank Ron Leprohon for his many valuable suggestions on the text.

The variety of images that accompany the text is due to the generosity and assistance of a great number of people including Christopher Naunton of the Egypt Exploration Society, London; Karen Exell of the Manchester Museum, University of Manchester; Christian Loeben and Christian Tepper of the Museum August Kestner, Hanover; Jaromir Malek of the Griffith Institute, Oxford University; Karen Manchester and Mary Greuel of the Art Institute of Chicago; Bettina Schmitz of the Pelizaeus-Museum, Hildesheim;

Christophe Thiers of the Franco-Egyptian Center at Karnak; Jean-Claude Golvin; Melinda Hartwig; and Florence Friedman.

Warm thanks go to my husband, Joe Cain, for his patience during my absences to work on the text, and especially to Beatrice Rehl, Publishing Director, Humanities and Social Sciences, at Cambridge University Press, who encouraged me and showed good-humored patience throughout the longer-than-anticipated preparation of this manuscript.

Chronology of Ancient Egypt

The history of ancient Egypt is divided into thirty-one dynasties. The individual dynasties are grouped into three kingdoms, separated by intermediate periods. A Predynastic Period preceded Dynasty 1. The division of Egypt's history into dynasties was devised by Manetho, a third-century BC priest-historian. In many cases, the divisions between dynasties are arbitrary. This chronology is based primarily on Shaw 2000.

All dates prior to 664 BC are approximate.

Early Dynastic Period (Archaic Period): Dynasties 1–2
3100–2686 BC

Consolidation of the Egyptian state.

Old Kingdom: Dynasties 3–8
2686–2125 BC

Dynasty 3: 2686–2613 BC. First large-scale stone funerary monuments for kings and stone mastaba tombs for nobility.

Dynasty 4: 2613–2498 BC. Construction of pyramids in Lower Egypt. Increase in documentation for religion and culture through wall reliefs and written texts.

Dynasty 5: 2497–2345 BC. Appearance of Pyramid Texts that explicate the king's afterlife. Elaboration of private tombs, wall reliefs, and tomb furnishings.

Dynasty 6: 2345–2181 BC. Height of Old Kingdom tomb decoration.

Dynasties 7–8: 2181–2160 BC. Many ephemeral rulers.

First Intermediate Period: Dynasties 9–11
2160–2055 BC

Fragmentation of the state and the rise of local power centers.

Middle Kingdom: Dynasties 11–14
2055–1650 BC

Dynasty 12: 1985–1773 BC. Rise of the god Amun at Thebes.

Second Intermediate Period: Dynasties 15–17
1650–1550 BC

Incursion of people from western Asia into Lower Egypt.

The New Kingdom: Dynasties 18–20
1550–1069 BC

The "Golden Age" of ancient Egypt; foreign conquest and great building projects in Egypt and Nubia. Detailed documentation of religious and funerary beliefs in decorated tombs, papyri, and funerary objects.

Dynasty 18: 1550–1295 BC. Period of great building and expansion of the temples in Thebes. Expansion of the Karnak Temple, construction of the temples at Deir el Bahri, the core of the Luxor Temple, the Small Amun Temple at Medinet Habu, and the Aten temples of Amunhotep IV/Akhenaton. Establishment of royal tombs in the Valley of the Kings and Valley of the Queens.

Dynasty 19: 1295–1186 BC. Expansion of the Karnak and Luxor Temples; construction of the Ramesseum (Ramesses II).

Dynasty 20: 1186–1069 BC. Construction of Medinet Habu (Ramesses III). Last period to use the Valley of the Kings as a royal cemetery.

Third Intermediate Period: Dynasties 21–25
1069–664 BC

Period of political decentralization of the country. During Dynasty 25, Egypt was ruled by Nubian kings. Period of fine coffins, elaborate mummification procedures, mythological papyri, and rise of animal cults.

Saite Period: Dynasty 26
664–525 BC

Period of renaissance in arts and building; construction of large private tombs at Thebes.

Late Period: Dynasties 27–31
525–332 BC

Period of native rule interrupted by two Persian dominations.

Ptolemaic Period
332–30 BC

Following the death of Alexander the Great, Egypt was deeded to his general Ptolemy after whom the Greek period in Egypt is named. Continuation of most religious traditions.

Roman Period
30 BC–AD 395

With Octavian's defeat of Antony and Cleopatra, Egypt was annexed to the Roman Empire.

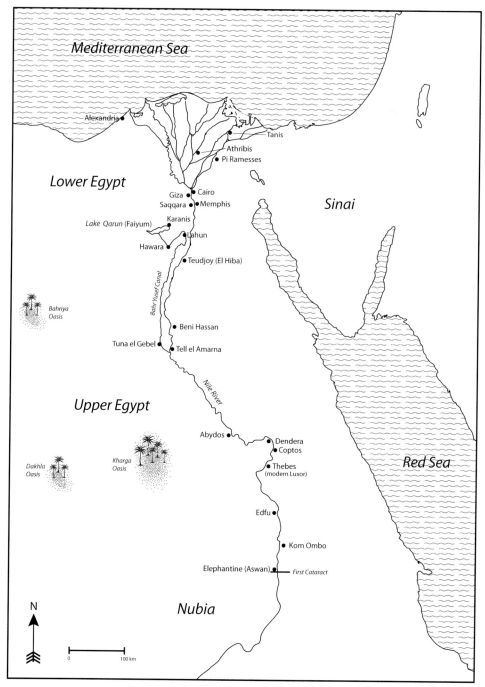

Map 1. Egypt

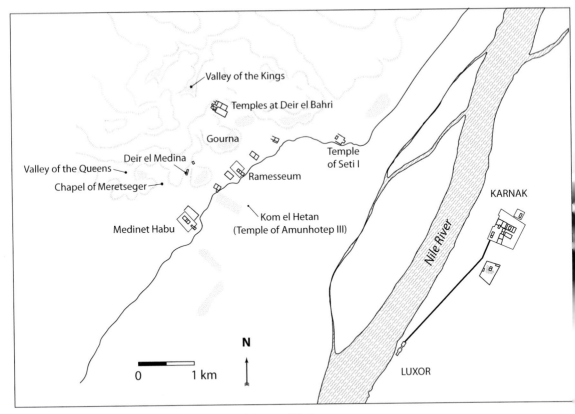

Map 2. Thebes

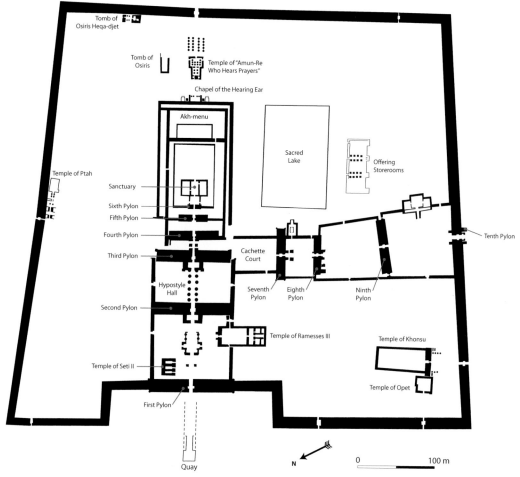

Tomb of
Osiris Heqa-djet

Tomb of
Osiris

Temple of "Amun-Re
Who Hears Prayers"

Chapel of the Hearing Ear

Akh-menu

Sacred
Lake

Offering
Storerooms

Temple of Ptah

Sanctuary

Sixth Pylon

Fifth Pylon

Fourth Pylon

Tenth Pylon

Cachette
Court

Third Pylon

Hypostyle
Hall

Seventh
Pylon

Eighth
Pylon

Ninth
Pylon

Second Pylon

Temple of Ramesses III

Temple of Khonsu

Temple of Seti II

Temple of Opet

First Pylon

N

0   100 m

Quay

Plan 1. The Karnak Temple

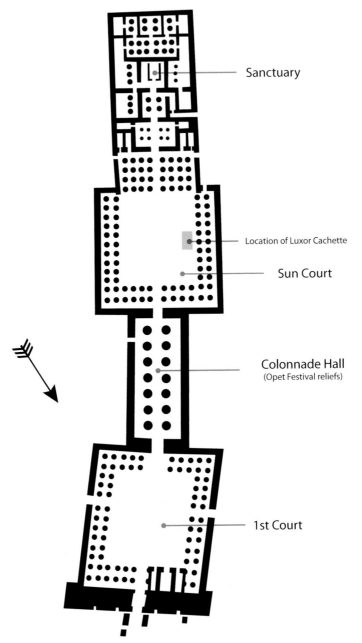

Sanctuary

Location of Luxor Cachette

Sun Court

Colonnade Hall
(Opet Festival reliefs)

1st Court

Plan 2. The Luxor Temple

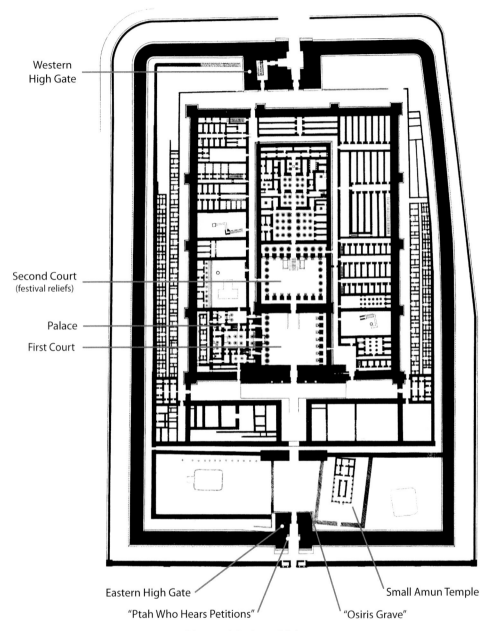

Western
High Gate

Second Court
(festival reliefs)

Palace

First Court

Eastern High Gate

"Ptah Who Hears Petitions"

Small Amun Temple

"Osiris Grave"

Plan 3. Medinet Habu

Introduction

Religion and the cult actions derived from those beliefs held ancient Egyptian society together and allowed it to flourish for more than three thousand years. This text does not start with the myths of Osiris and Isis or Horus and Seth, because there are many books that cover that well-trodden ground. Rather, my goal is to examine how the manifestations of religious beliefs were incorporated into the culture, how they formed the society, and what the impact of those complex beliefs and practices was on the people who lived in the Nile Valley thousands of years ago.

This book explores how the ancient Egyptians responded to their world. How did the Egyptian people relate to the great temples that dominated their cities? Did they even enter the temples? How did they regard and worship the gods? What was their attitude toward death, and how did they prepare for the end of life? What was the relationship between the realms of the living and the dead? How did religion color the most basic aspects of Egyptian life: birth, death, even commerce? These are among the questions investigated in the text that follows.

Whenever possible I have allowed the ancient Egyptians to speak for themselves by incorporating quotations from their letters, autobiographic texts, economic records, prayers, and inscriptions on tomb and temple walls. I have also brought paintings and reliefs, statues, and ritual objects into the discussion, for they are rich sources for exploring how religion was expressed.

It is hoped that this presentation of the reality of the religion practiced by the ancient Egyptians – what it meant for the people, and how it affected their daily lives – will make their culture less abstract and more understandable, which to me is the ultimate goal of studying and writing about the distant past.

The Egyptian Mind

They [the Egyptians] are religious to excess, beyond any nation in
the world.

– Herodotus

This book is about how ancient Egyptians related to and worshipped their
gods, and how religion affected their daily lives. It focuses on personal
involvement with religion, and how religion and the human response to it –
cult actions – formed the Egyptians' material and psychological culture. The
text explores what, in the most practical sense, their beliefs meant to the
early Egyptians and how they incorporated religion into their lives. A study
of Egyptian religious practice – of how religion permeated society and stimulated human action – must include an examination of what the people were
like, how they conceived of their gods, and what they apparently (reading
backward from their practices) "needed" from their religion, that is, how
they approached their own beliefs and responded to those beliefs.

   We are fortunate to have so many sources that describe both the impact
of religion on individual Egyptians and how these individuals incorporated
those beliefs into their day-to-day lives. Yet despite this wealth of sources,
it is still frustratingly difficult to understand what these people, so removed
from us by time, were really like. Did they cringe under the weight of the
long tradition of their religion, the manifestations of which were omnipresent

both physically and culturally? In many ways, ancient Egypt was one of the most theocratic societies in history. One could easily argue that there was no "secular" realm in Egypt because all aspects of the society and culture were outgrowths of religion. Reminders of religion and the gods were everywhere. Temples were the dominant feature of every landscape, and every good-size town had many of them. On the outskirts of towns, tomb chapels dominated the view (Fig. 1). Priests hurried back and forth between the temples and tombs, craftsmen relied on commissions from funerary cults, and dreaded annual taxes supported a government led by a semidivine king.

It is clear that religion and religious institutions underpinned the Egyptian society. The king, or pharaoh, was a semidivine ruler – the incarnation of the living Horus, the son of Osiris (Fig. 2). In some periods, if there were uncertainties about the succession, the king could be confirmed by divine oracle. There were few codified laws because the pharaoh was the highest judge in the land and all laws emanated from him. The dual props of the economy were land held by the temples and land held by the state, and there was often no clear division between the two.

Art and architecture were either outgrowths of religion or just its physical manifestations. The record is skewed by the durability of stone tombs and temples compared to domestic structures of mud brick, but it is evident that much architectural effort was devoted to structures that functioned in the context of religion. Art is a special case in ancient Egypt, for it was entirely intertwined with religion. Statues, paintings, and reliefs all served a religious purpose. Although the Egyptians certainly differentiated good art from bad, in their culture art was not created for its aesthetic value as it is in the Western tradition. To the Egyptians, a representation of an object was a counterimage – an actual substitute for the object portrayed. The statue of an individual, for example, had the potential to be imbued with the spirit of that person and to serve as his or her eternal double and surrogate. Statues were an essential part of mortuary cults because Egyptians believed that a person could not exist in the afterlife unless his or her image – in the form of a statue – was preserved among the living. The sculptures that now fill museum galleries, most of them carefully incised with the name of the deceased, were those eternal images that perpetuated the memory of the dead (Fig. 3). This was a practical and stunningly simple solution to immortality – as long as the individual was remembered on earth, that person had not died.

Writing too was a consequence of religion. The Egyptian language and its hieroglyphic script were referred to as *medjet netcher*, "words of the god."

Figure 1. Aerial view of the necropolis in western Thebes (modern Luxor). The hillsides are dotted with the entrances to tombs. Many of the tombs would originally have had walled courtyards at their entrance (*see lower right*), making the necropolis look more like a village. Photo: Emily Teeter.

Writing was believed to have been given to humans by the god Thoth. Writing always had a religious potency, and to write about a thing or a person, or to read a reference to an individual, was to call that thing or person into existence. Thus a prayer written on a tomb wall asking that the deceased be provided with a thousand of bread, beer, oxen, and fowl actually made those foodstuffs eternally available (Plate I). And because the script was pictorial, the hieroglyphs, like statues, were replicas, or counter-images, of what they represented.

The institution of the priesthood was another aspect of religion that influenced daily life. As indicated by genealogies that noted peoples' titles (at least for the elite for whom we have records), a large percentage of the population served in the temples or in funerary cults. The Egyptian tradition of religious service was quite different from its Western counterpart. In the dynastic period, and indeed until the third century of our era, there was no monastic tradition and the clergy was not cloistered. On the contrary, most Egyptian priests and priestesses lived in their own homes in their village or town and were free to marry and have families. The blurred

Figure 2. King Senwosert III of Dynasty 12. Kings were typically shown in an immobile and dignified manner. Here, the king is differentiated from his subjects by his striped headdress (*nemes*) and uraeus. His power is expressed by the bows of foreign enemies that he crushes under his feet and by the bull tail that hangs from his kilt (visible between his legs). Hierakonpolis. Brooklyn Museum 52.1 Charles Edwin Wilbour Fund.

Figure 3. Statue of
Nenkhefetka and his
wife, Nefershemes. The
statue was deposited
in the couple's tomb,
where it was to be an
immortal reminder
of them. Deshasheh
Dynasty 5. OIM
2036a-b. Photo: Jean
Grant. Courtesy of the
Oriental Institute of the
University of Chicago.

boundary between the clergy and the rest of the society is exemplified by the tradition of part-time priests (see further in Chapter 2), who practiced other professions when they were not on duty in the temple.

Using ancient texts and the archaeological record, this book explores how individuals functioned in ancient Egypt's belief-saturated world. One might think that the ancient Egyptians were oppressed and culturally limited by the weight of religious thought and obligation. Yet although they functioned in a nonsecular world, it is astounding how similar their basic moral principles and the patterns of their lives were to those of our current, more secular time. Their rhythm of life followed a trajectory that is familiar to us. Egyptian instructional literature advises the individual to have fun as a child, then to get an education and find employment, and, finally, to find a spouse and start a family. If the marriage does not work out, the person is advised to get a divorce and find another, more compatible, companion. Among the other admonitions in the Egyptian literature are do not lie or steal, honor your mother and father, care for and respect the aged, and show up for your job (but it is all right to cheat a little on the "time card"). Live a modest life – do not be a braggart, do not start fights, beware of prostitutes (they will "cut your purse"), and be obedient to your superiors. In addition, appearance and grooming were an important concern and investment for the ancient Egyptians. The status of Egyptian women was not all that different from women's status in parts of today's world either. At least in legal affairs, women were considered to be the equals of men – although exercising those rights socially was a more difficult matter; such legal equality has been achieved in only a handful of countries in the last half century.

The similarities between then and now are even more striking when the details of daily life are explored. Like us, the Egyptians had board games, tops, and other toys, and had collars for their pet dogs; they wrote romantic poetry; and parents wrote letters complaining about their children. We hear of adulterous couples, divorce, and money problems, and we see a familiar family structure (monogamous marriages and nuclear rather than extended families). The Egyptians expressed grief at funerals, and they named children after their parents or grandparents. All their routine trappings of life make the ancient Egyptians seem much more immediate, approachable, and appealing to us. Despite the millennia that have passed, what we know about Egyptian life is very recognizable.

It is also important, however, to be aware of the shortcomings of our documentation. The textual sources generally relate only what was socially desirable at the time. Thus the wisdom texts (written as models of proper behavior) give us the standards of *ideal* behavior. A more realistic picture can be gleaned from legal texts, from oracle texts, and even from informal notations on ostraca (usually more casual texts on bits of pottery or limestone) that tell us about community and family life and about social strife. In those sources, we get closer to hearing firsthand the people's complaints and pleas, and, especially, how religion and belief affect them daily.

Indeed, there are so many aspects of ancient Egyptian culture that we recognize that it is tempting to assume that the Egyptians were very much like us, just separated from us by many thousands of years. But despite these similarities, it is unlikely that we would recognize ourselves, for Egyptians had an approach to understanding the world around them that was fundamentally different from ours. The Egyptians were visually oriented and were tremendously keen observers of their environment. Their worldview was based entirely on concrete principles that they could see around them. One might characterize them as the most rational of people, for their response to their world was based on their observed reality. What may seem like odd reasoning, obvious contradictions, or absurdities to us are only strange because our reality is different from theirs.[1] Our reality is formed and informed by a host of different scientific (and often seemingly irrational) ideas, whereas the Egyptians explained all natural phenomena in concrete terms, avoiding speculative thought. This is not to suggest that Egyptians were not creative. On the contrary, their achievements in art and architecture, and the mythologies they created, all attest to incredibly fertile minds. But a major aspect of their psyche was that everything that was "unknowable" – the great mysteries of the prescientific age, such as why and how the sun crossed the heavens, and where the sun went when it set – could be explained in concrete and familiar terms. To them, the sun crossed the sky in a boat because people in the Nile Valley traveled by boat. Or the sun was a great orb that was pushed across the sky by a scarab, an analogy based on observations of the natural world. They made no attempt to explain what the sky was, or what the sun was, or the relationship between the two elements.

This sort of reasoning also accounts for the way that the Egyptians regarded death. Faced with a seemingly unfathomable event, they articulated a vision of the hereafter modeled entirely on their own lives, down to the details of food, household effects, entertainment, and activities. The afterlife was a perfect mirror image of life because it avoided abstractions and the unknown. The Old Kingdom tomb, called the *per djet*, or "house of eternity," physically resembled a house, complete with bedrooms; some even had bathrooms. The walls were covered with scenes that showed, and hence preserved and replicated, daily life activities and scenes of the natural world (Plate II). The unknowable was thereby made perfectly familiar, avoiding abstractions and uncertainty.

This reliance on observable and familiar patterns of daily life to explain the unknowable provided great comfort to the Egyptians. Everything was

Figure 4. The sun (Atum) in the form of a ram crowned with a sun disk crossing the underworld sky in a boat. The day sun was shown as a scarab, the night sun as the ram. Together they completed the cycle of dawn to dusk with the rebirth of the sun at dawn. Imitating human travel, the gods traveled by boat. Here Atum is protected by the coils of Mehen, a serpent, and flanked by Hw and Sia, the divine personifications of wisdom and creation. Tomb of Ramesses VI at Thebes. Dynasty 20. Photo: Emily Teeter.

related to recognizable life experiences. Conversely, to not know was frightening, and abstraction – the corruption of the natural world – was abhorrent to Egyptian thought.

The Egyptians' reliance on physical explanations for natural processes was a fundamental and persistent feature of their culture. There was apparently no motivation for early thinkers to look beyond the physicality of the phenomenon. This was a "rational response to the intellectual and social context" of their time.[2] As their society flourished and developed across three thousand years, alternate explanations for physical phenomena were developed. Yet new explanations did not displace old ones; for the Egyptians, a variety of explanations for a single phenomenon could simultaneously be held as true.[3] What we might view as contradictions were in fact parts of a series of complementary explanations that created a layered understanding. For example, consider the mythologies and religious texts that related how the sun was thought to cross the sky. In one version already noted,

Figure 5. The vault of the sky represented as the goddess Nut. The goddess's head is at the west and her feet are at the east, and the red orb of the sun can be seen traveling along her star-studded body to be reborn each morning. *Below*, the Lady Taperet adores Atum. Thebes? Dynasties 21–25. Louvre E 52-N3663 © 2008 Musée du Louvre/Georges Poncet.

the disk of the sun, or the two forms of the sun (the scarab day sun and the ram-headed night sun), crossed the sky in a boat, mimicking a human method of transport (Fig. 4). But the Egyptians also equated the heaven that the sun crossed with the star-studded body of the goddess Nut, who bent over the earth, her toes on the eastern horizon, and her outstretched hands on the west. Representations show the red disk of the sun traveling along the underside of her body, which was likened to the vault of heaven (Fig. 5). At dusk, the goddess swallowed the disk, hiding it from human beings in the darkness of her body until she gave birth to it again at dawn. In another version, the disk of the sun was pushed across the sky by a great scarab beetle (also the hieroglyph "to come into being").

The same variety of mythologies can be seen in the explanations for the origin of the gods, who in turn created humankind. One creation myth relates that a mound, called the *benben*, the prototype for pyramids and the apex of obelisks, emerged from undifferentiated waters personified as Nun. This image was taken from nature and was based on the mounds (*geziras*) that spontaneously appear in the Nile. In one version of the myth, a phoenixlike bird, "the great cackler" alighted on the mound. Its loud cries shattered the primordial silence and heralded the beginning of life. In a second version, the god Atum appeared on the mound. The Pyramid Texts relate that Atum created the first generation of deities, Shu and Tefnut, through masturbation; in other sources, he created them with his spit. In another variation on this myth, the first god, Nofertum, emerged from a water lily that emerged from Nun. Other myths recount that the virile ram god Khnum created humankind on his potter's wheel or that humans were created by the god Ptah, who simply thought of them. Similarly diverse explanations existed for almost every natural event. What is important is that the various explanations were all held to be equally valid and could be true at the same moment. Hence, a tomb could be decorated with two, three, or more different illustrations seeking to account for what happened after death. The ancient Egyptians based each explanation on readily observable physical features of the world that surrounded them, which helped reduce their angst in the face of the unknowable.

This relatively uncomplicated level of knowledge and understanding of the world, as limited and limiting as it was, was apparently adequate to satisfy the Egyptians' intellectual curiosity. The ease with which they could explain the world around them in concrete ways may be the reason why the Egyptians did not develop a tradition of more analytical thinking or question the processes that created the basic visual clues in their environment. This certainly limited their scientific progress. Although the Egyptians were remarkably adept at simple computations using basic geometry (which, after all, depend on easily visualized information), it was the Greeks – people of a distinctly different background and world outlook – who started to really question the world in theoretical terms. The famed university at Alexandria, where Aristarchus of Samos invented astronomy and where Eratosthenes computed the circumference of the earth, was staffed by Greeks who lived in Egypt – not by the Egyptians who favored allegorical rather than empirical thought. The contrast between the Egyptian mind and the Greek mind is startling. With their tradition of adversarial discussion, the Greeks would debate one theory against another to reach a new, single synthesis – a process that was alien to the Egyptians, who, through accretion, would layer one possible solution on another without discarding any.

Although the Egyptians' lack of inquiry about the world around them may seem to have been an intellectual dead end, what is startling, and illuminating, about Egyptian culture is its longevity. For more than three thousand years, the Egyptians maintained generally the same outlook on the world, making theirs one of the most conservative and unchanging societies yet known. Reverence for the past was a major feature of the Egyptian mind, and one that had enormous impact on culture and religion. Texts relate that the condition of the world "at the beginning of time" was fresh and perfect, because the gods created it so. To modify those early forms, or to discard them, was seen not as "progress" but as a corruption of the state of perfection. Recalling the past through physical imitation of its patterns was seen as an important element in preserving continuity and predictability and hence in preserving an orderly society. This perspective helps explain the remarkably faithful retention by the Egyptians of the earliest manifestations of their culture, such as the crowns and dress of their king, and the styles of their architecture and art, all of which emerged during the early Old Kingdom and continued to provide the framework for their culture, with modest modifications, for three millennia. Such persistence in emulating and championing the past was aimed at creating a safe and comforting environment because new objects and situations were potentially threatening.

These differences between the Egyptian and later modes and levels of inquiry about the world are striking and informative. We approach natural phenomena with an *acceptance* of abstractions that we cannot observe (molecules, atomic particles, big bangs), whereas the ancient Egyptians explained their world in concrete terms rooted in the observation of their surroundings. Yet by limiting inquiry to the obvious and predictable, and avoiding potentially frightening and culturally unsettling metaphysical debate, the Egyptians were able to create for themselves a comfortable environment. This approach may also have been responsible for an outpouring of symbolic art by the Egyptians, as they strove to decode and make sense of their surroundings and to explain the unexplainable in concrete terms. The Egyptians' worldview cannot be viewed as flawed or shortsighted – their civilization lasted for thousands of years and its architects and artisans, protected and encouraged by a vibrant society, produced innumerable masterpieces of art and architecture. Even today, the countless statues, temples, and wall paintings produced by the ancient Egyptians are among the most revered and immediately recognizable products of any of the world's cultures, past or present.

The chapters that follow explore how the ancient Egyptians expressed their faith and how religion shaped and affected their lives and culture. Chapter 2, "Priests," presents a study of the large percentage of the Egyptian population who served in the priestly institutions that brought men and women directly into the realm of the gods, and seeks to describe the impact of that service on people's lives. Chapter 3, "Inside the Temple," explores the cult duties of priests and the workings of the official state cult, outlining the elaborate rituals that the priests had to execute for the gods and for their semidivine king. The next chapter, "Festivals," discusses the cult rituals that were celebrated both inside and outside the temples, showing that religious experience was not limited to official settings and that religious rituals were a part of the overall community experience. In Chapter 5, "Contacting the Gods," the formal temple setting is left behind, and the discussion turns to the varied ways that men and women contacted their deities and what motivated them to initiate such communication. This is followed, in Chapter 6, by the other side of that relationship. "In the Presence of the Gods" explores the forms of personal religious experience that were initiated by the god rather than by the petitioner and how individuals dealt with their personal highly charged encounters with the divine. Chapter 7 deals with the practical aspects of death – How did funerary beliefs and the myriad requirements of the mortuary cult affect individuals socially and economically? What happened at funerals? The next chapter (Chapter 8) discusses communication with the dead – In what ways were individuals or groups who were deceased accessible to the living? What demands did the dead place on the living, and vice versa? Another important aspect of religion, magic, is the subject of Chapter 9. Was all Egyptian religion magic? This chapter also addresses sorcery in the dynastic period and the forms that conjuring took. The book ends with an evaluation of the much-discussed Amarna Period of Akhenaten and Nefertiti and explores what it actually meant for people at that time.

It is hoped that this book will make the ancient Egyptians truly live again as individuals interacting with and within a complex religious system that demanded their full attention and response. The richness of their experiences, whether serving as priests, calling on the gods or on the dead for assistance, or engaging in ecstatic festival celebrations, is proof that the society created by these Egyptians was vibrant and humane.

2

Priests

In one sense, we know a lot about priests in ancient Egypt. We have the names and titles of thousands of priests, and numerous biographies and autobiographies that describe their duties. Yet in some cases, we do not know exactly what differentiated one type of priest from another. Further, little is known about the training of priests, and there is much debate about some aspects of the priesthood, including priests' specialized knowledge, initiation, and mysticism.

Economic records indicate that the priesthood was a major institution in Egyptian society. For example, the funerary cult of Neferirkare (Dynasty 5) had between two hundred and fifty and three hundred individuals associated with it.[1] Even smaller temples, such as those of Anubis at the Fayum and in Teudjoy, employed between fifty and eighty priests.[2] Though we lack similar rosters for the major temples like Karnak, the number of priests they employed must have been enormous.

In contrast to the many written records and the statues of priests that survive from the dynastic period virtually no visual record of priests remains in the temples themselves. Instead, temple walls are covered with endless scenes showing the king carrying out religious ceremonies (Fig. 6), for, in theory, he was the sole officiate before the gods. But texts make it clear that many priests were actually engaged in the temple workings as proxies for the king. Only in the Greco-Roman Period do we find priests depicted on temple walls. However, even then the individuals, such as seen in the processions of priests in the stairways leading to the roofs of the temples of Hathor at Dendera and Horus at Edfu (Fig. 7), are nameless, In the dynastic era, priests were frequently depicted in the wall paintings of private tombs, where they are shown as participants in processions or enacting temple or funerary rites for the tomb owner, or as the deceased himself if he had been a priest during his lifetime (Fig. 8).

Priests were an omnipresent feature of the Egyptian society and economy, and few people who appear in the written record lack a priestly title. As a result, it can be difficult to determine what differentiated a priest from a nonpriest. In contrast to the later Western world, ancient Egypt had no monastic organizations (although Egypt was the birthplace of the Christian monastic movement in the third century AD). Ancient Egyptian priests were fully integrated into all aspects of society. They lived in the villages, married, and had children. They did not even commit to being priests for the duration of their lives. An analogy might be the Muslim imam of a small village, who is often distinguished from his neighbors only by his specialized knowledge and his service in the mosque. However, the ancient Egyptian priest, in contrast, was not expected to serve as an example of religiously dictated behavior. As one Ptolemaic text exhorts, "oh brother and husband, priest of Ptah, never cease drinking, eating, becoming intoxicated, making love, passing the time in merriment, following your heart day and night."[3]

Most priests were expected to serve the gods only part-time; they could revert to other professions, whether in government service or in the trades, when they were not at the temple. Their ability to combine jobs is clearly documented in the sequences of titles preserved in biographical texts. For example, Nebnetcheru (Dynasty 22) was a priest of Amun in Karnak, a supervisor of priests "of all the gods," a *sem* priest, and a priest of Maat, and also served as the "Chief of All the Works on All Monuments."[4] Onuris-mose (Dynasty 19) held the titles of God's Father, Chief of Seers of Shu, and High Priest of Onuris, as well as those of royal scribe and scribe of the elite troops of the king.[5] Three successive generations of a family at Dendera held the titles Mayor of the City and priest of Hathor. Men bearing the low-level priestly title *wab*, "pure one," also worked as scribes at local courts, copper- and goldsmiths, gardeners, and guardians. Other strings of titles listed priestly designations and military rank. Thus Hori (Dynasty 22) was both the Chief Priest of Amun Re at Karnak and the overseer of the

Figure 6. Ramesses IV offering a tray of food and four trussed cows to the god Khonsu. Such scenes are among the most common form of decoration in temples because they emphasized the role of the king as the primary connection between humankind and the gods. Temple of Khonsu. Dynasty 20. Photo: Emily Teeter.

military.[6] The combination of secular and sacred occupations for a single individual had a long tradition. Harkhuf (Dynasty 6), for example, was, among his other titles, the overseer of foreigners, the seal bearer of the king, and a lector priest.

Because of both the lack of strictures on the behavior expected of priests and the part-time nature of most priestly positions, identifying what characterized a priest is difficult. In most cases, there did not appear to be an official ordination or a special mode of dress marking the transition from commoner to priest. Only certain higher levels of the priesthood had some official commemoration or wore distinctive garb. When Nebwenenef (Dynasty 19) assumed the post of First Priest of Amun, his appointment was confirmed by an oracle, and he was given rings and a scepter that served to differentiate him from other priests. Qualification for the priesthood appears to have been based on the individual's knowledge of the priest's role and specific duties and, in some cases, on literacy. But the most important marker for the transition from nonpriest to priest was the ritual purification that was required before entering the temple.

Figure 7. Procession of anonymous priests carrying shrines, as depicted on a stairway wall in the Temple of Hathor at Dendera. Greco-Roman Period. Photo: Emily Teeter.

Types of Priests and Their Duties

Priests were organized into many different ranks, each with specific duties and privileges and having varying levels of access to parts of a temple. Some ranks worked in the temples, others worked exclusively in funerary establishments, and a few apparently worked in both spheres. A priest could serve several deities at the same time. For example, Harwa, an official of Dynasty 25, bore the titles embalmer's priest of Anubis, priest of all the God's Wives, steward of the *ka* priests, and priest of Osiris.[7] Priests were assisted by *semdet*, a nonpriestly workforce who acted in support of the temple as farmers, sailors, shipbuilders, or gold washers.[8] Priests could be fired from their jobs. An Old Kingdom text relates: "As for any soul priest ... who shall not make

Figure 8. Scene from the tomb of Khons showing him acting as a priest offering incense and liquid purification to the sacred boat of the deified king Thutmose III. The shrine that contains the statue of the king is covered with a billowing veil. Tomb of Khons at Thebes (TT 31). Dynasty 19. Photo: C. F. Nims. Courtesy of the Oriental Institute of the University of Chicago.

invocation offerings, I shall make him lose (or resign) his job."[9] Descriptions of the most important ranks of priests follow.

Wab. The majority of priests held the title *wab*, "pure one," which was the entry-level position in the priesthood. There were regular *wabs* and "great *wabs*" (*wab aa*). Numerous *wabs* were associated with each institution.[10] Many priests of other ranks started as *wabs* and worked their way up to more prestigious titles. This rank of priest wore no distinguishing dress or hairstyle. They served in both temples and tombs. In the mortuary context, the *wab* was responsible for carrying offerings in the funeral and thereafter for periodically supplying the tomb chapel with additional offerings.

Inside the temples, *wabs* were charged with carrying offerings, and they are frequently listed among the personnel involved in the daily offering service. However, the *wabs'* low level of purity meant that they had only limited access to the inner portion of a temple. At Karnak, they were not allowed in the *Akh Menu* of Thutmose III (see Plan 1), in contrast to the *hem netcher* priests who were. Despite the *wabs'* restricted temple access, New Kingdom legal texts contain references to *wabs* who were in possession of property stolen from the temple, suggesting that these particular *wabs* either had had greater access than has been assumed (at least to the temple storerooms), had violated admission rules, or had received stolen temple property from priests who did have greater access.

Despite their low rank, *wab* priests carried the sacred boat of the god during oracles. This was an important and delicate point of contact between the temple and the larger community, for it was the *wabs* who perceived (and controlled) the movement of the boat, which was interpreted as the god's approval or rejection of a petition.

Even though there were many *wabs*, the title was a prestigious one. New Kingdom records from the Temple of Khnum at Elephantine describe a conspiracy among *wabs* to eject one of their colleagues from their temple (they refer to him dismissively as "that son of that trader") and to bring three new members in and have them confirmed by an oracle (over which the *wabs* had some control).[11]

Hem-ka. The *hem-ka* (literally, "servant of the *ka*") (Fig. 9) were low-ranking priests who carried food and other offerings in funerary rituals. *Hem-ka* were not characterized by distinctive dress. They can be identified in the tomb reliefs only by their activity and by the captions that indicate their rank.

These *ka* priests acted as custodians of, and executors of, endowments left by individuals to ensure that offerings were left daily in the donors' tombs.[12] Records, especially from the late Old Kingdom, indicate the legal issues that the *ka* priests dealt with, the foremost being that they not transfer any of the endowment to another person's tomb. Perhaps not surprisingly, their duties had the potential to immerse *ka* priests in family disputes. A text from the tomb of Nyankhkhnum and Khnumhotep at Saqqara (Dynasty 5) contains instructions to its *ka* priests:

> With regard to these [priests] who deal with the invocation offerings for us and who act on our behalf in the necropolis: They shall not let our children, our wives, or any people have power over them.

Apparently there was friction among these priests, for the text continues:

> With regard to any [*ka*] priest who shall start proceedings against his fellow priests, whether it be coming forward with a complaint about his carrying duties or producing a document for the discontinuation of the invocation offerings of the owners of

this funerary cult: All of his share shall be taken from him and given instead to that [*ka*] priest against whom he started the proceeding.[13]

The rank of *ka* priest could be passed through the family. Texts specifically state that "they should pass on to their children what is their share [together with] the *ka* priesthood."[14]

Lector Priest (khery hebet). Lector priests were distinguished by their ability to read, and their main duty was to recite specialized religious texts in both temple and mortuary rituals. The lector wore a distinctive sash that crossed from the shoulder to the hip (Fig. 10). In the Old Kingdom, lectors were often members of the royal family, a sign of the prestige of this profession, but by the Middle Kingdom, the pool of eligible candidates had widened to include any literate man. Because they were literate, this class of priest was considered to be the keeper of specialized knowledge (referred to as *seshta*, often translated as "mysteries"). Book of the Dead Spell 15B instructs the deceased to do certain actions "without letting any man see, aside from the one who is truly your intimate and a lector priest."[15]

Lectors were an important part of the funeral service, as they were respon-sible for reciting the spells that guided the soul of the deceased from the time of death to its transition to an *akh* (transfigured spirit). In a Dynasty 6 tomb, the lector is credited with being the one "who shall carry out the rites of transfiguration for an *akh* in accordance with those secret writings of the skills of the lector priest."[16] In scenes of funerals, the lector is shown accompanying the coffin, often holding a papyrus from which he will read.

Lectors also played a crucial role in Egypt's administration. Texts that refer to the coronation of the king state that the lector priest was respon-sible for the announcement of the prenomen (the name pharaoh assumed on accession to the throne). A text from the time of Hatshepsut (Dynasty 18) records: "They [the lector priests] proclaimed her names of Upper and Lower Egypt, for the god caused that it should be in their hearts to make her names according to the forms which he had made them before."[17] The lectors were also charged with announcing the result of oracles, that is, whether the movement of the sacred boat (under the immediate charge of the *wabs*) indicated the favor or disfavor of the god.

God's Father (it netcher). The class of priest known as God's Fathers wore no distinctive garb. They are mentioned in both temple and mortuary

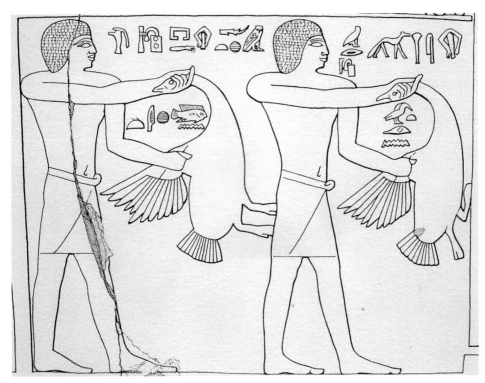

Figure 9. Two *hem ka* (*ka* priests), or priests who carried offerings in temples and tombs. The only way that they can be differentiated from nonpriests is by their activity and by the hieroglyphic caption that identifies them. Tomb of Mereruka at Saqqara. Dynasty 6. Courtesy of the Oriental Institute of the University of Chicago.

contexts, where they participated with other priests in the daily offering service and the offering for the soul of the deceased. Arranged in hierarchies bearing the ranks of First, Second, and Third God's Father, they are most commonly associated with the cult service of Min, Amun, and Ptah. The title is commonly encountered in New Kingdom temple administration texts (often with that of *wabs* and lector priests). God's Fathers are known from the Old Kingdom when the title was associated with men who were related to the royal family, being the father-in-law of the king, or more rarely, a son-in-law. By the late 18th Dynasty, the title designated a specific type of priest and no longer meant that the holder was a member of the royal family.

In New Kingdom administrative texts, God's Fathers are associated with the delivery of food and supplies to the temple and the inspection of temple property. Thus in one papyrus, they report to the king that some temple

Figure 10. Priests performing the Opening of the Mouth ritual. *To the left* stand a *sem* priest in a leopard robe and a lector (*khery hebet*) with a sash across his chest. *To the right*, another *sem*, dressed in a simple kilt and sash, stands behind the statue of Seti I, while a lector faces the statue. The two lector priests carry rectangular writing palettes, symbolizing their literacy. Tomb of Seti I at Thebes. Dynasty 20. Photo: Emily Teeter.

property has been stolen.[18] At least on occasion, this rank of priest was directly involved with the daily offering service; at Karnak there are references to their "opening the doors of heaven" (i.e., the shrine of the god),[19] and "uncovering the divine face,"[20] both important parts of the offering ceremony. They also provided offerings to statues within the temple. The autobiography of Nebnetcheru (Dynasty 22) calls on the God's Fathers to give water to his statue "every day, unendingly."[21]

Sem Priest. The *sem* is recognizable by his leopard-skin robe and by his hair, which is worn in a distinctive sidelock (see Fig. 10). Papyrus Jumilhac, dating to the Ptolemaic Period (ca. 300 BC), attempts to explain the significance of the leopard skin through a myth that relates the misdeeds of the god Seth. As told in the papyrus, Seth attacked Osiris and then transformed himself into a leopard. The god Anubis defeated Seth and then branded his pelt with spots,[22] hence the robe commemorates the defeat of Seth.

Sem priests are mentioned from the Early Dynastic era onward. They are attested in both funerary and temple contexts. Some *sem* priests were attached to specific gods; we have references to the *sem* of Anubis and of Khnum. The title could also be combined with other priestly titles. It was apparently a prestigious role, as suggested by the fact that Kaemwaset, a son of Ramesses II, gave his priestly title *sem* precedence over his title of "king's son."[23]

The *sem* presided over the Opening of the Mouth ritual at a funeral, in which he touched the face of the mummy with tools to revive the senses of the deceased in the afterlife. He performed the same ritual on statues, imbuing them with the spirit of the person they depicted and enabling them to act as surrogates for the one who commissioned the image.

Administrative texts of New Kingdom temples indicate that the *sem* was a prominent individual, for there appears to have been a single *sem* associated with each temple. From the middle of the Eighteenth Dynasty to the reign of Ramesses II (Dynasty 19), the *sem* acted as the First Priest (*hem netcher tepy*). He oversaw the temple lands, priests, and craftsmen. In the records of the workmen's strike that occurred during the reign of Ramesses III, it was the *sem* priest who made the unfortunate decision not to immediately grant the men their bread rations. The *sem* also served on the court known as the "Great Council of Thebes."[24]

Iwnmutef Priest. The *Iwnmutef* priest wears the same leopard-skin robe and sidelock as the *sem*. The name of this rank of funerary priest means, literally, "pillar of his mother," perhaps a reference to his supporting the sky goddess whose body formed the vault of heaven. *Iwnmutefs* were associated with both private and royal mortuary cults.

Hem Netcher. Until recently, *hem netcher*, which means "God's Servant," was rendered as "prophet," a translation that is now avoided because of its Judeo-Christian undertones. The more general translation "priest" is now preferred. The *hem netcher* priests cared for the materials used for the daily offering ritual. This function gave them considerable economic power, as the temples consumed massive amounts of food and other goods. The *hem netcher* priests were divided into escalating ranks of Fourth through First

Priest. Although there were several Fourth and Third Priests at one time, there were only one Second and one First Priest. There is also one example of a female First Priest of Amun, Nitocris of Dynasty 26. Known from the time of the Old Kingdom, the Chief Priest was usually the local governor, an indication of the economic power of the post. The *hem netcher* had access to the inner areas of the temple. Some of the First Priests had specific titles that specified the god they served. The First Priest who served Ptah, the patron of craftsmen, was called "Great Chief of All the Artisans." He wore a garment adorned with stars.

The lower ranks of *hem netcher* were responsible for duties within the sanctuary of the temple. Djed-khonsu-iwef-ankh, who was Fourth Priest of Amun, claimed to be responsible for robing the divine statue and preparing the chapel, and for being the chief incense bearer before the god.[25] Nebnetcheru (Dynasty 22), a *hem netcher* of Amun in Karnak, claimed to be in charge of opening the doors of the divine shrine "so that I saw his [the god's] form in light-land."[26]

In the New Kingdom and the Third Intermediate Period, the First Priest of Amun was among the most powerful figures in the land, often rivaling the king, because he administered the vast holdings of the god Amun that were spread throughout the country. He managed the temple's huge farms and livestock enterprises and oversaw the nonpriestly staff (*semdet*) who produced the goods that provided the economic underpinning of Amun's temples. When Ramesses II appointed Nebwenenef as the First Priest of Amun, he described the appointee's responsibilities thusly: "I have appointed to him [Nebwenenef] all the personnel of the court, the chief of the soldiers ... the priests [*hem netcher*] of the gods and the dignitaries of the house." The First Priest was to be "head of the double house of silver and gold, head of the double granary, chief of works, chief of all trades in Thebes ... the house of Amun was turned over to him as well as all its property and its people."[27] The political power of the post, even beyond the reference to the First Priest's being "the chief of the soldiers," is demonstrated by the fact that it was the Fourth Priest of Amun, Montuemhet, who surrendered the city of Thebes to the Assyrians in 663 BC. Many of the *hem netcher* of various ranks were able to amass huge personal fortunes, as indicated by their massive decorated tombs in western Thebes.

The First Priest of a temple was selected by the king. He commonly came up though the hierarchy of priests of the specific institution, but in some cases, he came from outside. For example, Nebwenenef (Dynasty 19) was appointed First Priest of Amun after having been First Priest of Onuris at Dendera. His appointment by the king was confirmed by an oracle, perhaps as a way of ensuring his acceptance by his colleagues. In his autobiography, another First Priest of Amun, Bakenkhonsu (Dynasty 19), stated that he had started as a lowly *wab* priest and after four years was appointed to the rank of God's Father. Twelve years later, he became Third Priest, and then, after fifteen more years, Second Priest, of Amun. After another twelve years, he was finally appointed First Priest, a post that he filled for twenty-seven years. He died after a career that spanned nearly seventy years.[28] Other priests had a slower career path. Amunemhet, who lived during the reign of Amunhotep II or Thutmose IV (Dynasty 18), was a low *wab* for more than fifty years before he made the rank of God's Father. A few years later, he was finally promoted to First Priest of Amun.[29]

Priestesses

Although ancient Egypt is well known for its gender equality, women did not play as active a role as did men in temple establishments. Women generally held higher positions in the religious hierarchy during the Old Kingdom than they did in later times. In the Old Kingdom, there were female *hem netcher* known as *hemet netcher*, who served the goddesses Hathor and Neith. In the Middle Kingdom, a few women served as *hemet netcher* of the gods Amun, Ptah, and Min and as *wabets* (female *wab*). Priestesses were divided into hierarchies similar to the men's. Ahmose Nofertari, the wife of Ahmose, held the title Second Priest in the early Eighteenth Dynasty. It was not until the Twenty-sixth Dynasty that a woman, Nitocris, held the title First Priest of Amun.

Female priestly roles were downgraded in the New Kingdom and the Third Intermediate Period. During those periods, women were almost exclusively singers (*shamyet* or *heset*) in divine choirs that accompanied priests in processions around and through the temple; the higher ranks apparently followed the priests into the area near the sanctuary. In Plate III, a woman is shown carrying a sistrum, the rattle whose tinkling sound was associated with Hathor, and a *menat*, a beaded necklace with an elaborate key-shaped counterpoise that produces a sound when shaken. Women bore titles such as "Singer in the Temple of Amun," or the more prestigious "Singer in the Interior [of the Temple of] Amun." They were under the supervision of a male or female "Overseer of the Singers." Other women appear as singers of Osiris, or dancers of the "Foremost of the Westerners" (i.e., Osiris) or Min. The erosion of female sacral titles is obvious in the Third Intermediate Period, an era in which many monuments were commissioned by women, or at least commemorated women. Among a group of forty-nine stelae dating to this period, only eleven lists a woman who bears a priestly title; most of the women listed either have no title or are simply referred to as "Mistress of the House."

The title God's Wife (also *hemet netcher*, but a different word than for the priestess's title mentioned earlier), which denoted a priestess of Amun in the Third Intermediate Period, is first attested several times in the Middle Kingdom. It appears more consistently in the early New Kingdom, when it is associated with queens and other royal women. In this early period, it may have been more closely related to succession than to any sacred function, but by the Third Intermediate Period, the post took on a new meaning and the God's Wife was charged with supervising the holdings of Amun in Thebes. In this era, the God's Wife became immensely wealthy and influential. As a part of her cultic role, she was thought to stimulate and please Amun, thereby evoking the concept of rejuvenation and rebirth (Fig. 11).

Although still debated, there is no direct evidence to suggest that priestesses of any rank were celibate. Many genealogies refer to mothers who held religious titles, and there is no reason to assume that even the God's Wives of the Third Intermediate Period were unmarried.

Becoming a Priest

How did one become a priest in ancient Egypt? Although little is known about their training, we do have some information about how priests were appointed. We know from autobiographical texts that some priests of the higher ranks were personally selected by the king. For example, Nebouay was appointed by Thutmose III, and Nebwenenef by Ramesses II. Clearly, family background and social status were often taken into consideration. Tutankhamun claimed that he installed priests "chosen from among the sons of the local dignitaries and the children of men whose names were known." Very often, a priest inherited his office from his father, or at least he was considered eligible because of the family's familiarity with the duties. Ramesses II promised Nebwenenef, "As for the temple of Hathor, queen of Dendera, it will pass into the hands of your son as well as the functions your father and the position that you occupy."[30] King Psametik

Figure 11. The God's Wife
Amunirdis embracing Amun.Chapel
of Osiris-Onnophris in the Persea
Tree at Karnak. Dynasty 25.
Photo: Emily Teeter.

(Dynasty 26) rewarded Petiese with the title of priest "in all temples where his father had served,"[31] and Nebnetcheru (Dynasty 22) claimed, "I saw my sons as great priests; son after son who issued from me."[32] The family of Wenennefer held the title of Chief Priest of Osiris at Abydos throughout Dynasty 19.[33] One of the best records we have of the inheritance of priestly titles is incised on a statue of a priest of Hathor named Basa (Dynasties 22–23) recording twenty-six generations of his family, most of whom were priests of Hathor at Dendera (Fig. 12). Fathers and sons sharing priestly titles was so common that the writers of genealogical texts used the shorthand *mi nw* ("ditto") to record the titles inherited by sons from their fathers. The inheritance of priestly office became so institutionalized that in the Persian Period (4th century BC) Somtu-tefnakht could claim, "He [the Persian king]

Figure 12. A priest of Hathor, Basa. The sides of the statue are incised with a genealogy of twenty-six generations of his family. Most of the men served as a priest of Hathor. Dendera. Dynasties 22–23. OIM 10729. Photo: Jean Grant. Courtesy of the Oriental Institute of the University of Chicago.

gave me the office of the Chief Priest of Sekhmet, in place of my mother's brother."[34] Herodotus (II:37) reported simply, "When a priest dies, his son is put in his place."

Once a man held a priestly title, he could advance through the various ranks. In some cases this was done simply on the basis of seniority, or by royal appointment. Promotions could be slow. As already mentioned, Nebwenenef (Dynasty 19) claimed that it took him forty years to reach the highest rank of First Priest of Amun.

There is considerable debate about whether there was a formal initiation ritual for priests in the dynastic period. Much of the uncertainty comes from our lack of knowledge about how priests were trained, if indeed they had any formal schooling at all. It is only in the very late period (2nd c. AD) that there is a reference (Papyrus Tebtunis II.291) to a test on religious matters that priests had to pass before assuming their posts. Throughout the dynastic period, references to "mysteries" (seshta) and "secret" writings can be found in both funerary and nonfunerary texts.[35] A tantalizing text appears in the tomb of Khentika (Dynasty 6) at Giza, instructing that incense be burned for the tomb owner according to those writings of "the secrets of the god's words of the skills of the lector priest. [There is nothing] kept secret from me in the writings of the house of the god's books, for I am a keeper of secrets … I know everything that an excellent akh should know … I know every way … for I am initiated into all the secret of the god's books of the palace."[36]

However, one should not associate the priestly tradition of the Egyptians with that of the later Greeks, which emphasized the mysterious, unknowable aspects of their religion. In that tradition, the seeker of knowledge underwent an esoteric symbolic death in order to experience the unknowable, culminating in the seeker's joining the solar cycle. In contrast, most references to "mysteries" in Egyptian texts are in the context of the acquisition of knowledge that will allow the acquirer to fathom the unknowable. Clues to the proper understanding of Egyptian mysteries are contained in the Book of the Dead Spell 148, which instructs, "This [papyrus] roll is a real secret. Nobody is to know it ever. It is not to be told to anyone, no one is to see it, no ear is to hear it … *except him* [the possessor of the papyrus] *and his teacher.*" In an inscription on a statue of the Ramesside Period, we see the same relationship of "secret" to knowledge. The official who commissioned the statue claimed to be "one who was discreet, reticent, with access to knowledge, open of ears, skilled in what is secret."[37] In these texts, the idea of "secret" or "mystery" does not mean unknowable; rather, it means specialized knowledge that may be restricted to certain types of priests through levels of literacy and knowledge. These sorts of texts emphasize the Egyptians' appreciation of knowledge as power, making it plausible that references in Egyptian texts to "initiation" refer to specialized training rather than to a mystical transformation.

Although we have no evidence of initiation rituals, there are hints that priests were ceremonially presented to the gods. Brief texts from the Temple of Karnak from the Third Intermediate Period refer to specific days on which priests were "introduced to the god" (the Egyptian term is *beset*), in an area of the temple to which access was restricted to those who possessed a certain level of purity.[38] One such text records that the priest Hori presented some sort of written credential that verified his rank.[39]

Purity and the Priesthood

The main feature that distinguished a priest from a nonpriest was the priest's state of purity. Unlike in other cultures where ritual purity might be a state of mind that resulted from knowledge or meditation, in Egypt purity was mainly an acquired transient physical state achieved by washing. Varying levels of purity characterized different ranks of priests. Although we do not know exactly which physical acts were involved, references to priests in an Old Kingdom tomb "who having not purified themselves according to the manner in which they should to enter a temple of a god,"[40] indicate that there was a standard preparation to attain the state or condition of purity. In New Kingdom temples, certain sections of the temples were restricted to priests who possessed specific levels of purity, weeding out the lower level priests from the higher. Some temple doorways had markings on their jambs warning that "everyone who enters here should be twice [or three or four times] pure" (Fig. 13). Herodotus (II:37) reported more generally that priests washed themselves twice a day in cold water, and twice again at night and that they rinsed their mouths with natron (a naturally occuring salt) and water. Other texts are more general, such as one that warns against "anyone who shall approach this statue in an impure state."[41]

Funerary priests purified themselves in a structure called the *ibw* (purification tent) or *seb-netcher* (god's shrine).[42] Most temples had a sacred lake within their enclosure walls that was accessible to the priests before they entered the temple itself. Some of the doorways of the Temple of Amun at Karnak that bear instructions about the requisite level of purity required to enter face the lake where the priests would wash themselves to prepare for temple service.

There are scattered references to other aspects of purity. Herodotus (5th c. BC) and Apuleius (2nd c. AD) record that priests were forbidden to wear wool. Although wool was known in the earlier eras, it was never common; linen was the primary textile for clothing. Apuleius also comments that priests were ritually installed after they had fasted for ten days, which is probably an exaggeration.[43] Scattered references to circumcision as a form of ritual purity also appear. King Piye (Dynasty 25) related that "the [rival] kings and counts of Lower Egypt could not enter the palace because they were uncircumcised … but Nimlot entered the palace because he was clean."[44] Although this quotation refers to a palace, the same strictures may have applied to the temple. In either case, it indicates some inconsistency

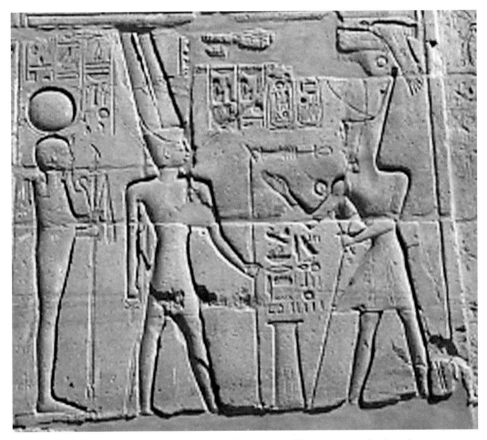

Figure 13. This doorway at the Temple of Amun at Karnak is marked with an inscription indicating that all who entered this part of the temple must be "four times pure." Dynasty 20. Photo: Emily Teeter.

in practice, because the mummies of Kings Amunhotep I and II appear to be uncircumcised.

Our understanding of whether purity was related to dietary restrictions is muddied by the contradictory comments of classical authors who often refer to forbidden foods that include cow, pork, sheep, and the head or feet of animals. Herodotus (II:37) commented, "As for beans, they cannot bear to even look at them," and "fish they are forbidden to touch." Plutarch included salt among his list of impure foods. However, comparing these suggested prohibitions to the lists of foods that were offered to the god (and then reverted to the temple staff) suggests a different reality. Offering lists and scenes from the New Kingdom include most of the foods that the later authors claim were prohibited. The Egyptologist Serge Sauneron attempted to resolve this discrepancy between the early and later sources by suggesting that some of the food prohibitions may have been localized, depending upon the chief god of the nome (administrative district). Animals associated with the nome's emblem or favored local god were considered taboo in that nome, but might be eaten freely in other districts. Sauneron cites a story in Plutarch describing a conflict between two nomes: "In our time, the people of Oxyrrhinchus [a district with a fish emblem], because the people of Cynopolis [the neighboring nome with a dog emblem] had eaten of the oxyrrhinque [fish] seized some dogs, and killed and ate them as victims. From this came a war in which the two towns both suffered very much."[45] The inscription of Piye (Dynasty 25) claims that the unclean ones were "eaters of fish." This is at odds with the archaeological evidence (fish bones in kitchens and garbage heaps) and with tomb scenes of food preparation that show fish being cleaned and hung to dry.

Though we do not know which specific foods were pure or impure, it is clear that as early as the Old Kingdom diet was a factor in priests' purity. A text in a tomb cautions those who "shall enter my tomb ... in an impure state, having eaten something abominable ... and who are not pure at the time when they should be pure as in the temple of the god" or those "having eaten the abomination which an *akh* [spirit] abominates."[46] A priest could reverse the effects of having eaten a taboo food, as is indicated by another text in an Old Kingdom tomb, which refers to individuals' "having consumed the abomination, and not having purified themselves in accordance with the manner in which they should be made pure."[47]

Associations between sexual activity and priestly impurity are rare, though they do exist. A heading for the Book of the Dead Spell 21 states, "This spell is to read by one who is pure and clean, without eating quadrupeds or fish and without being intimate with women."[48] A text in the tomb of Idu at Saqqara (Dynasty 6) warns one "who has had sexual intercourse with women" not to enter.[49] Herodotus (II:64) contrasts the Egyptians, who did not have ritual sex in temples, with other peoples who did (referring to them as "beasts"), claiming that the "prohibition against uniting oneself with women in the sacred places or entering there after leaving the arms of a woman without washing oneself comes from Egypt." Yet, in contrast, a text on a funerary stela to the wife of a priest from the Ptolemaic Period mentioned earlier contains the exhortation, "oh brother ... priest of Ptah, never cease drinking, eating, becoming intoxicated, making love ... following your heart day and night."[50] As this is from a funerary context, it may not describe the ideal behavior of a priest while on duty.

Organization of Priests

Throughout the dynastic period, most priests worked part-time, reverting to their other profession(s) when off duty. Systems of organization were devised for the orderly rotation of priests. One system was applied to priests classified as *wenut*, or "those who serve in their hour [*wenut*]." These "hour priests" made up most of the priests in New Kingdom temples.[51]

Another system divided priests among five (later four, then again five) service groups called phyles (*sau*). The names of most of the phyles were derived from nautical terms from the Coffin Texts, an association that led Egyptologists to conclude that the rotation of priests was based upon sailors' watches on board a ship. Now, it is thought that the phyle names, "Little," "Great," "Asiatic," "Green," and "Last" are derived from the names of early clans (Fig. 14). The phyle system was not exclusive to priests; it was also employed by police and other workers.[52] As with all aspects of priesthood, phyles were hierarchical, each being headed by an inspector (*shedj*). According to the phyle system, a priest served for one thirty-day month and then stepped down, serving one month out of five in a five-phyle system, and three months of the ten-month year in the four-phyle organization. There were four phyles in the Middle Kingdom, but the original count of five was restored in the Ptolemaic Period.

In the New Kingdom, priests became increasingly professional and full-time, but there was still a phyle system under which groups relieved each other in rotation.[53] It has been suggested that the greater number of full-time priests in the New Kingdom may reflect the fact that individuals belonged to several different priesthoods, their service to each being regulated by the phyle system. For example, Djed-khonsu-iwef-ankh (Dynasty 21) served as a monthly priest in the house of Amun of the third phyle, and also in the second phyle as the "Guardian of the Chest of the House of Amun." Some mortuary texts indicate that a large number of men could be regulated by a modified phyle system in which the men served only once. In one Old Kingdom text, priests who served in a private cult were listed for the entire year, yet the personal names of the individual priests were not repeated, suggesting that each served only once.[54] Priests worked both day and night,[55] but there was some flexibility in the system. Economic records indicate that priests were able to trade and sell days of their required service.[56] The danger that the regular and dependable services of priests might be disrupted by their enlistment in government projects (corvée)

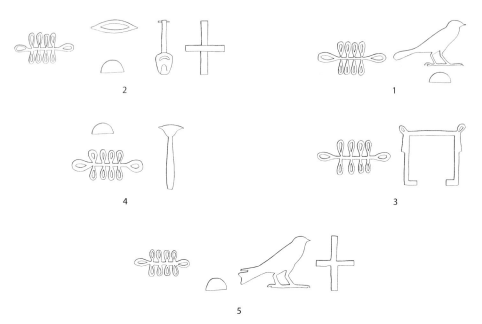

Figure 14. Signs that identify each of the groups (phyles) of priests who worked in rotation in the temples in the Old Kingdom. (1) Little Phyle, (2) Last Phyle, (3) Asiatic Phyle, (4) Green Phyle, and (5) Great Phyle. These examples are written from right to left. From the mastaba of Mereruka at Saqqara. Dynasty 6. Courtesy of the Oriental Institute of the University of Chicago.

was overcome by exemption decrees that protected the temple staff from transfer to other projects or duties.[57]

Remuneration of Priests

Priests were paid in kind from the offerings that were presented to the god or to royal or private statues in temples or tombs. These goods, referred to as "reversion offerings" (*wedjeb hetep*) because the food reverted to the temple staff, are attested in economic records from the Old Kingdom down into the Ptolemaic era. All classes of priests were paid by reversion offerings.

It is astounding to consider the huge number of priests who depended on the temples and tombs for their subsistence and the immense amount of food that circulated through the economy as a result. To ensure a steady supply of grain (the main medium of payment and the source for the most common offering, bread loaves), the temples had granaries that served much like ancient reserve banks. Crops raised on lands that belonged to the

Figure 15. Aerial view of granaries surrounding the Ramesseum in western Thebes. It has been estimated that they could store enough grain to feed thirty-four hundred families for an entire year. Dynasty 19. Photo: Emily Teeter.

specific temple, whether in the immediate area or elsewhere in Egypt, were brought to the temple for storage. The granary at the Ramesseum (Fig. 15), the Temple of Ramesses II in western Thebes, had a capacity of 226,328 sacks of grain, equal to 16,522,000 liters, an amount that would support thirty-four hundred families for an entire year.[58] This was only one of the temple storehouses in the region. The granary of the nearby Temple of Ramesses III at Medinet Habu held 56,972 sacks. A single offering table of Ramesses III at Karnak – one of many – received 20 sacks of grain a day, enough to feed one hundred ten families for a year.[59]

Offerings were made three times a day in the temples. "Heaps" (a term for a specific measure) of beer, fowl, vegetables, and bread would be left on altars before the cult statue. There is no indication of how long the food remained on the altar to be "consumed" by the god, but, considering that some meat offerings were raw, the offerings were probably removed fairly quickly. However, warnings were given about removing the food too hastily. A text from Edfu states, "Do not go freely to steal his [the god's] things. Beware, moreover, of foolish thoughts. One lives by the food of the gods, and 'food' is called that which comes forth from the offering-table(s) *after* the god has been satisfied with it."[60] Burnt offerings were not common in Egypt, probably for the practical reason that the food was to be passed along to the priests.

Priests were paid based on of a formula that divided the total offerings presented in the temple or tomb over 360 days in the year by the number of days the priest served, rather than the priest's receiving a percentage of the food presented during the duration of his rotation. This system apparently equalized the greater amounts of offerings that might be presented during festivals when a specific priest was not working. In concrete terms, an overseer of a Middle Kingdom temple at Lahun received sixteen loaves of bread and twenty-five jars of beer daily, certainly more than necessary to feed his household, leaving him extra to barter.[61]

All evidence suggests that being a priest was a desirable profession and occupation. As indicated by the hereditary passing of priestly titles, it was prestigious, and economic texts show that the priesthood paid well.

3

Inside the Temple

The World of the Gods

Temples were perhaps the most prominent features of the Egyptian landscape. Even today when people visit Egypt it is usually the temples – Karnak
and Luxor, Medinet Habu and the Ramesseum – that make the greatest
impression on the visitors. Thousands of years after they were built, these
structures still have the power and grandeur to astound the viewer.

The temples are enormous. The Temple of Amun at Karnak (see Plan 1)
is a complex of stone buildings that sprawls over 100 hectares of the town
of Luxor. The Hypostyle Hall is a veritable forest of ten-meter-wide sandstone columns that soar twenty-three meters into the air, like great reeds
in a primordial swamp. Pylon after pylon demark different sections of the
temple. The visitor is surrounded by innumerable scenes of the deities and
the king – everywhere one looks, the gods are present (Fig. 16). Today,
most of the walls are a soothing near monochrome of gray and tan, punctuated by a doorjamb or statue of red granite or a shrine of alabaster. Apart
from the visitors who are craning their necks to look upward following the
prompts of their guide, or are looking downward into their guidebooks, the
only sign of life is the scuttle of a beetle or a tiny gecko across the path, or
the stirring of the waters in the sacred lake.

The thousands of years have not stripped the temples of their grandeur,
but the structures have lost much of their humanity and color. Missing are
signs of activity. In ancient days, the temples were places of humans in

Figure 16. Wall at Karnak covered with scenes of King Ramesses II making offerings to various deities. To step into the temple was to enter the realm of the gods. Dynasty 19. Photo: Emily Teeter.

motion. Hundreds of priests passed through the halls, and porters carried heaps of offerings – incense, sacks of grain, bolts of cloth, and other objects needed for temple rituals. Groups of priests gathered to wash and prepare for duty. Doorkeepers lolled near their posts. The temples were always in a state of architectural flux, and so there would have been teams of workmen hauling blocks and the sound of workmen's chisels against the stone.

The smells of the ancient temples are also lost. Today, the temples are clean and sterile, but in ancient days, they would have been fragrant, and at times pungent. The odor of incense would have filled the air. But other smells were prevalent as well. One would have been aware of the cows that were kept nearby for sacrifice to the god, and of the hundreds of birds kept in the pens on the south side of the sacred lake. The Egyptians were never very good trash managers, and the houses of the priests within the Karnak Temple walls would have added their own scent to the atmosphere.

Light is also missing from the temples today. The light levels within the temples were carefully and dramatically controlled. Brightly lit open courtyards alternated with dim spaces. The Hypostyle Hall at Karnak was originally dim, but its great sandstone roofing slabs have collapsed, leaving it brightly illuminated. The original darkness of the space would have been broken by shafts of light from the grilled stone clerestory windows. These were positioned along the center of the hall, at the transition between the taller columns of the central row and the field of shorter columns that filled the rest of the hall. As one approached the sanctuary, the most sacred part of the temple, the light levels diminished. This is particularly noticeable in the Greco-Roman temples of Dendera and Edfu. There, the sanctuary is in almost total darkness; the only sources of light are small square window shafts, carefully positioned to allow slivers of sun into the ambulatory and chapels (Fig. 17).

The temples have also lost much of their color, for the carved scenes on the walls were once brightly painted with white, red, green, blue, and yellow pigments. Brightly colored pennants flapped from the top of the cedar masts that stood against the pylon faces (Plate IV). The temples, with all their exterior color, were surrounded and shrouded by tall, plaster-covered mud-brick walls. This somber outer face would have been a striking contrast to the brightly painted pylons visible on entering the temple grounds, a vivid reminder that one had entered another, very sacred, realm.

The Care and Feeding of the God

The temples were the dramatic settings for the performance of the rituals essential for the maintenance of the cosmos and that formed the main dialogue between the realms of humans and god. Most of these rituals took the form of offerings from the king to the gods and were meant to assure the dieties that the king was a just ruler who kept the forces of chaos at bay. The most important of these rituals was the daily offering service that was believed to satisfy the deity's, or in some cases, the deified king's, need for nourishment.

The most sacred part of the temple was the sanctuary, the "holy of holies" (djesr djesru) that was literally the bedroom of the god (Plate V). In that chamber stood a shrine (naos) that sheltered the statue of the resident god. Smaller temples dedicated to one god would have a single resident statue. But large temples, such as Karnak, were complexes of multiple shrines dedicated to Amun, Mut, Khonsu, Montu, and Ptah, each of whom was represented by a statue in its own sanctuary. Texts record that some temples on the Nile's west bank – such as Medinet Habu, dedicated to

Figure 17. The corridor surrounding the sanctuary at the Edfu Temple, with its carefully controlled lighting. Greco-Roman Period. Photo: Emily Teeter.

Ramesses III – had multiple statues in their sanctuaries. The naos was, through its construction and decoration, a focus of the temple.

Ironically, considering the number of statues that once inhabited the many temples, it is debated whether any has actually survived. However, we know something about their appearance from texts and representations. The cult statues from the great temples were made of a combination of precious materials. One of the earliest texts describing a divine statue appears on a stela of Ikher nofert dating to the later Middle Kingdom.[1] In that text, the statue of Osiris was described as being of gold, silver, lapis lazuli, amethyst, *sesnedjm*-wood, and true cedar.[2] The Restoration Inscription of Tutankhamun (c. 1335 BC) relates that the king "fashioned his [Amun's] holy image of electrum, lapis lazuli, turquoise and every precious stone." A statue of Ramesses VI is described as being "of good *nib*-wood and persea-wood, the torso colored and all of its limbs of faience like real red jasper, and his kilt of hammered [?] yellow gold; its crown of lapis lazuli, adorned with serpents of every color; the uraeus of his head of six-fold alloy inlaid with real stones; its sandals of six-fold alloy; its right arm bearing the *mekes*-symbol ... his left arm furnished with a scepter."[3] The use of gold, silver, and lapis lazuli is explained by other texts that describe the gods as having "bones of silver"; skin of gold; and eyelids and brows of true lapis lazuli. The emphasis on these materials was a testament to their value and scarcity. Although there were plentiful supplies of gold in the Nile Valley, silver was rare, and lapis even more so, as it had to be imported from Afghanistan. One statue that matches this general description represents Horus seated on a throne (Plate VI). It is forty-two centimeters tall, cast of solid silver (the god's bones), and overlaid with gold "skin." It has startling lifelike rock crystal eyes.

The statues were of various sizes, as suggested by variations in the interior dimensions of the naoi that enclosed the statues in the sanctuary. The wooden doors for a shrine of Thutmose III and Hatshepsut are 75 centimeters tall, indicating that the shrine contained a statue of considerable height. The interior of a naos of Shabako (Dynasty 25) is even more spacious (92 cm), and another, dedicated by Nectanebo (Dynasty 30), whose interior space is 1.43 meters high, would have accommodated a statue a meter or more tall.[4] Although most of the surviving naoi are somber stone enclosures, one is described as having a ceiling and walls of gold, a floor of "pure silver," door leaves of hammered copper, and "figured images in fine gold."[5] In the autobiographic text of Peftuaneith (Dynasty 26), the naos at Abydos is described as "one block of granite, [with] the august shrine of electrum, ornaments, divine amulets, [and] all sacred objects were of gold and silver, and all precious stones."[6]

How did the ancient Egyptians view the divine statues? Did they believe that the statues were representations of the gods or their actual manifestations? Texts that refer to their production indicate that the statues were considered to be just that, statues (*bes* or *sekhem*), rather than the actual god (*netcher*). The statue functioned as a transient receptacle for the presence or essence (*ba*) of the god. The *ba* was a powerful force that was always potentially present in nature. The divine statue was provided as a physical form (*ka*) in which the *ba* could reside so that human beings could communicate with it. The divine *ba* was omnipresent in the cosmos. Letters from the Ramesside Period call on "gods and any god by whom I pass to give you a long lifetime"; there are references from the same period to individuals' feeling the *ba* (or *bau*) of the god on them (see Chapter 6). The constant presence of the god's *ba* is also made evident by the multiplicity of places in which the *ba* of a single god could simultaneously be manifest. For example, each village and town had multiple shrines or temples to the god Amun, and Amun was thought to be present in each. The many hundreds of statues of different aspects of the goddess Sekhmet created for the royal temple of Amunhotep III at Thebes, all of which are thought to have been erected in the same temple, are another indication of how omnipresent the *ba* of the deity was – it enlivened each of these statues. Looking at these examples, one might equate the *ba* power of the god to a free-flowing emanation that could be summoned through, and for, cult rituals.

Because of their literal mindedness, the Egyptians described the *ba* power of a god not in abstract terms, such as energy, but concretely, as a golden falcon that had the power to travel from image to image, awakening each with the divine being. The *ba* of the god dwelled in heaven, for there are references to the *ba* that "came from heaven [to see] its monuments"[7] and the *ba* of the god "descending upon" cult statues.[8] Other texts give an even more physical description of the *ba*. The Bentresh Stela (Ramesside Period) refers to it as emerging from a shrine as a "falcon of gold,"[9] and a text at Dendera refers to the *ba* of Osiris as "flying out of the heavens like a hawk with glittering plumage. He soars like a falcon to his [shrine] at Dendera. He beholds his sanctuary. Then he sees his secret aspect [the cult statue] and installs himself upon his image [*sekhem*]."[10]

Once filled with and enlivened by the *ba* of the god, the cult statue became the *ka*, or physical form of the god. The Memphite Theology (Dynasty 25, but based on an earlier text) relates that after Ptah created the gods, he placed them in their shrines, and "the god [i.e., the *ba* power] entered into their bodies [i.e., the cult statue] [made of] every kind of wood, every kind of stone, having united the gods with their *kas*." This concept is even more explicit in texts at Edfu: "The god rests in his shrine after his *ba* has united with the image of his *ka*."[11] At Dendera, the entire reason for building the temple is explained as follows: "The king built the temple so that he [the god] might alight on his statue in the chapel ... so that when the *ba* of 'He-who-Shines-as Gold' has seen them [the cult statues] he may alight upon them."[12] The statues were treated with great reverence. A text on a stela from Thutmose I states that the statue "is less accessible than that which is in heaven, more secret than the affairs of the underworld, more hidden then the inhabitants of the primeval ocean."[13]

Because the gods were modeled on humans, they had a physical need for nourishment and a desire for adornment. These requirements were met by elaborate offering rituals. Texts indicate that it was the *ka* of the god that needed actual food and drink. For example, an inscription of Ramesses III relates that the food provisions of the temple were intended to "fill the storehouse of your temple with many things, and to double your offerings in order to offer to your *ka*,"[14] and a later text at Edfu contains the dedication "delivering a noble offering to his august father [the god], feeding his *ka* with millions of things."[15]

Did the Egyptians believe that the *ba* of the god was always present in the cult statues, or were human cult activities necessary to call the god to the image? This question is fraught with circular reasoning, for how could one tell if the *ba* of the god was present unless a priest was there to serve it? Certainly, in other contemporary ancient cultures, such as that of Anatolia, rituals such as the offering of thread and oil were enacted to draw the deity to the statue, for without such a ritual, the statue was believed to be dead.[16] In contrast, there are no Egyptian rituals for attracting the *ba* to the cult statue.[17] The text of Ramesses III just quoted seems to indicate that the pious act of building the temple and providing the cult statue was enticement enough. The texts are somewhat unclear as to whether the *ba* of the god spent the night in the statue or whether it flew back up to heaven until dawn. A text from Edfu states that the god Horus "sleeps in Edfu daily," and that Re "sleeps in it [the Edfu nome] until dawn," suggesting that the god stayed in the statue. But other texts suggest that the god migrated: "His [Re's] two eyes are fixed upon his cult statue. His living *ba* comes from heaven and rests upon his cult statue every day,"[18] or, "May your [the deified Imhotep] *ba* swoop from heaven every day to your house [i.e., temple or statue]."[19] A sequence of the daily offering ritual [discussed in the next section] was entitled "awakening the god," rather than something more explicit such as "spell for calling the *ba* to the statue." This suggests that the *ba* may have stayed with the statue overnight.

However, the Egyptians believed that they could not take the presence of the god for granted. The Bentresh Stela (Ramesside Period) tells the

Figure 18. Scene from the daily offering ritual in the Second Hypostyle Hall of the Temple of Seti I at Abydos. The king, dressed as a priest, applies perfume to the forehead of the statue of Amun Re. Dynasty 19. Photo: Emily Teeter.

story of a foreign king who was loaned a statue of the god Khonsu that was capable of "expelling disease demons." He failed to return it, hoping to keep the powerful image for himself. But the homesick god flew away from the cult statue "as a falcon of gold" toward Egypt. The gods could also turn their backs on Egypt when humans disobeyed their commands.[20] This was thought to be the cause of bad luck on the battlefield.

The Daily Offering Ritual

The cult statue of the god was the focus of the daily offering ritual. We have a wealth of pictorial and textual information about this ritual. The eastern interior walls of the Hypostyle Hall at Karnak, the chapels of the Temple of Seti I at Abydos (Fig. 18), the sanctuary of the Temple of Horus at Edfu, and the southern part of the Luxor Temple are all covered with scenes showing the ritual, although the order in which they are to be read is sometimes unclear. A remarkable papyrus, Berlin 3055 (Dynasty 22), contains the complete liturgy for the daily offering service for Amun, and two others (Berlin 3014 and 3053) have a similar liturgy for Mut. We also have many detailed lists of food and other materials that were required for the ritual, as well as economic texts that detail where the goods for the rituals came from and record their transfer from one temple or government agency to another.

The daily offering ritual was performed in every functioning temple three times a day, in imitation of human meal times. Texts are very clear about the timing and intent of the rituals: "Three offerings are conducted for them [the statues] daily, at every rising of the sun over the mountains."[21] The offerings given to the god are specifically referred to as "meals."[22] The offering ritual is known from the Old Kingdom, from the Pyramid Texts and the economic records of Neferirkare at Abu Sir, and it continued to be the essential temple ritual throughout Egyptian history.

The ritual consisted of the physical maintenance of the god, followed by the presentation of food and drink. All ritual actions were made in the name of the king, and it is he who is shown in the temple reliefs, although in reality a priest acted in his stead. Each morning as the sun rose, the temple staff would assemble for duty. The daily ritual involved a variety of ranks of priests – *wabs*, lector priests, and God's Fathers are specifically mentioned. The Chief Priest would be specially purified in a section of the temple called the *per duat* or "the house of morning."[23] There, he washed his body with water, was purified with incense, and rinsed his mouth with natron. Texts record, "There was performed for him all ceremonies that are performed for the king," transforming him from a priest into a proper surrogate for the king. He then joined the other priests, who had also undergone purification. They gathered the materials needed for the ritual and proceeded to the temple's sanctuary. Before entering, they began a series of recitations that accompanied their preparations – the utterance for lighting the fire; the utterances for taking the incense, putting the brazier on the censer (?), and putting incense on the fire; and, finally, the "utterance for advancing to the holy place." The sense that the ritual was in theory performed by the king is evident in the Chief Priest's first ritual words: "It is the king who sends me."

Each step of the ritual was highly symbolic, referred to mythic events, and was accompanied by a set liturgy. To begin the ritual, the priest awakened the god who slept in the sealed shrine. Holding a candle, he entered the sanctuary, chanting, "Awake in peace! May your awakening be peaceful!" He broke the seals of the door bolts of the shrine, and drew back the bolts – an action that was equated with removing the fingers of Seth from the eye of Horus. The priest then "opened the sight of the god" as he swung open the doors of the shrine, and he "kissed the ground," prostrating himself before the god's shrine. Each ritual step was punctuated with a specific recitation and an offering of incense and adoration of the deity. In preparation for removing the god from his shrine, the priest scattered pure white sand on the floor of the sanctuary, symbolizing the mound of creation from which all life sprang. He then recited a liturgy for "Laying Hands Upon the God," and removed the statue from the shrine, placing it on the sand. After more purifications, the priest removed the deity's outer linen garment and jewelry and wiped away the unguents from the previous day's ritual. Once the statue was suitably cleansed, the priest offered the god lengths of red, white, and green cloth that symbolized the blood of Isis, the uraeus, and fertility. This was followed by the presention of green and black eye cosmetics. The god was adorned with bracelets, a broad collar, and anklets, and given the appropriate scepters and headdress. The statue was then wrapped in his "great garment," probably a linen wrapper such as those that were found with the divine statues in the tomb of Tutankhamun.[24]

Now fully awakened and ready for the day, the god was presented with flowers, food, and drink. Economic texts specify that the food offerings consisted of grain, vegetables, wine, and cuts of meat and fowl. When the god was considered to be done, an interval that is not specified in the texts, the food was taken away and the god was readied for sleep. After further purifications, the god was returned to his shrine, the doors closed and sealed. As a final ritual, the king performed the "Bringing of the Foot," in which he grasped a broomlike *bad*-plant and backed out of the sanctuary, sweeping his footprints from the room. This procedure not only left the sanctuary in good order, but, it was believed, also prevented evil from approaching the god, presumably by following the footprints of the priest-king.

A version of this ritual was repeated at midday and in the evening. The evidence for how elaborate these other two daily rituals were is inconclusive, but it is clear that the morning service was the most complete. The evening service may have been essentially food offerings, but the shrine was not opened, and the activity took place in the antechamber rather than directly before the god.

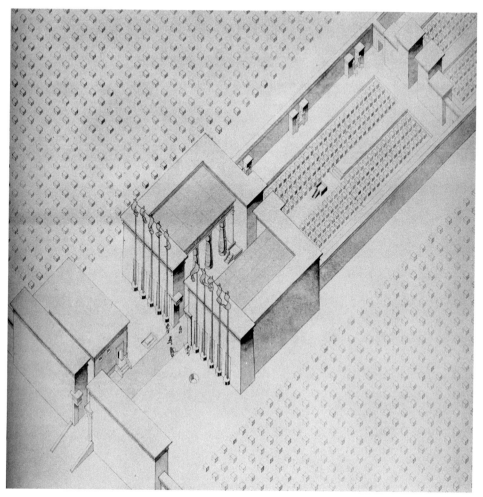

Figure 19. Temple to the Aten at the city of Akhetaten. Because the Aten was a noncorporeal sun god, his temples were open to the sky, allowing the sun's rays to pluck offerings off the hundreds of small altars in the courtyards. Dynasty 18. Courtesy of the Egypt Exploration Society.

The daily offering service was such a fundamental part of Egyptian religion that it continued during the Amarna Period, although in a slightly modified form (see Chapter 10). Because the Aten, the god of Akhenaten, had no corporeal form, there was no cult image to maintain. Since the Aten was the sun and its light, the ritual moved from the dark sanctuary of a god to the open courtyards of the Aten temples, which were filled with hundreds of offering tables on which food and flowers were placed to be "consumed" by the rays of the sun (Fig. 19). The ritual also became more public. The traditional images that showed the king performing the service alone were

Figure 20. Gods often left their sanctuaries during festivals and for other purposes. The statues of the deities are inside the veiled shrines on the boats. The gods can be identified by the texts and by the heads on the bow and stern. The upper boat is Khonsu's and the lower is Mut's, his mother. These vessels, joined by those of Amun and of the king, would process around and outside the temple. Medinet Habu. Dynasty 20. Photo: Emily Teeter.

replaced by scenes of the king and the queen, or even of larger groups that included their daughters, ladies-in-waiting, dwarves, and other court officials, laying food on the altars. During this period, flowers became a more prominent feature of the offerings, perhaps because the Aten was a more abstract deity, who, it was thought, was not able to actually consume food offerings.

The King's Offering Cult

The king had his own cult, which was functionally similar to that of the gods. In the New Kingdom, the king's cult was celebrated in the temples in western Thebes called "Mansions of Millions of Years." These temples had shrines to the gods, but they also had a false door or an altar where the king, and often the cult of the king's father, was celebrated. The wall reliefs in the second court of the Temple of Ramesses III at Medinet Habu (and elsewhere) show that a statue of the king joined the divine statue in processions and festivals (Fig. 20).

These offering cults for the king were celebrated during his lifetime and apparently were intended to continue long after his death. A few kings, including Thutmose III, Amenhotep III, Seti I, and Ramesses II, were worshipped during their lives. In an extraordinary scene from the Temple of Seti I at Abydos, Seti is shown making an offering to himself. The cults of some kings continued to be active long after the death of the celebrant, while others were short-lived. An official at the end of Dynasty 18 prayed that he "might smell the incense of the offerings when there is a gathering [?] in the temple of [Thutmose III]," who at that time had been dead for 150 years. The cult of Thutmose I was still active more than five hundred years after that king's death.[25] We do not know why some kings' cults were more popular and long-lived than others. Some apparently were discontinued shortly after the death of the king out of sheer disinterest. In the case of Thutmose III, the cult was probably abandoned in Dynasty 21 after rock falls from the nearby cliffs demolished his temple.

Knowledge of Temple Ritual

Was there a sense of mystery to the daily offering ritual? Did the people of the village have any understanding of (or concern about) what went on in the temple? Based on the later Greco-Roman traditions of mystery religions, it has been assumed that the temple rituals of the dynastic period were also shrouded in mystery and that the rituals were the exclusive domain of a small fraternity of priests. However, it appears that the Egyptian situation was quite different and that the general population had a good sense of what went on inside the temple. Texts indicate that the priests who assisted in the daily offering service were drawn from the ranks of *wabs*, lectors, and God's Fathers, all of whom, in some time periods, were part-time priests (see Chapter 2). They served "in their time," that is, for a month, and then reverted to their other occupation(s). Because these ranks of priests were drawn from the community, many men had firsthand experience with temple ritual. Scenes of the rituals enacted in the sanctuary were also used to decorate the interior walls of the temples. At Karnak, these occur on the east wall of the Hypostyle Hall. This area of the temple was accessible to ordinary people, as indicated by inscriptions on the architraves that say that it was a place of popular assembly where people could adore the king and the gods. One could guess that even people from the lower levels of society – the men who produced the goods needed for the ritual, the women who wove cloth offerings and garments for the god, and the porters who carried the many sacks of grain into the temple – had some idea of the purpose of their tasks.

The daily offering ritual provided the structure for the temple day and employed huge numbers of people. Along with the priests, who were engaged in the ritual and who received food from the "table of the god" as part of their wages were temple porters and craftsmen in the workshops where the heaps of incense were processed and the pottery jars and other ritual objects manufactured. The amount of food required for the ritual is simply astounding. Our most complete records come from Thebes. One text specifies that the daily requirement of grain for the small Temple of Ramesses III in the forecourt of the Karnak Temple was twenty sacks, which amounted to more than fifteen hundred liters. Another list at Karnak specifies a daily order for twenty-one sacks of grain, six fowl, two or three measures of wine, fourteen baskets of fruit, four (or more) baskets of incense, four measures of honey, two measures of fat, ten bunches and ten baskets of flowers, and one hundred bunches of vegetables.[26] We have many other similar lists, giving us a good idea of the impact of the offering cult on the overall economy.

In this context, the temple service can be seen as affecting a huge percentage of the population, for it took a vast and sophisticated infrastructure to provide the goods consumed in the temple rituals. The food was raised on land that belonged to the "domain" (economic holdings) of a specific god. The various gods' landholdings were documented in detail. These farmlands were often far away from the temple that ultimately received their grain or other goods. For example, the Temple of Amun at Karnak had huge landholdings in the north and south of Egypt. Ostracon Gardiner 86 purports to be an inventory of the staff of the northern estates of Amun. It records 8,760 farmers, each responsible for producing 200 sacks of barley; a number of cowherds, each in charge of 500 animals; 13,080 goatherds; 22,530 bird keepers, each in charge of 34,230 birds (pity the lowly official who supposedly had to count the birds!); 3,920 donkey drivers, each with 870 animals; 13,227 mule drivers, each with 551 mules; and an unspecified, but surely enormous, number of fishermen.[27] This was only one of the domains of Amun. Produce was then funneled to the Amun temples for the daily service. The resources of the temples were linked to each other. For example, the Ramesseum in western Thebes functioned as a great redistribution center, gathering the produce from throughout the Nile Valley and then distributing it to temple cults in the area. It has been estimated that the Ramesseum's granaries (see Fig. 15) could hold 226,328 sacks of grain, enough to support thirty-four hundred families for an entire year.[28] Today, we tend to view the temples in binary terms, funerary (i.e., the west bank "mortuary" temples), and "festival" (the east bank), when these in fact were linked economically through shared employees and by shared resources, for daily offerings were celebrated in both west bank and east bank temples.

What Happened to the Cult Statues?

What was the fate of the cult statues on which so much attention was lavished? Where have they all gone? They seem to have met a variety of fates. We know that some were carried off into captivity by foreign invaders. A text of Ptolemy II relates that he rescued statues: "Having gone off to the province of Asia and reached Palestine, he found numerous gods [i.e., statues] there. He returned them to Egypt." Likewise, the Canopus Decree of Ptolemy III refers to the recovery of cult statues that had been stolen by Persians: "The divine images that the doomed ones of Persia had removed from Egypt, his majesty ... rescued them. It was to Egypt that he returned them to their proper places in the temples from which they had previously been removed." His successor, Ptolemy IV, claimed:

> He [the king] took every care for the divine images which had been taken out of Egypt to the province of Syria and the province of Phoenicia in the time when the Medes [Persians] devastated the temples of Egypt. He commanded that they be searched for carefully. Those which were found, apart from those which his father had returned to Egypt, he had them returned to Egypt, while he celebrated a festival and offered sacrifices in their honor, and had them brought to the temples from which they had previously been taken.[29]

Although the Assyrians were famous for snatching statues from their enemies, there is little evidence that, even during Ashurbanipal's sack of Thebes in 663 BC, statues were specifically targeted. In his annals, Ashurbanipal refers to obelisks and "booty" but not specifically statues. In an earlier text, Esarhaddon, who advanced no further south than Memphis, claims to have taken "the spoil of Egypt and Ethiopia [Nubia]," but again, not specifically statues.[30]

Were the cult statues melted down by the Egyptians in order to recast them into newer cult statues? Although recycling metal statues was common among the Greeks and Romans, it is doubtful that this was a common practice in Egypt. The idea of casting a deity's body (or anyone's other than an enemy's) into a fire would have been terrifying to an Egyptian, for one of the great horrors of the Egyptian underworld was a consuming fire that left one without a bodily form. Perhaps a stronger argument against the Egyptians' melting down their own cult images is their well-documented practice of burying unneeded cult images. One example is the so-called Osiris Grave near the Eastern High Gate at Medinet Habu. When excavated in the 1920s, it was found to contain hundreds of bronze statues of the god Osiris. Though these were smaller statues deposited by individuals, they, like temple statues, were incarnations of Osiris and therefore had been buried, returning them to the god's underground realm. Other groups of buried statues are known from Thebes. One is the Karnak Cachette, an enormous cache of statues discovered in 1903 that was buried in the courtyard that separates the south side of the Hypostyle Hall from the Seventh Pylon (see Plan 1). The group consisted of more than seventeen thousand small statues and pieces of temple furnishings, and approximately seven hundred fifty larger stone statues of deities, kings, and individuals. The latest of these statues has been dated to the early Ptolemaic Period, suggesting that either Ptolemy III or Ptolemy IV was responsible for their burial. Another such find was made in 1989 in the Amunhotep III sun court of the Luxor Temple (Plan 2). That group consisted of twenty-six stone statues of deities and the king, some of them in an almost perfect state of preservation. Pottery found in the cache indicates that the material was buried in the fourth century AD.[31] None of the statues from the Karnak or Luxor cachettes match the surviving descriptions of the cult statues, but they do shed light on how the Egyptians dealt with sacred images. In the case of the Karnak and Luxor cachettes, the statues had apparently been fixtures of the temples. When they were deemed to be obsolete, or (perhaps in the case of the Karnak Cachette) when they simply became too numerous to be accommodated in the temple hallways, they were buried in the temple's precinct, rather than destroyed.

There is direct and sobering evidence that some of the last surviving cult statues met their end at the hands of the early Christians. Just as so many of the wall reliefs of temples were defaced by Christians who feared the potency of the images, so too were the temple statues often destroyed by them. A biographical text of Bishop Theophilos (AD 391–2) records,

> When the trouble [religious riots] had ceased, Theophilos and the eparch assisted each other in burning the altars; the idols they melted down into vessels for the needs of the church. This they arranged according to the emperor's wish. But one image, a statue, they left unmelted; for mockery they put it in an inappropriate place for their admonition.[32]

A sad end for a statue that must have received so much veneration during its cultic use.

The cult practices that were enacted inside the temple had an impact on society well beyond the temple grounds. A large percentage of the population socially far removed from the priests – farmers, fishermen, herdsmen, and potters and other craftsmen, including those who concocted incense, perfumes, and eye paint, or who wove cloth – all owed their livelihoods to the demands of the daily offering services. The cult actions reinforced the rhythms of the Egyptian universe, creating a comforting, predictable pattern. The rituals reinforced the status and authority of the king and created a network of economic supply and demand that tied the mortuary and festival temples together, creating an economic engine that assured Egypt's prosperity.

4

Festivals

Festivals structured the practice of ancient Egyptian religion and gave ordinary people a chance to be actively involved in cult celebrations. The most sacred cult functions enacted in temple sanctuaries (see Chapter 3) excluded common people and even the lower ranks of priests. By contrast, religious festivals allowed for broad and direct public participation. Egyptians celebrated hundreds of festivals, both local and national, at regular intervals; most were held once a year. Records at Karnak from the reign of Thutmose III indicate that 54 days of each 365-day year were dedicated to festivals. By the reign of Ramesses III, the number had increased to 60. Each of these festivals provided an opportunity for the public to see and honor the god. Commoners could participate by witnessing a sacred performance, by communing with the gods through prayer and oracles, or simply by singing, dancing, and feasting. For ordinary Egyptians, festivals were a time of sensory stimulation through sound, movement, scents, and the nervous anticipation of being in the company of the divine. Festivals were community affairs, a time for the residents of a village or town to abandon their daily tasks and come together in celebration. These periodic, regularly recurring events helped mark the passing of the seasons in the agricultural calendar. Their repeated commemoration was part of the rhythm of life, providing security through predictability. This was particularly true of the celebrations marking the renewal of the king (such as the Opet or the

Decade Festival), which symbolized the victory of order over chaos. Their important structural role was demonstrated and reinforced by the festivals' longevity. For example, festivals of Osiris were enacted for more than two thousand years, from at least the Middle Kingdom until the Roman era.

Festivals also served to bolster state control and promote royal ideology. Although in theory the king was the primary officiant for all festivals, in practice he was represented by a High Priest. The Opet and Sed (jubilee) festivals specifically commemorated the renewal of the king's power. Festivals also illustrated how little separation there was between the concepts of funerary and nonfunerary practices. For example, festivals of Osiris, the god of the afterlife, were celebrated in the Karnak Temple and recorded in detail at the Temple of Hathor at Dendera, structures that are not usually associated with mortuary cults.

Festivals presented logistical and economic challenges. They required huge amounts of bread, beer, wine, and precious incense, and the preparation for the larger festivals involved massive mobilizations of people and resources. If the king was to attend, the additional needs of the members of the royal court had to be met. This apparently meant that citizens could be subject to an unreasonable requisitioning of supplies. The Edict of Horemheb (Dynasty 18) expressly forbade the "agents of the queen's estate" from harassing "the local mayors, oppressing them and searching for the [supplies] for the trip downstream … each year during the [festival of Opet]." According to the decree, "The agents of the royal quarters would approach the mayors saying 'give the supplies which are lacking for the journey, for look, pharaoh is making the trip to the festival of Opet.'"[1]

Some festivals are known only from brief references in letters or graffiti. Others are recorded in considerable detail in texts and in representations on the walls of tombs and temples. For example, the walls of the second court of Medinet Habu are covered with scenes of the rituals of the festivals of Min and Sokar. Scenes of the annual Theban festival of Opet, when the gods and king traveled from Karnak to Luxor (Map 2), appear in the Temple of Ramesses III at Karnak, in the colonnade hall of the Luxor Temple, and on the upper terrace of the Temple of Hatshepsut at Deir el Bahri in western Thebes.

Private tomb scenes and personal texts provide a more individual perspective on festival participation. Autobiographical texts refer to individuals taking part in festivals, and duty rosters record when workers were required to work during a festival or were given time off to join the celebration. Yet, even with this amount of information, the records have a certain hollowness because we lack the more intangible aspects of festivals – the noise of peoples' shouts; the music; the aromas of roasting meat, incense, and perfumes; and the general atmosphere of excitement that we would recognize today. A text from the Temple of Horus at Edfu gives a vivid impression of the sensory aspects of festivals:

> There are all kinds of bread in loaves as numerous as grains of sand. Oxen abound like locusts. The smell of the roast fowl, gazelle, oryx and ibex reach the sky. Wine flows freely throughout the town like the Nile bursting forth from the Two Caverns [its supposed source]. Myrrh scattered on the brazier with incense can be smelled a mile away. The city is bestrewed with faience, glittering with natron and garlanded with flowers and fresh herbs. Its youths are drunk, its citizens glad, and its young maidens are beautiful to behold; rejoicing is all around it and festivity is in all its quarters. There is no sleep to be had there until dawn.[2]

These festivals were greatly anticipated events in the community calendar. They were times to see and adore the god and also opportunities to join the community in celebration, breaking the routine of the work week – but in an ordered, predictable, unthreatening way.

Festivals of Osiris

Osiris, the primary deity of the dead and the legendary first ruler of Egypt, was a god who symbolized eternal rebirth through the story of his own resurrection. His festival was celebrated in the fourth month of inundation, from the twelfth to the thirtieth day, when the Nile receded and crops began to sprout – a potent natural symbol of resurrection. The festival is known as Khoiak, after the name of the month in which it was celebrated. It is known from Middle Kingdom texts (the Ikhernofert stela and texts of King Neferhotep) and from a great number of private stelae and Middle Kingdom monuments from Abydos. Though we lack the overall "script" for the festival, because the earlier records refer only to isolated events, later records, including Roman-era texts from the walls of the rooftop chapels of the Temple of Hathor at Dendera (Fig. 21), provide a fuller account of the Khoiak festival.

Khoiak celebrated and reenacted the "mysteries of Osiris," a cycle of myths that recounted the god's death and resurrection. In this story, of which several versions exist, Osiris was murdered by his treacherous brother Seth. Seth dismembered Osiris and scattered the fourteen (some accounts

Figure 21. Relief in the chapel on the roof of the Temple of Hathor at Dendera recounting the "script" of the festival of Osiris in the month of Khoiak. Osiris is shown in his usual mummy form on a funerary bier. His sisters, Isis and Nephthys, respectively, stand at the head and foot of the bed. Greco-Roman Period. Photo: Emily Teeter.

say sixteen) parts of his body throughout Egypt. Isis, the wife of Osiris, traveled throughout the land gathering the parts of her husband which she bound together with linen wrappings (the prototype of a mummy). Once reassembled, the life force of Osiris enabled him to impregnate Isis (Fig. 22), who then gave birth to a son, Horus. This act became the archetype of life following death; Osiris's story became the basis of Egyptian mortuary beliefs.

Unlike the localized Opet or Decade festivals, which were celebrated only in Thebes, the Khoiak Festival was celebrated throughout the country. The broad geographic spread of the festivities commemorated the dispersal of the parts of Osiris's body across all parts of Egypt. However, the festival was not restricted to those sites originally linked to the myth; we know from Dendera texts that Khoiak was celebrated there, although Dendera was not one of the places mentioned in the original myth.

The festival had two major components, both of which provided opportunities for public participation. The first part of the festival was a dramatic

Figure 22. Osiris, on his funerary bier, impregnating his wife, Isis, who descends on him in the form of a kite. The postmortem conception was the symbol of eternal birth. Greco-Roman Period. Photo: Emily Teeter.

reenactment of the death and resurrection of Osiris and the defeat of his foes. This was performed before the public, much like a Christian passion play. At Abydos, where the festival is first recorded, it was enacted against the backdrop of the hundreds of tombs and shrines that lined the route to the tomb of King Djer of Dynasty 1, which was thought to be the actual burial place of Osiris. The religious drama followed a set script, laid down on a papyrus scroll that kings could cite to prove the authenticity of the festivals they held. King Neferhotep (Dynasty 13) claimed that he retrieved a papyrus from the library inscribed with "the writings of the Temple of Osiris – Foremost of the Westerners, Lord of Abydos," that gave instructions for the enactment.[3] The second aspect of the festival was the manufacture, procession, and ceremonial internment of Osiris figurines. New images of Osiris, his ennead (the eight gods associated with him), and the jackal god Wepwawet were made, and sacred boats, sledges, and shrines were constructed to convey the divine statues through the necropolis.

During the festival, the king was supposed to play the role of Horus, the faithful son who avenged the murder of Osiris. However, Middle Kingdom accounts indicate that the king appointed a surrogate to represent him during the festival, just as the First Priest of the god acted on behalf of the king in daily temple rituals (see Chapter 3). At Abydos, the priests claim to have played the role of deities, but we do not know whether they donned costumes or simply stood as representatives of the gods. Some parts of the ritual enactment took place in the temple to which the public had no access. Other parts took place where the gathered crowds could watch and participate.

The festival began with the arrival of the royal delegation. Within the dark confines of the Osiris Temple, a priest offered myrrh, wine, and other "divine products" to "Osiris, in all his identities." The official Ikhernofert claimed that within the temple the statue of Osiris was embellished with lapis, turquoise, gold, and "all precious stones" and was clothed with garments. The statue was then placed in a new naos of gold, silver, copper, sesnedjem-wood, and cedar. Construction of the naos and of the god's boat was overseen by Ikernofert himself.

These preliminary acts complete, the procession set out from the temple and made itself visible to the waiting throngs. It set out through the necropolis, led by the statue of Wepwawet (especially appropriate, because his name means "Opener of the Ways"), who acted as the protector of the god. Dramatic tension was fueled by a reenactment of the attack on Osiris by the company of Seth, which retold the story of Osiris's murder on "the sandbanks of Nedit." Several autobiographic texts refer to their authors' involvement with this part of the festival. One, on a stela of Rudjahau, states that Rudjahau acted as a "great rebel slayer."[4] One can imagine the screams and groans from the assembled onlookers as the two factions clashed and Osiris was slain. As in passion plays, this sequence always concluded with the triumph of good, as the priest representing Horus defeated Seth's company. In his speech of victory, he proclaimed: "I avenged Wennofer (Osiris) on that day of great fighting, and I felled all his enemies in the sandbanks of Nedit."

The victory of Horus was followed by a "great procession" simulating the sorrowful funeral of Osiris.[5] The body of the god, drawn in the elaborate neshmet barque, traveled toward his "tomb." In their autobiographical texts, Middle Kingdom authors recall "seeing the beauty of Osiris and Wepwawet in the great procession."[6]

Once at the tomb of Osiris, participants enacted the funeral rites and recited an invocation to Re – "Come down to me!" – to bring the life-giving forces of the sun back to the dead god. Several references to dancing suggest that some sort of ritual dance, perhaps to celebrate the victories of Horus and Thoth, was performed. Finally, the procession returned to the Osiris Temple, and the statue of the god was restored to its shrine.

The public participated in the festivals of Osiris through their observation of the procession presented during Khoiak but also in more personal and intimate ways, especially through the creation and manipulation of images of the mummiform god. These images were made of a variety of materials that alluded to different aspects of the god's cult and also reflected the affluence of the person who commissioned or used the statue. One type, generically called a corn mummy (Fig. 23), was usually about thirty centimeters long. They were most commonly made of soil (symbolizing the fertility of the land) mixed with grain and wrapped in linen. Some were outfitted with a green wax mask, and others wore the *atef* or white crown of Osiris. Some corn mummies were ithyphallic, referring to Osiris's ability to conceive a son after his own death. The earliest pictorial record of how corn mummies were made appears in the tomb of Neferhotep at Thebes, which dates to the end of Dynasty 18. At first glance, the scene looks like an embalming scene, but it is captioned by a corrupt version of Coffin Text Spell 1 that refers to "moistening the malt and spreading the [embalming] bed" and to a "formula for enchanting the bed." A further reference to the "fourth month of inundation" (the month of Khoiak) decisively links the manufacture of these corn mummies with the Khoiak rituals of Osiris.

Some of these figurines were made during the Khoiak Festival, kept for a year, and then ritually buried, whereas others became a part of an individual's funerary equipment. The texts in the rooftop chapels of the Temple of Dendera have specific instructions for the statues' manufacture, saying that on days twelve to twenty-one of the month, for example, figures of Khenty-Imentyu (a form of Osiris), Sokar (another funerary deity), and the "Divine Members" (*sepy-netcher*, a group of other gods) were to be made.[7] A woman who played the role of the goddess Shentayit (who was associated with Isis, the wife of Osiris) was instructed to "take a bushel basket and take a quart of seeds ... divide it into four parts. Soak [the seeds] in five pints of water from the sacred lake until the sixth hour arrives." This was mixed with sifted sand. The figure of Osiris was formed in a two-part mold of gold lined with cloth. Once filled, the mold was sheltered under reeds (also called a "garden") and watered daily, allowing the grain to germinate. Nine days later, the two halves of the figurine were removed from the mold, joined, and tied together with papyrus strips. There are variations on the instructions; one states that the

Figure 23. A corn mummy, a replica of the mummy of the god Osiris, made of sand and grain wrapped in linen. Corn mummies were made in conjunction with the annual festival of Osiris celebrated in the month of Khoiak. Late Period–Ptolemaic Period. Museum of Fine Arts, Boston, Hay Collection, Gift of C. Granville Way, 72.4829. Photograph © Museum of Fine Arts, Boston.

figure was to be left in the sun, which was thought to magically enliven the figure because of the symbolic association of the sun with renewed life. The following day, the figure was placed on a model boat, one of thirty-four that carried small images of the gods. After an outing on the sacred lake, the figurine was returned to the temple. The next day, it was wrapped in linen and placed in a miniature anthropoid coffin ornamented with a tripartite wig, divine beard, and scepters.[8] At the commencement of the next year's celebration, the year-old figurine was buried, and a new one was made.

Osiris figurines were put to a variety of uses. In recent years, excavators at Karnak have discovered small structures at the east side of the complex, dating from perhaps Dynasty 21 to the reign of Ptolemy IV, that were dedicated to the burial of Osiris figurines. The main structure, a rectangular building

Figure 24. The Osiris catacombs at East Karnak consist of a series of small niches that were intended to receive figurines of Osiris. Ptolemaic Period. Photo: Emily Teeter.

dating to the reign of Ptolemy IV, contains three hallways, each lined with small plastered niches stacked on top of one another to form a miniature columbarium (Fig. 24).[9] At the time of excavation, some of the niches still contained plastered mummiform figures made of sand and wrapped in linen, wearing the tall crown of Osiris. One well-preserved example was found placed on a bed of sand accompanied by tiny replicas of canopic jars (containers in which the embalmed viscera was stored). Texts from other sources indicate that this group of structures was thought to be "the tomb of Osiris." The archaeological remains suggest that this was a place where, over five hundred years, individuals deposited figurines of Osiris. The impressive number of niches in the Ptolemaic structure indicate that this was not the repository for the single figurine made annually mentioned in the Dendera texts. It seems likely that this was a more widespread cult, available to a larger group of participants. The location of the Karnak Osiris tomb – outside the temple proper and near the Chapel of the Hearing Ear (Plan 1, and see Chapter 5) – supports the suggestion that this was a place of more popular appeal, where members of the community could come during the festival of Khoiak to deposit images of the god, seeking renewal of their own lives through the promise of Osiris's rebirth.

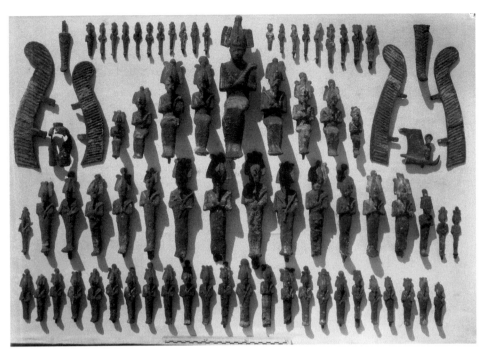

Figure 25. Bronze Osiris figurines deposited in the "Osiris Grave" at Medinet Habu as part of a cult honoring the god. Third Intermediate Period. Courtesy of the Oriental Institute of the University of Chicago.

This symbolic burial of Osiris figurines is also documented in western Thebes at Medinet Habu. Near the Eastern High Gate was a pit that the excavator dubbed the "Osiris Grave." Hundreds of bronze figurines of Osiris were left in this pit, presumably by worshippers. The figurines are small (Fig. 25), and many of them are near duplicates of one another, suggesting that they were being made in quantities at or near the site and sold to pilgrims. The pit probably represented the subterranean realm of Osiris. As a part of their devotions, individuals would purchase a small bronze and deposit it into the pit, symbolically returning Osiris to his realm and thereby accruing favor with the god.

In the Greco-Roman Period, the burial of Osiris figurines became more elaborate. Some statuettes were placed in wooden coffins with a falcon head, a reference to the deities Sokar or Horus, both of whom were associated with Osiris.[10] By contrast, other examples recovered from the Wadi Qubbanet el-Qirud (Valley of the Monkeys) in western Thebes, and dated to the Late or Ptolemaic periods, had no coffins. They were simply buried in shallow graves in the valley floor, perhaps because the water that periodically

Figure 26. Brick representing the sarcophagus of the god Osiris. The recess, in the form of the figure of Osiris, would have been filled with soil and grain. Third Intermediate–Late Period. Hildesheim, Pelizaeus-Museum 4550. Photo © Roemer-Pelizaeus-Museum, Hildesheim.

flowed along the wadi would moisten the figurines and cause the grain in them to germinate, symbolizing the renewal of life.[11]

Pottery bricks with the silhouette of Osiris carved in a recess on one side were another type of Osiris figurine that may have been used in festivals (Fig. 26).[12] The recess in the brick was filled with soil and grain. Although they look like molds, the bricks themselves were finished products, probably intended to represent the coffin of the god. Osiris bricks and corn mummies were roughly contemporary (Third Intermediate and Late periods),[13] and like some corn mummies, bricks were sometimes deposited in the desert to be watered by periodic floodwaters.

The festivals honoring Osiris allowed individuals to publicly and personally participate in the cult of the god. In the annual Khoiak Festival, they witnessed the dramatic reenactment of the murder of Osiris and his burial, allowing them to share a communal outpouring of grief. The production of figurines of Osiris was another way in which individuals could personally be involved in the symbolic rebirth of the god.

Feast of the Valley

The "Beautiful Feast of the Valley" was celebrated only in Thebes (Map 2). Like Osiris's festivals, the Feast of the Valley was closely associated with funerary beliefs. Egyptians believed that the cliffs on the west bank of the Nile housed vast underworld realms, populated by the deceased and protected by Hathor, the guardian goddess of the necropolis. Scenes in Theban tombs show the goddess in her cow form, emerging from the hills (Plate VII), reinforcing the Egyptian belief that the spirits of the dead remained physically close to the realm of the living.

The Feast of the Valley was observed once a year, on the first day of the second month of summer in conjunction with the appearance of the new moon. It lasted for two days. The first record of the feast dates to Dynasty 11. The festival was most popular in the New Kingdom, the Ramesside Period, and Dynasties 25–26, but there are references to the festival as late as 117 BC during the reign of Ptolemy VIII. By that time, however, the festival had likely changed character, taking on more Osirian overtones.[14] Today's Hispanic Day of the Dead celebration has strong similarities to the Feast of the Valley; both mark festive meetings between the living and the dead designed to blur the boundaries between life and the afterlife. The meeting of the living and dead also reflected the Egyptians' ingrained sense that time was cyclic and brought with it life, death, and rebirth in an unending repetition. Both Muslims and Christians in Egypt still visit the tombs of their ancestors to eat and distribute ceremonial foods; it is very likely that the Feast of the Valley was the distant ancestor of these surviving cultural practices.

The focus of the festival was the parade of statues portraying the gods and deceased royalty (Plate VIII). The festival began on the east bank of the Nile at the Karnak Temple where, after purification ceremonies, the statue of Amun was removed from its dark sanctuary, placed in its portable shrine, and loaded onto a ceremonial boat. Priests carried the god from the temple to the Nile, where it was placed aboard an elaborate barge called Userhat ("Powerful of Prow"), whose topsides were covered with gold and ornamented with scenes of the king before the gods. The procession, led by the king, was accompanied by throngs of priests who carried the great fans signifying the presence of the deity and by huge crowds of locals. The passage from east to west symbolized the transition from life to the land of the dead.

The composition of the divine procession changed over time. In the Eighteenth Dynasty, it consisted of a single divine image of the god Amun. But by the Nineteenth Dynasty, as shown in tomb paintings, Amun was joined by Mut, Khonsu, and statues of dead kings and queens.

Graffiti note that priests watched for the procession from the heights of the west bank. It must have been an exciting and prestigious duty, for some of the priests recorded that they stood lookout for several years in a row.

Once the flotilla was spotted, mobs of people who lived on the west bank joined the crowd that had followed the procession from the east. Everyone was dressed in his or her finest white linen clothing, clutching flowers and food offerings as they greeted the "divine arrival"[15] as it moored on the west bank.

According to scenes in Theban tombs, some of the statues were unloaded from the boats and dragged across the sand on sledges. This grand procession, trailed by entire families, set off from the Nile and traveled by road and canal through the cultivated lands to the great western necropolis in order that Amun might visit the temples of the deceased kings. People crowded around the pageant clamoring for a view of the gods. One can imagine the roadways and canals of the west bank lined with people laden with bouquets of flowers and baskets of offerings, and crying out in honor of the gods.

The clearest explanation of the procession's function comes from an inscription on a stela from the Temple of Amunhotep III at Kom el Hetan. The inscription states that the temple was considered to be a "resting palace of the Lord of the Gods at his Festival in the Valley in Amun's procession to the West to visit the gods of the West when he will reward his majesty with life and dominion."[16] Other texts confirm that during the festival, the god Amun visited ("rested") in the temple of the current king, and that the temple was a place of "receiving Amun (and) extolling his beauty." As a result of the divine visit, the spirit of the king was revived and "reward(ed) with life and dominion." All the great temples on the west bank – the Ramesseum, Medinet Habu, Deir el Bahri, and the others (Map 2) – shared the duty of receiving Amun when he traveled to the West, for during this commemoration, the union of the god and king ensured the king's eternal existence.

In the Ramesside Period, the procession visited the memorial temples of the ruling king and his predecessors. Evidence for each temple's incorporation into the festival is often subtle; brief texts in temples may not even explicitly mention the feast by name. For example, reliefs on a false door of Seti I in his temple at Gourna show the king offering great bouquets of flowers to the sacred boats. The divine boats and the act of offering large floral bouquets to them are hallmarks of the festival. Scenes in the second court of Medinet Habu (Ramesses III) show a similar composition. Brief texts on the architraves of the Temple of Ramesses II (the Ramesseum) are more explicit, indicating that this temple too was a stop on the processional route, for it is called a "resting place of the Lord of the Gods [Amun] in his Beautiful Festival of the Valley."[17] Each of these temples had a small version

Figure 27. View of the three temples at Deir el Bahri. *From bottom left*, Mentuhotep II (Dynasty 11), Thutmose III, and Hatshepsut (both Dynasty 18). The cliff separated the temples from the royal burials in the Valley of the Kings. Photo: Emily Teeter.

of a palace on its south side. As indicated by the inscription on the stele of Amunhotep III, the soul of the king was thought to be revived by the presence of Amun. The architectural plans of the temples, best preserved at Medinet Habu (Plan 3), positioned the "palace" along the route of the procession, allowing the spirit of the king, enthroned in his palace, to encounter the reviving presence of the god.

During the first day of the festival, the procession wound its way through the necropolis. The musicians and onlookers made – intentionally – a lot of noise, for according to the texts, those buried in the western necropolis harkened to the sound of the procession. The clamor enlivened them and caused them to emerge from their tombs to see Amun and to meet with their families.

By late day, the procession headed toward Deir el Bahri, a bay in the cliffs of the western plateau (Map 2; Fig. 27). These cliffs, in which Hathor dwelled, were equated with the hidden *duat*, or realm of the dead. In the Middle Kingdom, the procession spent the night in, or near, the Temple of Mentuhotep Nebhepetre – the only structure at Deir el Bahri at that time. A graffito of the priest Neferibed (Dynasty 12) records, "Praising Amun and kissing the earth before the Lord of the Gods in his summer festival when he crosses over to the valley of Nebhepetre."[18] Although the temple is very poorly preserved, the remains of the floor plan and pillars indicate that the interior space was quite restricted. Either the sacred boat of Amun used during the Middle Kingdom was smaller than later iterations, or the boat did not actually enter the temple sanctuary.

During the night, Amun in his ithyphallic form was thought to spend the night with Hathor, their union evoking re-creation and rejuvenation. By the middle of the Eighteenth Dynasty, temples built by Hatshepsut and Thutmose III were added north of the earlier structure of Nebhepetre, making a dramatic setting for the reception of the divine procession (see Fig. 27). The three-room suite area for Amun in the Hatshepsut Temple was embellished with four monumental statues of the queen – garbed as Osiris – to guard the visiting god.[19] The sexual union of Amun and Hathor that symbolically took place that night symbolized renewal, and as a result, the shrine at Deir el Bahri became a place of pilgrimage for those seeking cures or fertility charms. The "basketsful" of wood votive phalluses and clay figurines of women and Hathor recovered from the site were left there by individuals who wished to take advantage of the fertility created by the divine union.[20]

For the public, the Feast of the Valley promised the rebirth of their deceased relatives and the same happy future for themselves. A text in the tomb of Neferhotep (Dynasty 18) implores, "May you give me a place in the necropolis so that I may see Amun when he visits [the temple of Thutmose III]."[21] Another asks, "May the revered one [i.e., the deceased] be refreshed on this day! May what the funerary prayers call for be given to him!"

During the festival, priests could participate by carrying the divine boat or walking alongside it, holding the broad fans that announced the divine presence. A much larger number of ordinary people took part as well, by observing the procession and enacting rituals at the family tombs. For them, the most important aspect of the Feast of the Valley was the sensual communion between the living and the dead that took place at the tombs. Throughout the first day and evening of the festival, the living visited, and were visited by, their deceased relatives. This part of the festival is recorded pictorially in many Theban tombs.

Also on the first day of the festival, members of the community, still dressed in their finest white linen, draped with broad *weseh* collars made of fragrant flowers (Plate IX), followed the divine procession through the necropolis, and then went to the tombs of their ancestors, which were called "the houses of joy of the heart." The souls of the dead had been summoned by the joyous noise of the procession and by Amun's presence. In physical terms, the deceased were represented by statues that could be removed from the tomb and placed among the living celebrants. The union of the living and dead was thus both physical – through the three-dimensional representation of the dead family member – and also mystical and intellectual, a meeting achieved through heightened stimulation of all the senses. The properties of smell, sound, and taste were thought to be capable of transcending the barrier between life and death to reach the deceased and bring him or her into the celebration. These senses were further stimulated by copious amounts of beer and wine, which created an ecstatic state and brought the living closer to the dead. The revelers called on Hathor, addressing her as the "Lady of Drunkenness." The families encouraged each other: "For your *ka*! Drink the intoxicating drink! Celebrate a beautiful day ... may your heart be refreshed in your house [i.e., tomb]."[22]

The necropolis was filled with activity, noise, smells, and music. Fueled by alcohol and the excitement of the festival, the living recited hymns to their ancestors' statues to encourage the spirits of the deceased to enliven them: "Emerge from the earth! Behold Ra and follow Amun in his beautiful Feast of the Valley!" The spirits were encouraged to join the procession: "May you be in the crew of the royal boat and may you hear the clamor in the temples in western Thebes. May you see Amun in the Beautiful Feast of the Valley and follow him to the temple precincts."[23]

Bands of musicians circulated through the necropolis visiting individual tombs. Women shook beaded necklaces (*menat*) and clanged their metallic rattles (sistra) (see Plate III) both instruments sacred to Hathor, while male musicians clapped and sang, creating a hypnotic rhythm that reverberated among the tombs. Their refrains continued into the night, celebrating Amun's presence at Deir el Bahri: "Praises are in heaven, jubilation is in the Great House and celebrations are on earth because Amun in his Userhat boat is at Djeser-akhet [the temple of Hatshepsut]! His heart is joyful, heaven and earth are happy."[24]

The odor of food filled the necropolis. The dead were presented with fragrant roasted birds and meat. Sweet myrrh oil was poured on the meats, making the scents even more alluring. The chants continued: "May your voice be true ... and [may you] enter the earth among the august spirits who are before Osiris. May you eat the offerings and participate in the repast like the gods of the netherworld. May you be called into the presence of Wennefer [a form of Osiris] like those who follow Horus, unhindered like one of them. May your name endure."[25] This song, sung by the living, referred to essential aspects of funerary ritual, that is, justification before Osiris and the divine tribunal (being "true of voice") and the recollection of the deceased by the living that assured the former's immortality.

Another source of sensory stimulation was the enormous, fragrant bouquet of flowers, called an *ankh* (a pun on the word *ankh* that also means "life"), that each family presented to its deceased ancestors (Plate X). The flowers symbolized freshness, rejuvenation, and rebirth, as indicated by a text in the tomb of Rekhmire (Dynasty 18): "Take scented flowers which I have brought you from the best of the plants which are in the garden. Behold! The servants carry produce, shoots and fragrant stems of all kinds that you may be satisfied ... and that your heart may partake of its tender growth, and that you may do whatever your spirit desires for ever and ever."[26]

All these rituals were enacted to produce an ecstatic union of the dead and the living – to bring the living into the realm of the dead and the dead back to the living. This reminded people of the closeness of death and also of the unending cycle of rebirth. The sanctity of the dead as a true transfigured spirit (*akh*) was proclaimed, and his or her eternal life associated with the undying cycle of the god Re was affirmed. This is summed up in a text in the tomb of the official Puimre that implores the deceased to

> receive the ornaments of the Lady of Heaven [Hathor], Lady of Drunkenness ... They open the road in heaven for you. They throw open the doors of the *duat* so that you may go forth, you appearing as a god, becoming a perfect *akh* in heaven and taking shape in the *duat*. Your sins are expelled by Re. You are raised high by Osiris.[27]

Several tombs show an additional ritual, in which the statue of the deceased was placed on a boat in a pool somewhere near the tomb. Some scenes show the pool surrounded by a lush garden and ringed with date trees. In one scene, as the son offered incense to his deceased father, the boat was towed around the pool, perhaps symbolizing the renewed mobility of the deceased.

The desire to participate eternally in the Feast of the Valley motivated the Theban elite of Dynasties 25–26 to build their tombs along the path of the procession leading to Deir el Bahri. Up to that time, few tombs had been built on top of the three east–west causeways that led to the temples at Deir el Bahri (Map 2; Fig. 27); the necropolis administration probably prohibited development in this area because of its important cultic function. In the Late Period, earlier tombs in the cliffs to the north of the causeways, with their panoramic views of the processional route, were usurped and refurbished. On the plain to the south, the elite built enormous tombs whose entrance pylons were oriented north to the causeway, giving the tomb owner an unhindered view of the procession of Amun. Thus, the soul of the tomb owner, when summoned by the noise and invocations of the festival, could leave its tomb and join with the gods in eternal rebirth.

The Festival of Amunhotep I

Not all Egyptian festivals were celebrations of joy and rebirth. The festival of Amunhotep I, celebrated by the residents of Deir el Medina on the Theban west bank, commemorated the death of King Amunhotep I. It was a somber occasion, akin to the Shiite Muslim commemoration in the month of Muharram of the death of Imam Hussein.

Amunhotep I, the second king of Dynasty 18 (ca. 1526–1505 BC), was especially revered by the workmen of Deir el Medina. He had instituted the state-supported organization of those workmen who, under his successor, Thutmose I, settled in the village in western Thebes. The festival of Amunhotep I is attested from the reign of Amunhotep III (ca. 1350 BC), and it continued to as late as Dynasty 25. The festival started on the accession day of Thutmose I – the day his father, Amunhotep, died. The festival lasted for four days, with each day dedicated to a different activity. Although the festival focused on the workmen and on their association with Amunhotep, the texts clearly indicate that the men's wives and children also took part.

On the first day of the festival, Amunhotep's statue was brought out of its shrine on the west bank to "greet" the public. The next day was devoted to a feast in the necropolis. This was followed by a "feast of meditation" as the residents of the village reflected on the deified king and his death. The last day was for the "appearing" of the king; it was probably on this day that the statue was transported to the Valley of the Kings. Scenes of the procession show the statue being carried or dragged over the sand on a sledge pulled by four pairs of men; one of these men wears a leopard-head ornament on his cloak. Two other priests, holding the large feather fans that indicated the divinity of the image, stand beside the statue. Other scenes show a larger procession made up of twelve men.

The deified Amunhotep had a variety of forms. A wig with either a ribbon or a blue crown adorned the one celebrated in this festival, known simply as "Amunhotep of the Village."[28] Some images of the king portray him with a black face, evoking the underworld realm in which he dwelled.

As the procession passed the onlookers, they struck their faces with their hands and wept, intoning: "They make mourning for you oh, Amunhotep the one for whom it is blessed to weep!"[29] Texts from Deir el Medina indicate that this was an official holiday for the workers, and they were issued special rations of cream and fat. As with the Feast of the Valley, copious amounts of beer and wine were consumed over the four days of the festival.[30]

An important part of the festival was the consultation of the oracle of the deceased king (see Chapter 6). The close association of the villagers of Deir el Medina with Amunhotep made the deified king a trusted mediator of local disputes. In the community, the deceased king was referred to as "the vizier who looks into hearts, whose abomination is falsehood."[31] The oracle of Amunhotep took the form of a statue of the king, and so – unlike most other oracles housed in shrouded shrines – Amunhotep's oracle was especially approachable.

The royal statue as oracle was used to determine administrative issues, such as the appointment of officials. In such a small community, the oracle may have been perceived as an impartial way of making such decisions. In one case, the oracle was asked to select the new inspector of divine offerings. It picked the son of a former inspector, thereby forestalling any charges of nepotism.[32] The oracle of Amunhotep was frequently consulted about the ownership of land and tombs. In one example, a workman named Kenna claimed an abandoned tomb and renovated it. His claim was disputed by a man named Mery-Sekhmet (who occurs in other texts in an unflattering light), who stated that "the god … told me to share it with you [Kenna]." Kenna chose to bring the dispute before the oracle of Amunhotep through the intermediary of the necropolis scribe. In front of a large group of witnesses, the god declared, "Give the chapel back to Kenna, its owner!" In a similar case, the divine oracle was called on to decide the legality of an issue as practical as granting an easement.[33]

Amunhotep and his mother, Ahmose Nofertari, were also the focus of a popular cult on the west bank at Thebes. A small chapel near Deir el Medina was dedicated to their memory. It became a popular place of pilgrimage in the reign of Ramesses II,[34] and images of the son and his mother were recipients of votive offerings.

Festivals were an important part of Egyptian life and religion. They afforded people the opportunity for personal involvement in religious life through feasting and communicating with the gods and with deceased ancestors. On a community level, the celebrations provided socially appropriate and sanctioned ways of showing emotion – from the ecstatic meeting of the living and the dead to public drunkenness, dancing, and singing. The involvement of the entire community also created social solidarity through participation in a communal experience that validated shared religious beliefs and cultural traditions.

5

Contacting the Gods

The Egyptians had an intensely personal relationship with their gods whom they constantly approached with prayer, offerings, and requests for assistance. The deities were beneficent, sympathetic, and often responsive to the pleas of their devotees. The diverse ways in which they could appeal to the gods reflected people's confidence that the gods were accessible and could be trusted to assist them in matters of concern both large and small. Gods were revered, but they were also seen in practical terms as patient problem solvers and mediators who could be counted on for help as long as they were revered, maintained by offerings, and shown proper respect though prayer and veneration.

A remarkable feature of their contact with the gods was the confidence and boldness with which the Egyptians approached their deities, a reflection of the intimacy between humans and gods. The texts show that the people were motivated to contact a deity by their desire for help with a range of personal issues, from the major – infertility, illness, grief – to the relatively minor – complaints about a neighbor or the theft of small items. The gods were always there for the petitioners, and they were a constant comfort to their flock. The gods were rarely consulted on philosophical issues – practicality was the motivation for communication. In keeping with this practicality, prayers were often offered with a brisk, businesslike directness. Some texts show an individual trying to cajole a deity into action or even stretching the truth to get a god to act. In a letter from late Dynasty 20, one man dared to scold a god who had been unwilling to help him:

> When I was looking for you to tell you some affairs of mine, you happened to be concealed in your sanctuary ... See, you must discard seclusion today and come out in procession in order that you may decide upon the issues involving seven kilts belonging to the temple of Horemheb and also those two kilts belonging to the necropolis scribe.[1]

Places of Prayer

The immediacy and ease with which Egyptians communicated with the gods is astounding, especially in contrast to societies in which communion with the deity was restricted to temples or churches. The Egyptians developed a wide variety of ways by which virtually anyone, at any time, could have contact with the god. Many instances of communing with a god took place within the temple in which the deity lived and had a constant, predictable, presence. But what sort of access did ordinary Egyptians have to these structures that dominated their towns and villages? One might even ask what relevance the temple had for ordinary people. Did they visit the local temple at all, or was it the exclusive domain of priests?

Reliefs and inscriptions in temples indicate that there were parts of the structures that were commonly accessible to any worshipper whether in a state of priestly purity or not. This contradicts the widely held assumption that common folk were cut off entirely from access to temple interiors. Although devotees were barred from the inner section of a temple, they were allowed entry, even if just on certain occasions, to temple courtyards and some interior spaces.

Evidence for what parts of the temple people could visit is relayed in references found in the texts and reliefs that decorate temple walls and ceilings. For example, the architraves of the Hypostyle Hall of the Temple of Amun at Karnak (Plan 1) bear inscriptions stating that the area was "a place in which Amun is made manifest to the people," indicating that people were allowed, at least at certain times, to adore the god in that space. The triple shrine of Seti II (at the time of its construction, not yet enclosed within the walls of the later court) (Plan 1; Fig. 28) was likewise a place of assembly, being labeled as a "place of reverence, honoring, and praying to all the gods."[2] The first court of the Luxor Temple (Plan 2) was, according to the texts on its walls, a place where people could petition the gods, and the Mut

Figure 28. Triple shrine of Seti II at the Karnak Temple, which was a place of prayer for the common people. The middle chapel, dedicated to Amun, bears an inscription indicating that it was "a place of praying to all the gods." Dynasty 20. Photo: Emily Teeter.

and Khonsu chapels of the triple shrine of Hatshepsut in that court were also sites of assembly and prayer for the faithful.

The indication of which areas of a temple were places of public prayer could be subtle. Some temple walls had holes drilled in them to support dowels from which fabric was hung to shield particularly sacred reliefs (Fig. 29). These shrouded reliefs most commonly depicted Amun or the Theban triad of Amun, Mut, and Khonsu. The drapes signaled the special potency of these images and apparently provided privacy for the devotee who prayed before them. The Karnak Temple has many of these sacred spots. On the exterior north wall of the Hypostyle Hall, an area accessible to the general population, the scene of Amun, Mut, and Khonsu is surrounded by the telltale holes. In the second court at Medinet Habu, some of the reliefs depicting the sacred boats received the same treatment. In some cases, only the divine shrine on board the boat was shrouded, leaving the rest of the vessel uncovered. The holes often were drilled through adjacent texts, suggesting that some drapes were added after the wall was originally carved; perhaps certain reliefs only developed popular appeal over time.

A temple's exterior doorway – the transition point between the sacred and temporal spheres – could be entered even by those who did not have

Figure 29. Reliefs that were considered to be especially holy or potent were hidden behind drapes or within a wooden booth where one could pray in private. The holes that supported that covering can be seen around this scene of Ramesses II offering the hieroglyph for "jubilee" to Thoth. Karnak. Dynasty 19. Photo: Emily Teeter.

authorization to venture further into the temple. As a result, these portals were also associated with especially approachable gods. At Medinet Habu, for example, some representations of Amun at the doorways are identified as the place where one might meet "Amun Re in the Thickness of the Door" ("thickness" referring to the space created by the threshold).

Other structures in and around temples were devoted specifically to enabling people to appeal to the god(s). One type is called a "chapel of the hearing ear," referring to the ear of a god who hearkens to prayer. These chapels are known from the Middle Kingdom and continued to be founded and patronized into the Roman Period. Anyone hoping for divine assistance could approach the shrine and recite his or her petition. In most cases, the figure to whom the petitioner appealed was a god, but in some cases, the appeal was made to the god and the king or, in rare instances, to the divine king alone.

These chapels (generally referred to as contra-temples) were usually located on the exterior back wall of a temple, allowing people easy and private access without having to enter the temple itself. The east side of the Temple of Amun at Karnak has several of these chapels. One is an

Figure 30. Alabaster (calcite) "shrine of the hearing ear" at Karnak, with large statues of Thutmose III and Amun. Located outside the temple proper, it was place where people could come and ask the gods for assistance. Dynasty 18. Photo: Emily Teeter.

enormous alabaster naos carved into the form of two seated figures, probably Thutmose III and Amun (Plan 1; Fig. 30). The king and god sit, their arms linked, ready to jointly hear the petitions of devotees. Thutmose's dedication of the naos states, "My majesty erected for him [Amun] a proper place of hearing." Later, the shrine was associated with Amun, his consort Amunet, and an obscure deity called "Amun of the Date Palm," perhaps a form of the deified Amunhotep I.³ This temple was in continuous use for more than one thousand years. In the last stages of its life, petitions were heard not by a god but by the deified king Ptolemy VII. Just to the east is a larger temple built by the First Priest of Amun Bakenkhonsu in the reign of Ramesses II (Plan 1; Fig. 31). The god who dwelled in this temple and who heard petitions was called "Amun-Re Who Hears Prayers."⁴

Another such chapel can be found at the Eastern High Gate at Medinet Habu in western Thebes (Plan 3). The chapel was built, as was usual, on the perimeter of the temple, where it could be easily and discreetly approached. In a niche on the south interior side of the gateway was a large image of the king presenting Maat, the goddess of truth, to Ptah (Fig. 32).

Figure 31. The Temple of "Amun Who Hears Petitions" at East Karnak, also known as "the place where Ramesses hears petitions." Like most such places of popular supplication, it was located outside the temple so that anyone might approach it. Dynasty 19. Photo: Emily Teeter.

Figure 32. Scene on the High Gate at Medinet Habu showing Ptah "Who Hears Petitions" and Sekhmet inside a shrine. Members of the community would come before this relief to ask Ptah to hear their pleas. Ptah's skullcap was originally filled with bright inlay to make the image stand out from the surrounding reliefs. To emphasize the justness of Ptah, Ramesses III is shown presenting a figure of Maat, the embodiment of truth, to the god. Note the square holes above and around the scene that supported some sort of chapel or drape, an indication of its sanctity. Dynasty 20. Courtesy of the Oriental Institute of the University of Chicago.

Contacting the Gods

Figure 33. Exterior back wall of the temple at Kom Ombo decorated with the ears of the god that were thought to be able to convey prayers and requests directly to the deity. Maat, the goddess of truth, appears above the composition. Greco-Roman Period. Photo: Emily Teeter.

Holes above the scenes allowed for a drape or perhaps for a small wooden booth to be mounted to give the petitioner privacy. The hieroglyphic texts referred to Ptah as a god who "hears petitions." The headdress of the god was inlaid with blue faience to make his image stand out from the surrounding reliefs.[5] These chapels must have been popular, as numerous examples have been identified in western Thebes. The Small Temple at Medinet Habu (begun in the reign of Hatshepsut and added onto successively thereafter) had an inscription from King Hakoris (Dynasty 29) designating it as a place for prayer and petition.[6] Like other shrines, a Roman-era shrine at the Temple of Kom Ombo was located on the back exterior wall of the temple for easy and unfettered access. Reflecting the Egyptians' preference for concrete images rather than abstract concepts, large ears were carved on either side of the shrine's central niche (Fig. 33). Winged protective genies flanked the composition, and above the ears was a large figure of Maat, the personification of truth, reassuring

Figure 34. Stela incised with the ears of the god who would hear petitions. This example does not have a text that identifies what god was being addressed, but others refer to the god Ptah. Medinet Habu. Dynasties 22–26. OIM 16718. Courtesy of the Oriental Institute of the University of Chicago.

the petitioner that the god would listen to those who have conducted themselves morally and hearken to true concerns.

Outside the Temple

There were many ways through which the Egyptians could contact their gods outside the temple. One means of communication was through stelae of various sizes (many, ironically, about the size of a mobile phone) engraved with images of ears that were thought to receive prayers and transmit them to the deity. There might be one ear or several pairs (Fig. 34). Although few of these stelae had inscriptions, some bore a brief label, such as "Ptah, Lord of Maat," or less commonly, "Hathor," indicating the deity to whom the petitions were being sent.[7] One stela was carved with a scene of a man named Seti-er-neheh and his family adoring Amun Re and statues of the god Ptah and King Ramesses II (Fig. 35). Behind the statues were the god's ears, ready to receive the family's requests. Some of these ear stelae have been excavated from houses, indicating that they were kept at home as private lines to the god that could be activated at any time.

People could also approach the gods at village shrines. One of the best known is dedicated to the cobra goddess Meretseger, one of the patron

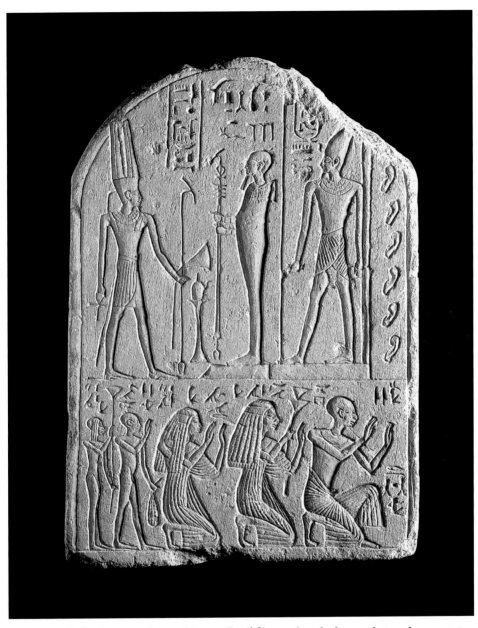

Figure 35. Stela showing the god Amun Re (*left*) standing before a shrine that contains statues of Ptah and Ramesses II (*right*). The back of the shrine is incised with the ears of the god. Some monumental statues of the king, such as the one depicted here, were the focus of popular worship because the king was considered to be an intermediary who could convey petitions to the gods. In the lower register, Seti-er-neheh and his family adore the deities shown above. Qantir. Dynasty 19. Hildesheim, Pelizaeus-Museum 375. Photo © Roemer-Pelizaeus-Museum, Hildesheim.

Figure 36. Shrine to Meretseger, a goddess to whom prayers were addressed. The shrine is located in a natural cliff formation in western Thebes. The rock surfaces were carved with inscriptions and offerings, and stelae were left there in honor of the goddess. New Kingdom. Photo: Emily Teeter.

deities of the workmen who lived in the village of Deir el Medina. This little shrine, called "the beautiful hillock" or "the great promontory of western Thebes," is located within an outcropping of limestone near the path to the Valley of the Queens. (Map 2; Fig. 36) A series of large reliefs chiseled into the rocks imitate stelae in their depictions of individuals adoring the goddess. People would come and pray to Meretseger asking her for health, wealth, or protection. Smaller stelae dedicated to the goddess (Fig. 37), many of them decorated with images of the devotee kneeling before snakes (one of the forms of the goddess), were left at the shrine in thanks for her help. Many more of these small devotional objects have been recovered from the village at Deir el Medina.

Ear stelae and nontemple shrines to the gods are good reminders that religious experience in ancient Egypt was not limited to the temple spaces. On the contrary, piety could be expressed anywhere and everywhere. It is this multiplicity of places and means of expression that enlivened ancient Egyptian religion and allows us a better glimpse of how Egyptians actually expressed their beliefs.

Contacting the Gods

Figure 37. Votive stela in honor of Meretseger, showing Lady Tarekhanou adoring the goddess, who is in the form of a large snake with a crown. A series of serpents, additional representations of the goddess, appear in the lower part of the stela. Dynasty 19. Louvre E 13084. Réunion des Musées Nationaux/Art Resource, NY.

Votive Offerings

Figurines of women, animals, and gods that were used in worship are collectively called ex votos or votive figurines (Fig. 38). They have been excavated by the hundreds from the remains of houses, temples, and tombs. Although

Figure 38. Baked clay figurines in the form of women. Such statuettes have been recovered from tombs, houses, and temples, attesting to their broad association with fertility and rejuvenation. Medinet Habu. Dynasties 22–23. OIM 14594, 14583, 14613. Photo: Anna Ressman. Courtesy of the Oriental Institute of the University of Chicago.

they seem to have functioned in various ways, votive figurines were generally offered to the gods in thanks for divine intercession or in the hope that they would spur the god to act on behalf of the petitioner.

Votive figures were common in all periods of Egyptian history from the Early Dynastic Period through the Roman and Byzantine eras, although the forms and materials from which they were made, and their specific function (as well as it can be understood), changed over time. Some forms of figurines, such as models of women, were found in houses, tombs, and temples. Others, such as images of the god Osiris, were more commonly associated with temples or symbolic burials. The recovery of votives from both funerary and nonfunerary contexts attests to the lack of separation between those spheres. The enormous quantity of votives is a testimony to their perceived efficacy and to the most practical aspect of human–divine relations in which the individual established a quid pro quo with the deity, offering the god a votive to stimulate divine intervention.

Deir el Bahri provides a good illustration of the use of votive figurines. This area, nestled in the western cliffs that rise up from the Nile floodplain in western Thebes, was equated with the entrance to the realm of the dead. In Thebes, Hathor was the patron of this western entrance to the beyond. From Dynasty 11 through the Roman era, shrines within larger temples dedicated to Hathor were established in the rocky bays of the cliffs. The most important of these shrines were those within the Temples of Mentuhotep (Dynasty 11), Hatshepsut, and Thutmose III (Dynasty 18). The offerings left for Hathor included figurines of women, some nursing a child; plaques showing cows; models of ears, eyes, and phalluses; and beads and amulets. It seems that the shape of the votive was more or less associated with the request being made to the deity: female figurines and phalluses in reference to fertility and health; ears, like the hearing ear stelae, probably to encourage the god to hear one's plea; plaques and figurines of cows and faces of Hathor in honor of that goddess. Most were simply crafted, and while the majority were made of clay, some were of faience, and the small stelae could be of faience, baked clay, or limestone. Most were produced in molds, making it easy to manufacture multiple copies, another indication of their popularity and relatively low cost. But the simple materials from which they were made should not be taken as an indication that votives were worthless. A good analogy has been drawn comparing the relative cost of a votive candle in a Catholic church to its cultic value; the same could be said for clay votive figurines in ancient Egypt.[8]

Women seem to have been particularly active in the cults of Hathor, perhaps because they may have been less busy in the fields and workshops than the men were, but probably more so because Hathor was associated with particularly "female" issues – fertility, childbirth, and love. Although the details are not entirely clear because there were no instruction manuals and few depictions of people engaged in cult activities using votive figurines, it appears that votives were left in the Hathor shrines during festivals and processions related to the goddess. The excavator Charles Currelly reported finding "basketsful" of wood votive phalluses in the Hathor shrine in the Temple of Thutmose III in 1905, indicating some sort of community or group ritual or at least a sustained cult. But votives have also been found singly, indicating that they were left by individuals seeking help.

It is difficult, if not presently impossible, to closely describe the rituals in which votives were used. Female figurines were the most common form of votive (Fig. 38). Because most were depicted nude and emphasis was placed on the breasts and pubic area (sometimes at the expense of any detail of the face, hands, or feet), female votives were initially interpreted as "concubines for the dead," a rather odd conclusion considering that they were also found in the graves of women and children. The general consensus now is that these female figurines were associated with fertility in its broadest sense, encompassing good health, long life, and rebirth, as well as reproductive fertility. Some were specifically associated with the desire for children, as indicated by the inscription on the back of one that read, "May a birth be given to your daughter Seh."[9] Only a few examples were inscribed, and all of those inscriptions expressed a wish for children.

Clay votive figurines in the form of rectangular boxes that imitated elaborate beds (Plate XI) are even more difficult to interpret. One side of the bed was usually decorated with the representation of a woman seated in a boat playing a lute while another woman plucks papyrus from the marsh, or of a standing woman who holds plucked reeds. Bes appears on both sides of the scene. The papyrus-plucking scene is known from Old Kingdom and later tombs and temple decoration to be linked to Hathor, who was the focus of so many other cults employing votive objects. The association of the bed, Hathor, and Bes suggests that the objects were related to female fertility or the safeguarding of children, but the exact purpose of these objects is unknown. They have been found with female figurines, but there is no evidence that the latter were directly associated with the beds, so the question of whether other figurines were placed on the bed's surface, as on a small altar, cannot be answered. Because votive beds have been recovered from both houses and temples, they may, like so many other types of votives, have been dedicated generally to Hathor or Bes to stimulate fertility and to safeguard the family.

Another category of votive that is difficult to interpret (and even harder to date with any certainty) depicts animals. Some of these – cats, dogs, snakes, and falcons – can be related to the cults of gods or goddesses (Sekhmet or Bastet, Sothis, Renenutet, Horus or Re), but others are more mysterious because the animal has no apparent association with a deity. For example, a great variety of votives in the form of nonraptor birds was excavated from the ruins of houses at Medinet Habu. In the absence of a clear connection with a deity, they may simply have been toys.

Mummified animals were another type of votive offering. This practice is known from the late New Kingdom, and it became very common in the Third Intermediate through the Ptolemaic periods. The mummies include virtually every animal that walked, slithered, or flew in the Nile Valley, including falcons, ibises, cats, crocodiles, baboons, jackals, snakes, mongeese, bulls, and various insects. Each animal was associated with a particular deity – the baboon with Thoth, the crocodile with Sobek, the cat with Bastet or Sekhmet, the mongoose with Re, and the ram with the Apis bull. The animal was thought to represent the *ba* or the soul of the deity and to serve as an intermediary between the god or goddess and its devotee. Priests would raise flocks or herds of the animal that represented the temple's resident deity, then kill and mummify them. X-ray and CT examinations of cat mummies, for example, reveal that most of them were about ten months old when they were sacrificed, which indicates that they were culled from breeding stock. The mummification process was, in the case of most of the animals, rudimentary. The animal was usually not eviscerated but only desiccated using natron (naturally occurring salt compounds including sodium carbonate or bicarbonate) and then coated with resin or bitumen. In the Persian Period (6th–5th c. BC) the process was further abbreviated. Many of the birds at Tuna el Gebel from that era were simply coated with a sort of sweet-smelling turpentine to mask the smell of the decomposing flesh.[10] The wrappings of many of these animal mummies, by contrast, were quite elaborate, showing geometric patterns created by different colors of linen (Plate XII). Some animal mummies were placed in wood, bronze, or stone coffins. Once prepared, the mummies were sold to pilgrims, who, in turn, restored them to the priests to be deposited in the temple's catacomb. At the ibis catacombs, officials called "carriers of the ibis" were responsible for taking the mummified birds to their burial site. Before being stacked in rows in side chambers hewn from the rock, the birds were anointed with oils and unguents in an abbreviated version of the "Opening of the Mouth" ritual (see Chapter 7) intended to revive the bird and its divine nature in the afterlife. The excavators of the ibis catacombs at Tuna el Gebel could still see the stains of the sacred oils on the stairway of the room where this ritual was performed.[11]

Inscriptions on some of the animal mummies or coffins indicate that, as with other types of votives, the donor of the mummy expected this action to motivate a god to favor him. An example from an ibis mummy from Tuna el Gebel is typical; it says, "Thoth – twice great, lord of Hermopolis, he may give life, prosperity, and sanity and the lifetime of Ra and a high and beautiful age for the general Petosiris, son of the general Nakht-ef ..."[12]

The dedication of animal mummies was a common practice. It is estimated that there are four million birds in the falcon catacomb at North Saqqara and "hundreds of thousands, if not millions" of ibis mummies at Tuna el Gebel,[13] and these are just two of the many animal catacombs in the Nile Valley. The excavation of the chambers for the mummies was a grueling task. The falcon catacomb at North Saqqara is a network of axial corridors some fifteen meters underground. Although not all the Saqqara catacomb is accessible, the areas that are measure more than six hundred sixty meters in length. The demand for animal mummies was so great that excavators have found many examples of "false mummies," consisting of packets of sand and sticks or other debris wrapped to resemble an authentic animal mummy.

Statue Cults

As already mentioned, not all people were allowed entry into the temples, and even those allowed in were not allowed into the most sacred areas where the god dwelled. These restrictions, combined with the desire to be near the gods at all times, gave rise to private statue cults. Individuals commissioned statues of themselves to be placed in a temple where the statues functioned as surrogates, allowing the individual to be eternally present. These statues were commissioned especially by the devotee, or they could be purchased from the stock of a sculptor. In the latter case, it did not matter whether the statue's face resembled that of the purchaser, it became him when it was inscribed with his name. Because statues were made of stone rather than clay, they were expensive. Their cost, combined with the inscription that mentions the occupation of the person represented, suggest that statue cults were a phenomenon of the mid and upper elite.

Although limited to the wealthier segments of Egyptian society, the establishment of a statue in the temple was a common practice throughout most of the dynastic period. The popularity of this practice at the Temple of Amun at Karnak is documented by a spectacular find (called the "Karnak Cachette") of more than seventeen thousand statues and votive objects that were excavated in the courtyard between the Hypostyle Hall and the Seventh Pylon between 1903 and 1906 (Plan 1). Among the objects were approximately seven hundred and fifty stone statues of worshippers, kings, queens, and deities. The statues once crowded the temple, where they had been placed to absorb and transmit the prayers and sanctity of the rituals and processions to their owners. The Hypostyle Hall must have been choked with statues – standing against the walls, resting on the column bases, and placed between the aisles. Eventually, for some unknown reason, perhaps due to overcrowding, they were cleared from the hall. Because they were pious objects, and in fact surrogates for worshippers, the statues were given an honorable burial in the temple precinct. The statues reflect artistic styles ranging from Dynasty 11 to the second century BC, representing two thousand years of piety.[14]

Texts incised on some of the statues from the Karnak Cachette, as well as texts from other sources, give us a good idea of the workings of these statue cults. Among the earliest references to a statue of an individual being set up in a temple (as opposed to in one's own tomb) is in a decree of Pepi II (Dynasty 6) that refers to a statue of his vizier that was established in a temple of the god Khenty-Imentyu at Abydos along with images of the king and his family. The decree instructs that the vizier's statues were to be given half an ox, a *meret*-jug of beer, and another one-eighth portion of an ox during every festival celebrated in the temple, indicating that, like the statues of gods in temples, they were the focus of a cult that provided food for them.[15] A slightly later text of Idi the son of a man named Shemai (Dynasty 8), refers to a statue in the Temple of Min at Coptos: "your [Shemai's] statues, your offering tables, your *ka* chapels … which are in any temple of the temple precinct."[16]

By the Middle Kingdom, especially at Abydos, there is rich information about private cults that were established in connection with the cult of Osiris. Abydos, thought to be the burial place of Osiris, was among the most sacred sites in Egypt. The tomb of King Djer of Dynasty 1 became equated with the tomb of the god. Because of the sacredness of the site, Abydos became a place of pilgrimage. A great processional route wound its way from the Nile through the wadi to the god's tomb. It became the tradition to establish a cenotaph (symbolic tomb) or to erect small chapels along the processional route. These were embellished with stelae that memorialized an individual, a family, or an entire household. The wadi became crowded with a forest of small whitewashed chapels whose niches held the stelae and statues.

As with the practice of placing a statue in a temple, the proximity of these shrines to the processional route allowed the individual to be near the god for eternity. As stated on one stela, "Then I made this offering chapel at the terrace of the Great God so that I might be in his company."[17] Establishing a stela at Abydos was also thought to allow the dedicator to actively partake of the festivals rather than be a passive viewer. One text wishes that the individual be greeted by the "magnates of Abydos, and that there might be given to me hands in the *neshmet* barque [the boat of the gods used in the processions of Osiris] on the festivals of the necropolis," assuring him that he would be able to join the gods on board the sacred boat. Another text states that the dedicator will share in the offerings presented in the Osiris temples: "It is in order to receive offerings and that I might inhale incense that I made this memorial offering chapel at the terrace of the great god." Another explains, "I made this offering chapel ... so that I might receive pure offerings which come forth in the presence of the Great God after his *ka* is satisfied with them." A decree of Senwosert I (Dynasty 12) indicates that in some instances chapels were gifts from the king to individuals as a reward for state service.[18] As with the large temples, these little shrines were served by their own ranks of priests. A stela from the Abydos chapel of a man named Hor relates his financial arrangement for priestly services in his chapel: "I have given payment to the *hemw netcher*, and to the great *wabs* who are in the temple of Osiris, Foremost of the Westerners in order that my name shall live at Abydos."[19] *Wenut* (hour) priests and "overseers of the house of the offerings" who served in the chapels are also mentioned.

Statue cults of private individuals continued through the New Kingdom and became increasingly common in the Third Intermediate Period. There are hundreds of statues from those eras whose inscriptions indicate that they were set up in temples to be in the presence of the god. Some are inscribed with texts that specifically relate the statue's function. That of Panehsy (Dynasty 19) reads,

> Oh my likeness, may you be firm for my name, the favorite of everyone, so that people will stretch out their hands to you bearing splendid bouquets, that you may be given libations as the remainder of your lord, and then my *ba* will come fluttering so that he may receive offering with you for the *ka* of ... Panehsy.[20]

As with the Abydos chapels, some of the statues were gifts from the king. For example, Senenmut, a high official of Hatshepsut, claimed that one of his many statues was "given as a favor of the king's gift."[21] The inscriptions on many statues emphasize their role in perpetuating the name of the donor, thereby granting him or her immortality, such as "may my statue endure as one of his [Amun's] followers. May my *ka* [i.e., physical form] be remembered in his temple night and day. May I renew my youth like the moon. May my name not be forgotten in after years ever."[22] Other dedications stress the importance of the statue as a recipient of food offerings that came from the main sanctuary and were temporarily placed before the statue before being distributed to the priests. A statue (one of eight) of the official Harwa (Dynasty 25) bears the text: "Oh prophets, divine fathers, priests. The whole temple-priesthood of Amun, Everyone who passes by this image: That *ba* who is in Thebes shall live for you, The august god [i.e., Amun] who presides over his secluded place, If you will say: 'A thousand of bread, beer, and all good things, For the *ka* of the one honored by the God's Hand [title of the God's Wife], the King's friend Harwa ..."[23] Another part of the text stipulates that the food will be given to the statue only "after the god is satisfied with it."

Many of the statues that were set up as surrogates in temples were in the form of a cube, or block, whose broad flat upper surface formed by the bent knees and crossed arms of the individual was perfectly suited to serve as a platform to hold food. Some block statues emphasize their desire for offerings by assuming a pose of begging for bread or water, cupping the hand to the mouth (Fig. 39). Texts indicate that offerings were left not only by priests but also by pious visitors to the temple.[24] They were implored by a text called "the appeal to the living" to recite "a thousand of bread, beer, oxen, and fowl for the soul of the individual" thereby symbolically creating those provisions. The inscription on a statue of the official Roma-roi (Dynasty 19) relates. "My statue upon which my name is engraved forever, that bread, beer, and offerings shall be placed before it during every offering service of the One Who is in Thebes [Amun]."[25] A statue of the priest and official Nebnetcheru (Dynasty 22) reads, in part, "O priests and divine fathers of Amun ... Do not remove my statue from its place ... Perform the royal offerings for my *ka* every day, with everything leftover from Amun, bread, beer, wine, and oil from the table of the Lord of Thebes, for the *ka* of this excellent noble!"[26]

There was concern that the statues established in the temples might become dirty, worn, or damaged, thereby reducing their efficacy. Texts on some New Kingdom and Third Intermediate statues instruct people who come into the temple to speak the name of the dedicator, to wipe dust from the statue with a cloth, and to remove old offerings before they decay: "May you speak my name when you bring water, may you remove any corruption, dirt or refuse [?] from me. May you take away all that is dirty from me that may come for me for eternity."[27]

Intercessory Statues

Statues of private individuals could act as intermediaries, interceding on someone else's behalf to contact the gods. Much like the *akh ikr n Re* in the funerary realm (see Chapter 8), the dedicators of these intercessory statues were considered to have a special relationship with the god (or the deified king) that made it possible for them, as a third party, to relay petitions and prayers more effectively to the gods than the petitioners themselves could. Intercessory statues were more common in the New Kingdom and onward. Most bore an inscription that detailed what service they could perform and what was expected in return. One example, a statue of the *is* priest (a rank of priest who wore a distinctive tonsure) Amuneminet (Dynasty 19) recovered from the ruins of the Temple of Thutmose III at Deir el Bahri, has the inscription:

> I am the *is* priest of the goddess [Hathor], the messenger of his mistress. Anyone with petitions, speak ... to my ear, then I will repeat them to my mistress in exchange for offerings. Give to me *bnqt*-beer upon my hand and *srmt*-beer for my mouth, sweet and pleasant oil for my shaven head, fresh garlands for my neck. Pour out for me with wine and beer ... If there is no beer, give to me cool water.[28]

The best-known intercessory cults, in a fitting testament to the Egyptians' reverence for the building arts, focused on two deified architects – Imhotep and Amunhotep Son of Hapu. Imhotep was the architect for King Djoser's Step Pyramid complex (Dynasty 3). The cult of Imhotep is best attested at Memphis and Saqqara but only from the beginning of the New Kingdom, some one thousand years after his death. Imhotep is most often shown as a man wearing a skullcap and long gown. In the Late and Ptolemaic periods, innumerable bronze figurines were made showing Imhotep seated with a papyrus on his lap (Fig. 40), a reference to his wisdom and literacy. Someone who wished to venerate the diety would buy a statuette, inscribe his or her name upon it, and leave it in a shrine to the god. In the Late Period and afterward into the Roman Period, Imhotep was associated with doctors,

Figure 39. Statue of Peraha with his hand to his mouth in a gesture of begging for offerings. Dynasty 19. E 501. Photo © The Trustees of the British Museum.

and he was venerated as the son of Ptah. The Romans equated him with Aesclepius, their god of medicine.

Amunhotep Son of Hapu was the architect of the mortuary temple of Amunhotep III (Dynasty 18) in western Thebes. He is shown in standard New Kingdom garb with a full-cut layered wig. His cult began soon after his death and continued into the Roman Period. Its popularity is indicated by a find of ten nearly identical life-size stone statues of him sitting cross-legged in the attitude of a scribe, hand poised to write any appeals. Two of the statues were found side by side at the Karnak Temple's Tenth Pylon, near a twenty-meter-tall quartzite statue of the architect's patron, Amunhotep III (Fig. 41). They were positioned just outside the temple, where they were easily accessible to the public, lined up like a row of ancient pay phones

Figure 40. Statuette of Imhotep shown seated with a papyrus unrolled on his lap. In the Late Period, some two thousand years after his death, Imhotep was deified and revered as a healer and as an intermediary who could convey individuals' requests to the gods. Ptolemaic Period. 1935.200.0559. Photo: Christian Tepper. Courtesy of the August Kestner Museum.

with a direct line to the god. One of these statues has a long inscription that addresses the passerby:

> You people from Upper and Lower Egypt, with your eyes watching the sun, you who are all coming to Thebes downstream and upstream in order to implore the lord of the gods, come to me! I will transmit your words to Amun in Karnak. Give

Figure 41. Two statues of Amunhotep Son of Hapu in the guise of a scribe (*right*). Amunhotep was considered to be an intermediary who could transmit personal requests to the gods. The statues (along with two of Paramesu, the future Ramesses I, *to the left*) were found just outside the enclosure wall of the Karnak Temple where they were accessible to people who wanted Amunhotep's assistance reaching the gods. Photo © CNRS-CFEETK.

me an offering and pour a libation for me, because I am an intermediary nominated by the king to hear the requests of the suppliant, to report to him the desires of Egypt.[29]

The inscription, incised on the stone papyrus roll that the statue holds, has been worn nearly smooth as a result of thousands of pious hands touching it as people told the statue their troubles. As indicated by the inscription, the statue was visited by people from all parts of Egypt when they came to the Karnak Temple; perhaps it was one of the stops that ancient tourists would make. Amunhotep was also revered as a healer. One request from a woman of Dynasty 26 reads, "Oh noble Amunhotep Son of Hapu, true of voice. Come, good physician! I suffer from my eyes. May you cause that I be healthy at once." An ostracon from the reign of Ptolemy II that was recovered from Deir el Bahri has a testimonial to the success of Amunhotep's power (in the text he is referred to as Amenotes):

> But I had heard from different sides that the miracles of Amenotes were numerous, and that he was merciful and that the hopeless were numerous who had found curing by him. Being a hopeless case, I went along to the sanctuary of Amenotes as a supplicant. Amenotes helped me, and cured by him by a vision and having regained my health, I wish to express to him and the other gods sharing in his altars and cults their miraculous power in written words for those who visit the temple enclosure of Amenotes that they may see the power of this god when they are taken by any illness.[30]

Although not common, there are also texts that indicate that living members of the community too could act as intermediaries with the gods, because they had a sensitivity to the presence of a god much like a modern "medium." These individuals (all known examples are women), were called *rekhet* – "the knowing one," or "the wise one." In one text, a *rekhet* is consulted about the death of two children: "Consult the Wise Woman about the death the two boys suffered: was it their fate or was it their lot? And consult them for me, and also see about my own life and the life of their mother."[31] The ability to be a *rekhet* apparently was carried through families. These people had the special ability to sense the presence of a god and particularly to determine whether the god had placed someone under a spell, or *baw* (see further in Chapter 6). In one text, a member of the community, who apparently had been searching for an explanation for some evil events in the life of a friend or relative, recounts, "I have gone to the wise woman and she told me, the manifestation (*baw*) of Ptah is with you,"[32] suggesting that the individual had committed some wrong that had been noted by Ptah. In another text, the seeker is told, "She [the *rekhet*] told me [it is a] *baw* of [the god] Nemti. And you should ..." The rest of the text is unfortunately lost.

Trances and Dreams as a Means of Contacting the Gods

The Egyptians considered sleep, especially while dreaming, to be a state of being alert in another realm, allowing the dreamer to access things and people who were faraway. Dreams enabled people to pass into the realm of the gods, or at least to stand at the threshold of their realm. These contacts with the gods were not considered frightening, which perhaps reflects the confidence people had in the benevolent nature of their deities.

One of the best-known tales of contact with a god through a dream is the account of Prince Thutmose (later King Thutmose IV), who took a midday nap under the chin of the Sphinx at Giza. The Sphinx spoke to him and promised that if he cleared the sand away from it, he would become king. As with so many examples of human interaction with the gods, here again is a quid pro quo – the individual received something in exchange for a service to the god. In the autobiography of the priest and official Dheutyemheb (Dynasty 19), recorded in his tomb at western Thebes, Dheutyemheb recounts how he was contacted by Hathor "while I was in a dream, while the earth was silent in the deep of the night." In a brief text from the Ptolemaic Period, a man named Ptolemaios related that he invoked the god though a dream: "I dreamt that I called upon the great god Amun to come to me from the north with his two consorts [Isis and Nephthys], until finally he came."[33]

The practice of incubating dreams in order to contact the god is rare in the dynastic period. Most accounts of dreams, such as Dheutyemheb's, state that the god simply came to the sleeper without preparation or warning. An amulet of Ramesside date is inscribed, "Are the dreams which one will see good?" suggesting that it was associated with planned dream contacts, but otherwise there is no tradition of invoking dreams. Only in the Greco-Roman Period are there records of people spending the night in a temple to deliberately incubate dreams in which they would communicate with the god.

Other texts refer to individuals who saw the gods in a trance rather than in a dream. A text on a stela of Ipuy (Dynasty 18) claims that Ipuy saw Hathor: "I saw the Lady of the Two Lands in a dream." His reaction was ecstatic. He recorded that he was "bathed and inebriated by the sight of her," and that the wonders worked by the goddess "should be related [to the] ones who don't know it [the wonders] and the ones who know it." His tone is that of a recent convert proselytizing for the deity. This event could be taken as an account of a memorable dream, had not Ipuy stated, "It was on the *day* that I saw her beauty,"[34] indicating that he was awake, not sleeping. The tone of his response and the fact that he chose to record the dream on his stela signifies the magnitude of the event for him.

Self-Dedication to the God(s)

The Egyptians were always aware of the presence of the gods. Letters of the New Kingdom start with a version of the formula "I call upon Amun, Mut, Khonsu, Sekhmet, and *any* god by whom I pass to give you a long life," indicating that people invoked and relied on a whole cast of deities. However, we have a few texts that reflect a special devotion to a single god, or an almost fanatical attachment at the expense of a person's integration into the broader society and perhaps a foreshadowing of true monasticism. In a biographic text, a man named Simut (also known as Kiki, Dynasty 19) claimed to have had a revelation about the goddess Mut. He recorded that "she recognized him as a child," apparently meaning that he had known since his youth that he had a special relationship with her. In the text he claimed that he had "placed himself in [her] hand," meaning under her protection. This unusual text resembles a description of a modern cult follower. As occurs in some contemporary stories, Simut's actions had repercussions on his family, for in confirmation of his exclusive relationship with the goddess, he transferred all his worldly goods to Mut's temple, thereby disinheriting his entire family.[35]

A similar kind of devotion, but perhaps less specific, can be seen in oracular decrees of the Third Intermediate Period in which individuals refer to themselves as *bak* or "servants" of a particular god. It is unclear what this really meant, and whether it indicated that these servants had an obligation to the god beyond a simple sense of devotion and humility. More specific levels of devotion and duty to a god are found in demotic texts of the Ptolemaic Period in which individuals claimed to be a "servant" (again the term is *bak*). These individuals seem to have been voluntary recluses who stayed within the temple. In one example from the second century BC, a man proclaimed himself to be the servant of the god and pledged his service to the god for ninety-nine years. As with the autobiography of Simut, this service entailed a financial obligation to the temple; the man pledged to pay a sum to the temple each year in thanks for the god's protection.[36] Another self-dedication text dating to the second century BC echos Simut's religious fervor. In this example, a woman named Tanebtynis swore,

> I am your [Sobek's] servant [*bak*] together with my children and my children's children. I shall not be able to be free in your temple precinct forever. You shall protect me, you shall keep me safe, you shall guard me, you shall keep me sound, you shall protect me from every male spirit and every female spirit, every sleeping man, every epileptic [?], every drowned man … every incubus [?], every dead man, every man of the river, every madman [?], every fiend, every red thing, every pestilence whatsoever. I will give you 1 1/4 *kite* [a unit of weight] … for my rent of service every month from year 33 until the completion of 99 years … and I will give it to your priests monthly.[37]

Egyptian religious practices provided a great number of ways through which devotees could have immediate contact with the gods. Although ordinary people were denied entrance to the sanctuaries of temples, other areas were designated for public use and assembly. Chapels of the Hearing Ear, located in areas of public access, were devoted to relaying requests to the gods. A devotee could establish a permanent presence in the temple by dedicating a statue or stela of himself to act as a surrogate and eternally absorb daily rituals and prayers. Portable stelae decorated with ears, as well as dreams and trances, made it possible for individuals to contact the god without even entering a temple. If one was not personally capable of contacting the god, intermediaries could help.

Most contact with the gods was motivated by a search not for philosophical knowledge or even counsel but rather for the resolution of everyday matters, especially issues of health. A characteristic feature of contact with the divine was its almost mercantile character. The petitioner gave something – prayers, food offerings, or a votive object – in confident expectation of stimulating divine action. The ability of people from all strata of society to turn to their gods at any time and for any reason underscores the immediacy of religion and the ways in which faith was incorporated into all aspects of Egyptian life.

6

In the Presence of the Gods

How the Gods Communicated with Men

The Egyptians' gods were ever present – and not only as passive deities called to action by the prayers of their devotees. On the contrary, the Egyptians believed that their gods were active players who could – and did – interfere with affairs of daily life at any time. In order to make sense of the immediacy of the divine in Egyptian life, it is necessary to explore how the gods made their presence and will known.

Texts indicate that Egyptians believed that they could sense the presence of a god through smell, sight, and intuition. For example, Queen Hatshepsut claimed that her mother, Ahmose, had determined that the figure who appeared to be her husband was in fact the god Amun by the sweet odor of incense that emanated from him. But more frequently, the presence of a god was conveyed through a vague sense that ill heath or some unfortunate event had been brought about by divine action. In many cases, a person who recorded an unpleasant encounter with a god admitted that some personal fault or action precipitated the god's action. While the divine–human encounters described in the previous chapter planned and invoked by worshippers were often positive, unsolicited meetings with a god could be a frightening event warning of the impending wrath of the deity on account of some personal misstep or shortcoming.[1] Most of those sorts of encounters appear to be instances in which an unfortunate occurrence, combined with a guilty conscience, spurred an individual to confess some wrongdoing to the gods, who would then be placated, allowing the individual to recover. This idea that people were responsible in some way for harmful actions of the god is in keeping with the belief that the gods were generally benevolent – it was not a part of their character to harm humankind, unless provoked or unless they intended to send a sign of reprimand.

Controlled Contact with the Gods

Most examples of invoking a god were done for practical reasons, primarily to ask the deity to serve as an oracle to adjudicate some civil matter. Because the pronouncements of divine oracle carried legal weight, oracles were consulted in the course of processions and festivals (see Chapter 4) when a significant number of witnesses were present thereby increasing the community's acknowledgment of the decision. The oracle was perceived as being a fair judge. In one text, the oracle is called "the vizier of the feeble, who does not take bribes from the guilty and [never] says 'bring written evidence.'"[2] Oracles are first known from the Middle Kingdom, but they became common in the New Kingdom and even more so in the Third Intermediate Period. It has been suggested that the increasing popularity of oracles was due to a rise in corruption in the local courts. However, the frequency of texts that refer to the use of oracles may be because a generally higher overall number of texts survive from that later period,[3] or because certain types of routine matters, especially those dealing with property, were taken to the oracle rather than to the court.

Oracles were used to decide every possible sort of issue, from the completely mundane, such as whether it was advisable for an individual to travel a short distance to the next town or consumer queries ("Is this calf good so that I may accept it?"),[4] to matters of theft. Examples of the latter charge include: "Is one of my goats with Ptahmose or is it the soldier who stole it?"[5] Although oracles were used to investigate theft and bureaucratic (and even royal) appointments, the most serious crimes, such as murder, were referred to the official judicial system. Only the king, or his vizier or a panel of judges especially designated for the task, could pass a sentence of death.[6]

On the day that the oracle was to be consulted, the god's statue was removed from its naos in the temple sanctuary and placed in a shrine on

Figure 42. Scene of a procession during the Opet Festival when the gods traveled from Karnak to the Luxor Temple. The veiled shrine containing the statue of the deified king is enclosed in the shrine on board the boat. It is carried on the shoulders of a double file of priests. In the course of these processions the god could be consulted as an oracle. Dynasty 19. Luxor Temple. Photo: Emily Teeter.

a portable sacred boat. The boat was placed on carrying poles that were lifted by a team of white-clad priests (Fig. 42). In the New Kingdom, it was more common that the shrine of the god was covered with billowing fabric (Fig. 43) that shielded it from the eyes of the public who approached it as it moved through the community. It is not known how the number or types of questions put to a single oracle were controlled. Perhaps the highest-ranking priest in the procession acted as the master of ceremonies, determining who among the crowd could consult the god. The Instructions of Ani

Figure 43. In some periods, the shrine enclosing the god's statue was covered with a fabric veil, perhaps to increase the sense of the god's sacredness. Here, the boat of Amun, identified as such by the ram's head on the bow and at the stern, is at rest in a kiosk. The smaller boats of Khonsu and Mut are shown to the right. Medinet Habu. Dynasty 20. Photo: Emily Teeter.

(Dynasty 21) advised about general protocol: "Do not disturb the oracles. Be careful, help to protect him, let your eye look out for his wrath and kiss the ground in his name. He gives power in a million forms."[7] Herodotus, who was writing much later, reported that the procedure for consulting oracles differed from place to place in Egypt (II:83). Certainly, those who wished to consult the god must have waited with nervous anticipation in the days prior to the event.

Those who could not wait for a scheduled procession might demand the presence of the god. A letter from Dynasty 20 contains this astounding exchange:

When I was looking for you [the god] to tell you some affairs of mine, you happened to be concealed in your holy of holies, and there was nobody having access
to it to send it in to you. Now as I was waiting, I encountered Hori, this scribe of the
temple of [Ramesses III], and he said to me, "I have access." So I am sending him in

Figure 44. Flake of pottery (ostracon) inscribed with a text read before an oracle: "Shall I bring the maid-servant?" The god would probably have made a favorable ("yes") decision by his sacred boat moving toward the ostracon. Dynasty 20 (?). OIM 18876. Photo Anna Ressman. Courtesy of the Oriental Institute of the University of Chicago.

to you. See, you must discard seclusion today and come out in procession in order that you may decide upon the issues involving seven kilts ...

The writer further complained that the oracle judged in favor of a woman, and then he continued his criticism of the god: "but now it happens that your pronouncements no longer come forth as though [confined] in the netherworld for a million years."[8] This letter shows how intimate and down-to-earth the relationship between humans and the gods was. The would-be petitioner scolded the deity for his seclusion when his services were needed, and then he complained about the god's effectiveness. The nature of their exchange seems no different than one that might take place between fractious neighbors.

When the time of day that the oracle is to be consulted is mentioned, it is always "morning." Presumably, on an invitation from the priest, each petitioner would approach the boat of the god and either state his question or submit it in writing for a priest or some other literate person to read to the oracle. Brief questions are also preserved on scraps of papyrus and flakes of limestone or pottery (Fig. 44), and one letter refers to papyrus rolls being placed before the oracle.[9]

The god then gave a decision, yes or no, which was transmitted to the priests who carried the deity. They then translated the god's directive through movement. In cases where two alternative petitions were placed before the god, the oracle "took" one, presumably, stopping before or approaching the one that it favored. In other cases that required a positive or negative answer, a "no" response was indicated by the god's "walk[ing] backwards emphatically," meaning that the god caused the priests to step away from the petitioner or the petition.

In other examples, the god was said to become "heavy," as the priests who supported the bow of the boat were pressed down by the will of the god. Still other texts relate that the god "nodded," indicated by a brief dip of the divine boat's bow. The most emphatic and frightening reaction was when the god became "very wrought," causing the entire boat to shake. Although the oracular process might seem farcical from a modern perspective, it is clear that the direct participants and onlookers truly believed that the movement of the sacred boat and the attendant priests indicated the will of the god. One text mentions that the boat "draws toward" the petitioner "by [the power of] the great god." An account of an oracle from a later period confirms that the priests who carried the god on their shoulders "go without their own volition wherever the god directs their path."[10] A modern parallel might be the faith that some ascribe to messages from a ouija board.

In order to fully understand how oracles worked, it is essential to appreciate their public nature. Oracles were held not just before those directly involved but also before members of the community who passively observed the proceedings. In the cases in which the oracle was asked to indicate the perpetrator of a crime, it is likely that the identity of the guilty party was well known to the members of the tight-knit community. The use of the oracle avoided the awkwardness of having a single member of the community stand in judgment of another. Rather, guilt was established by the god – a being who was above reproach. It was the perfect social mechanism for maintaining community peace through public consensus, presented as the word of the god. Any conflict of interest in letting the priests who bore the oracle present their own petitions was avoided by forbidding those priests from submitting petitions while on duty.[11]

While most oracular texts refer to the god's decision being conveyed through movement, some mention other modes of communication. Hatshepsut claimed that the god Amun directed her to Punt (an incense-rich land south of Egypt) when the sacred boat that held the god was at rest on a pedestal where it could not be manipulated by priests. The text specifically states that she "heard" the "order" of the god. The physical evidence confirms that the god communicated by voice. A large granite statue of a falcon (Fig. 45) of the Late Period has a hole drilled through its body from its head to its tail that may have enabled it to give audible oracles. Two

Figure 45. Falcon that may have been used as an oracle. A hole bored from the beak to the top of the head and from the top of the head through the body to the tail may have enabled it to transmit sound, or perhaps allowed the crown (now missing) to move in response to questions. Dynasties 26–31. OIM 10504. Photo: Jean Grant. Courtesy of the Oriental Institute of the University of Chicago.

other examples date to the Roman Period. The first, found at the temple at Kom el-Wist (near Alexandria), is an oracle statue in the form of a bull that was connected by a bronze tube to an adjacent room, where, it is presumed, priests could sequester themselves to relay the wishes of the god. The other speaking oracle is a statue of the god Re-Harmachis dressed as a

Roman soldier; this statue likewise was connected to what may have been a speaking tube.[12]

Appointments to civil or clerical positions could be put before an oracle for confirmation, a neat way of avoiding any hint of favoritism on the part of the administrators who made such decisions. There are written petitions about advancement, such as, "Will I become foreman?" or "Shall Seti be appointed as priest?"[13] When there were multiple candidates, the oracle simply stopped before the successful one.

Oracles could even be used to select, or at least to confirm, a new king. Both Thutmose III and Ramesses IV claimed to have been selected by a god. Thutmose III recorded that the sacred boat of Amun traveled around the Karnak Temple and "settled" before him, indicating that he was the divine choice for the throne. Amun also confirmed that Ramesses "should be ruler of the Two Regions." In the Third Intermediate Period, oracles were routinely used to proclaim the legitimacy of the king.[14]

If dissatisfied with an oracle's decision, people could submit their petitions to another oracle, much like appealing a legal verdict. One letter from the Ramesside era asks, "Submit my case before the oracles of Amun-United-with-Eternity and Amunhotep, and ask them, 'Will you bring them back alive?'"[15] One case concerning the theft of five tunics involved multiple appeals. The accused, a man named Pa-chay-m-di-Amun, protested his innocence, saying, "It is false. It was not I who stole them." This contradiction of the oracle was met with an immediate response from the god, who became "exceedingly wroth." Pa-chay-m-di-Amun, apparently unbowed by the reaction of the god, then went before a different oracle, that of Amun of Ta-Shenyt, saying, "I am now before my own god, whereas I was before the other [oracle]." Yet this supposedly more favorable god confirmed his guilt: "It is he who took them." And again Pa-chay-m-di-Amun proclaimed his innocence: "It is false." The case was then directed to a third oracle, Amun of Bukenen, "in the presence of many witnesses." Before the gathered crowd the accused proclaimed, "'Help me Amun of Bukenen, my beloved lord! Is it I who took the clothes?' And the god nodded very greatly saying 'It is he who took them.'" This final rejection of his innocence made Pa-chay-m-di-Amun confess, and he was given a hundred blows with a palm rib and made to swear that if he recanted his confession, he would be thrown to the crocodiles.[16]

Oracles continued to be an important part of religion and administration into the Roman Period and beyond. However, the practice clashed with

Roman law, resulting in several edicts that attempted to outlaw their use. One decree, issued in AD 199 by the local Roman governor, warned:

> ... in order that no danger should ensue upon their foolishness, clearly herein to enjoin all people to abstain from this hazardous superstition. Therefore, let no man through oracles, that is, by means of written documents supposedly granted in the presence of the deity, nor by means of the procession of cult images or suchlike charlatanry, pretend to have knowledge of the supernatural, or profess to know the obscurity of future events ... If any person is detected adhering to this profession, let him be sure that he will be handed over for capital punishment.[17]

But, oracles were such an engrained part of Egyptian religion and society, even in this late period, that this decree and others like it did not put an end to oracles but instead forced the practice underground, from temple court-yards into private spaces.

Uncontrolled Contact with the Gods

Less controlled, or completely unsolicited, contact with the gods was usu-ally a bad omen that was attributed to the god's displeasure. Although the Egyptian gods were generally benevolent and approachable, they also had an unpredictable and malicious side. When this side made itself known, the gods had to be appeased through offerings and prayers and sometimes by physical devices, such as amulets.

Unsolicited contact with the god usually manifested itself by some mis-fortune rather than by direct indication of the god's displeasure. A number of texts refer to a force called the *bau* that Egyptians understood as a sign of the god's anger, intended to direct or redirect human action. The *bau* could be manifested as a sense of guilt, a spell cast on an individual to cause him or her to act, or something vaguely evil, but in all instances, the *bau* is nega-tive, an indication of the god's displeasure. Most examples of the *bau* of the god involve only the deity and the affected party. However, there are a few examples that involve the king who, because of his special association with the gods, could direct the *bau* of the god against his enemies. One instance is found in the text of the Hittite Marriage of Ramesses II that records that the *bau* of Seth was upon the Hittites because they did not revere the Egyptian king. Another example occurs in a literary text that relates that because the Hittites would not submit to Egyptian power, Ramesses sent the *bau* of Seth against them, creating a famine.[18]

One stela neatly illustrates how a god's *bau* could force individuals to reconsider their actions. A man accused of a crime swore to his innocence before the local authorities but then returned to the court several days later to declare, "I am a man who had said 'it is true ...' in a wrong manner to the lady of the house, Nefertiti. A manifestation [*bau*] of the god has come about. I say to the light, to ... the moon, to Ptah, Thoth, to Amun, 'be merciful to me.'" The negative effect of the *bau* was enough to motivate him to recant his false statement and plead for mercy. In another instance, a man felt not only the *bau* of the god but also the "power" (*pehty*) of the god, causing him to warn others of the dangers of incurring a god's wrath: "I will relate your manifestation [*bau*] to the fishes of the river to the birds in air. And so will they, to the children of their children."[19]

Another account records that the power of the god descended upon a man probably because of a theft: "The *bau* of the god was upon him ... because of the cow." Another brief text from Deir el Medina relates that a woman who stole bread during the festival of the birth of Taweret felt the "divine anger" (*bau*) of the goddess.[20] The threat of being under the *bau* of a god was a frightening proposition. A man who stole a statue of Taweret worried that his misdeed might bring a *bau* of Seth against him.[21]

Sometimes the divine *bau* encouraged humans to reconsider their actions by creating physical symptoms. In two cases, blindness was attributed to the displeasure of the god. In the first example, from Deir el Medina, a member of the community who swore a false oath became blind. He claimed that his blindness was a sign (*bau*) from the god:

> I am a man who swore in a lying way to Ptah, the Lord of Truth. He caused me to see darkness by day. I shall tell of his manifestation [*bau*] to him who ignores it and him who recognizes it ... Be careful in regard to Ptah ... see, he does not set aside a fault of anybody.[22]

Those acknowledged to be under a *bau* were considered to be impure. A text on a doorway at the Ptolemaic-Roman temple at Esna lists what should not be brought into the temple. In addition to certain plants and animals, it includes people who are under a *bau*. Those individuals are instructed to go to "the space of the surrounding area of the temple."[23]

Gods could also make their presence known through dreams. Sleep was considered to be a liminal state in which the sleeper was between the realms of the living and the dead. Sleep, and especially dream sleep, gave humans access to realms and methods of communication inaccessible to the alert, facilitating communication with the gods. In a text in the tomb of Dheutyemheb at Thebes, the tomb owner related a dream in which Hathor appeared to him and instructed him where to build his tomb:

> I have come to you O mistress of the Two Lands, oh beloved one. Behold, I am in praise before your beautiful visage and kiss the earth before your *ka*. I am truly a servant of yours, and am at [your command]. I do not reject the speech of your mouth. I do not disregard your teaching. I am on the way that you have ordained, on the path that you yourself have prepared. Blessed be he who knows you! He who beholds you is blessed. How happy is he who rests at your side, who enters into your shadow. It is you who prophesied my tomb at the beginning when it was first planned. What you said has been realized through you, a place for my mummy has been founded ... It is you who spoke to me with your own mouth: ... "I have come to instruct you. Behold your place, seize it for yourself" ... while I slept and the earth lay in silence in the depths of the night. In the morning, my heart was jubilated, I rejoiced, and I went to the western side [of the river] to do what you said. You are a goddess whose word must be carried out, a lady who must be obeyed. I have not dismissed your words and I have not ignored your plan. As you have said, so I do. Give me your countenance, let me praise it, grant your beauty, that I may gaze upon your form in my tomb, so as to proclaim your power, so as to let posterity know of your might.[24]

Other people claimed that the god directed their lives. Somtu-tefnakht, a priest of Sekhmet who lived in the turbulent times of the Persians and the subsequent conquest of Egypt by Alexander the Great, left a fascinating text on his stela. He related that the god Harsaphes protected him in the battles between the Persians and Greeks and that his own success in finding favor with the administration was due to the god's special favor. He was motivated to make a dangerous return to his hometown by a dream in which the god appeared to him: "Thereafter I saw you [Harsaphes] in my sleep. Your majesty saying to me: 'Hurry to Hnes, I [will] protect you!' I crossed the countries all alone, I sailed the sea unfearing, Knowing that I had not neglected your word, I reached Hnes, my head not robbed of a hair. As my beginning was good through you, So have you made my end complete. You gave me a long lifetime in gladness."[25]

Some of the most vivid records of the unpredicted havoc that displeased gods could wreak on humans are contained in the oracular amuletic decrees of Dynasties 22–23. These refer to the evil that the gods could cause, but they also provide protection against that evil. These amuletic decrees are slips of inscribed papyrus that were folded up and placed in a small container that was worn as a talisman around the neck of the individual who sought divine protection (Fig. 46). They refer to a dizzying array of divine dangers. One decree claims, "We [the gods] shall keep her safe from the gods who bring about an [evil] state of affairs although no [evil] state of affairs should exist. We shall keep her safe from the gods who make a demon against someone." Another promises, "I shall keep him safe from ... every action of every god who does wrong." According to another decree, people were never far from the clutches of the gods: "I shall keep her safe from the gods of the southern region and I shall keep her safe from the gods of the northern region ... [from the] western desert edge, the gods of the sky, the stars ... I shall keep her secure from their hands."[26] These brief texts indicate that gods with evil intent lurked everywhere. There is a reference to "demons of a canal, demons of a wall, of a river, of a pool left by the inundation," all of whom posed potential danger. The gods appear to have delighted in meddling with humans, in some cases making their lives miserable, as related by another decree: "I shall keep her safe from their [god's] manifestations ... from their accusations, [from their] wrong doings, from their vexations."[27]

Seeking Protection from the Gods

The same amuletic decrees that spelled out the dangers posed by the gods offered protection, often provided by other deities. These and other types of amulets could defend against all sorts of mishaps – miscarriage; the sting or bite of reptiles, crocodiles, and scorpions; accidents that might occur while riding in a horse-drawn vehicle, traveling by boat, or walking along the river bank; and thunderbolts and collapsing walls. One decree mysteriously offers protection against bearing twins.[28]

Another form of protection was afforded by a *weret* ("great one [feminine]," or "great thing"). Only a few texts refer to the *weret*, but it was clearly considered to be a potent protection against the *bau* of a god. In one text from Deir el Medina, a man pled, "Please make a *weret* for me, for the one you have made for me has been taken by theft. So she [or it] may make a *bau* of Seth against me."[29] Although it is nowhere specified what a *weret* was, it was probably some sort of physical object, perhaps a figurine.

For those afflicted by illness owing to divine displeasure, temples were considered to be places of healing. The sanctuary of the Temple of Queen Hatshepsut at Deir el Bahri in western Thebes was among the places where

Figure 46. Papyrus inscribed with an oracular decree from the goddess Nekhbet promising to protect a little girl named Taibakhori from dangerous gods, demons, and spirits; from snakes and scorpions; and from "every accident ... by ship, horse or on foot." The papyrus was tightly folded up and placed in a container that was hung around the girl's neck. Dynasties 22–23. OIM 25622a-d. Photo: Anna Ressman. Courtesy of the Oriental Institute of the University of Chicago.

individuals who were sick came to pray to the gods, seeking their intercession against whatever evil spirit had brought them illness. As a reflection of the practical nature of the relationship between humans and gods, those who sought help from the gods left offerings to influence them to help. Many of

Figure 47. Baked clay votive
offering in the form of a woman's
vulva. It may allude to the
desire for children or perhaps
for a cure from a gynecological
illness. Medinet Habu.
Dynasties 21–24. OIM 14598.
Photo: Betsy Kremers. Courtesy
of the Oriental Institute of the
University of Chicago.

these offerings were in the form of votives, usually small wood or pottery
figurines. Some of the votives were shaped like specific body parts (Fig. 47),
much like the figurative metal *milagros* that are a feature of Hispanic religion.
The oracular decrees, already referred to, could also be used to ward off
illness, for some of them ensured that the god(s) would not attack a part of
the body for a specific time period or for eternity. Another text from Deir
el Medina indicated that demons were thought to cause epilepsy as well as
a vague sense of "dread."[30]

Some Egyptians chose to protect their children from divine wrath by
giving the newborn child a name that invoked the gods. These apotropaic
names were a long-standing Egyptian tradition rooted in the Old Kingdom
practice of bestowing simple names such as Seneb, the "Healthy One." By
the New Kingdom, personal names incorporated the names of gods, such
as Thutmose (Born of Thoth), Ramesses (Ra Bore Him), and Bakenkhonsu
(Servant of Khonsu). Increasingly, and especially in the Third Intermediate
Period, theophoric names that refer to the protection or patronage of a
specific god were common; examples include Djed-khonsu-iwes-ankh
(Khonsu Said That She Will Live), Pay-chaw-em-awy-Amun (His Air [i.e.,
breath] Is in the Hands of Amun), and Ptah-irr-disu (Ptah Is the One Who
Made Him).

The numerous records of direct divine intervention in their daily life are
vivid reminders of the Egyptians' deeply rooted faith in the reality, power,

and presence of deities. Contacts between gods and humans were marked by their practicality. The gods were an integral part of the legal and social system, and their omnipresence underscores the lack of division of sacred and secular in ancient Egypt. But the ease of human–divine communication also meant that the gods could, on their own volition, interfere with people's lives – and not always in fair or beneficial ways. As indicated by the texts that refer to the *bau* of the god descending upon those guilty of perjury, most evil from the gods appeared in response to improper human action. But other texts, such as the oracular amuletic decrees, reflect the dangerous and capricious evil that the gods could inflict without cause. However, even in those examples, religious practices such as the wearing of amulets provided relief and protection, reaffirming the fundamental fairness of the universe. It is this sort of symmetry and compassion that makes the Egyptians' ancient religious beliefs fascinating and palatable. Even with the complexity of those beliefs and the risk of danger from unseen forces, humans could hope for a peaceful coexistence with the gods. This balance between potential harm from the gods and the methods the Egyptians developed for alleviating or mitigating it illustrates the practicality of Egyptian religious beliefs. Over the millennia, these customs gave believers support and hope, and ways for the realms of the human and the divine to exist together. This functionality was certainly a factor in the longevity of religious beliefs, for they created a cycle of human need and divine response, and fostered a sense of personal responsibility for correct social behavior that was enforced by the ever-present gods.

Death and Funeral Rites

Death is one of the most prominent features of Egyptian religion. Graves, whether pyramids, vast fields of rectangular mastabas, or tombs cut into the hillsides of the Nile Valley, remain a prominent part of the landscape. A large section of ancient Egypt's economic base was devoted to preparing for death. Groups of men excavated the tombs, designed them, and planned and executed their decoration. Craftsmen designed and created the coffins and statues required by the funerary cult. Other artisans formulated incense that was used for purification rituals, threw the vessels that were used for offerings, wove the lengths of linen used to bandage the mummy, and grew the food that provisioned the deceased. Men and women made their livings serving as priests in mortuary cults. Most people, in one way or another, directly or indirectly, were associated with the industry of death.

The Egyptian Attitude Toward Death

How did the Egyptians manage to live with the grim specter of death always around them yet still enjoy life? Despite their preoccupation with death, they did not look forward to dying. Rather, texts indicate that they hated and feared the end of life. The Old Kingdom sage Hordjedef wrote, "Depressing for us is death – it is life that we hold in high esteem." An inscription that appears in many tombs sums up the relative merits of life and death: "Oh you living ones upon earth, who love life and hate death …" The inevitability of death is related in the lament of a man over his dead wife: "All humanity in one body following their fellow beings [to death]. There is no one who shall stay alive, for we shall all follow you."[1] The Egyptians left vivid descriptions of the realm of the dead and the sadness therein. The autobiographic text of a young woman named Taimhotep (1st c. BC) related the sadness of the end of social contact with her family:

> The west [the realm of the dead] is a land of sleep. Darkness weighs on the dwelling-place. Those who are there sleep in their mummy-forms. They awake not to see their brothers. They see not their fathers, their mothers, Their hearts forget their wives, their children.

Death was a place of unnatural occurrences and deprivations. Taimhotep continued, "The water of life … It is thirst for me. It comes to him who is on earth, [but] I thirst with water beside me."[2]

As with other unknowable phenomena, such as how or why the sun crossed the heavens, the Egyptians developed a conception of life after death that was rooted in what they could see around them and what they experienced during life. Life after death was not significantly different from life itself; existence was simply transferred to another, more remote realm. The closeness and familiarity of the afterlife was comforting because the routines therein provided answers about the unknowable in terms that were entirely understandable. Those grieving the loss of a family member could envision where the deceased was, and even in their grief they could take some solace in knowing what life after death was like for the deceased. Additional comfort came from their knowing that the dead were accessible to the living. The dead were not gone; they were merely away.

Despite the close parallels between life and death, Egyptians did not view the end of life casually. They feared death, mourned lost loved ones, and exerted great effort to prolong life. Letters record familiar scenes. Someone became ill; the family called for the best doctors available; they prayed for the patient's recovery. And when death conquered life, the friends and family grieved, often for years. Indeed, some widowers claimed that they did not remarry out of loyalty to their deceased wives' memory.[3]

The Egyptians' mortuary theology was based on the idea that all those who lived their life morally would be reborn in the afterlife. Rebirth was contingent on how one conducted one's life, not on one's wealth or social standing. The belief that moral rightness would eventually trump wealth is reflected in the tomb of Petosiris (3rd c. BC): "The west is the abode of him who is faultless, Praise god for the man who has reached it! No man will attain it, Unless his heart is exact in doing right." The text continues with a reference to social equality in the beyond: "The poor is not distinguished there from the rich, only he who is found free of fault by scale and weight before eternity's lord."[4] The Late Period text of Setna elaborates on this theme when the poor but just man died and was rewarded with riches taken from the unjust rich man.[5] The expectation of equality after death explains the wide variation in quality evident in Egyptian funerary provisions. Shabtis (funerary figurines that were thought to be able to perform work for the deceased) range in quality from crudely molded clay figurines to finely carved stone examples. Regardless of their relative cost, they were considered to be equally effective for serving the deceased in the afterlife. The less well off must have derived some comfort from knowing that in the afterlife they would be equal to the members of the elite whose wealth and prestige they must have envied. This equality of the rich and poor before the gods, even if only at the end of life, may have alleviated social conflict and ultimately contributed to the stability and longevity of the culture.

Building the Tomb

What did the parallelism between life and death mean in practical terms? Because the deceased would have had the same physical needs in death as in life, he or she would need shelter in the form of a tomb, food and drink, pleasurable activities, and all the trappings of everyday life. These requirements entailed a tremendous expenditure of resources before death. The tomb was a major expense. Whereas houses, meant to be inhabited for only a person's lifetime, were constructed of relatively inexpensive mud brick, tombs had to last for eternity, and so they were built of durable but costly stone. The physical location of the tomb was important for the prestige of the deceased. Some tombs were grouped in specific areas because the tomb owners shared the same profession. Other owners received their tomb sites as a reward from the king. One Old Kingdom autobiographical text relates, "Regarding this tomb which I made in the necropolis; the king gave me its location … for I always did what his lord favors." Another inscription refers to the individual "requesting" that the king grant him a sarcophagus and burial.[6] Not all royal favors seem to have been the result of faithful service – some were more casual. The official Debehen (Dynasty 4) recalls. "With regard to this tomb of mine; it was the King of Upper and Lower Egypt Menkaure who gave me its place while he happened to be on the way to the pyramid plateau to inspect the work being done on [his] pyramid."[7] There was, at least in some cases, concern that the tomb not be located on a previously developed site and not encroach on other tombs: "I made this tomb of mine where there was no tomb of any man, so that the property of one who has gone to his *ka* [died] could be protected."[8] But often, tomb sites, and entire tombs, were usurped. If this occurred after the tomb had been abandoned by the family of the original owner, then it could be refurbished. For example, in the Late Period, the mayor of Thebes, Nespakashuty, renovated a Middle Kingdom tomb near Deir el Bahri, lining the walls with fresh new limestone slabs that were then carved with funerary scenes. Less noble was the outright usurpation of a tomb. In that case, the original inhabitant might be cast out of the burial chamber and the names on the walls changed to reflect the new owner.

Until the Third Intermediate Period, when group tombs became common, a tomb was usually commissioned for a man and his wife, unless the woman was of very high social rank, in which case she would have her own tomb, or at least her own wing of a double tomb. Children were expected to build their own tombs, but there were exceptions. A man named Djau recalled why he had chosen to share the tomb of his father, also named Djau: "I saw to it that I [Djau Jr.] was buried in one tomb along with Djau [Sr.], because of the desire to be with him in one place, and not because of the lack of means to build a second tomb. I did this from the desire to see Djau [Sr.] every day."[9]

An individual would normally contract with a professional architect for the design and with draftsmen for the decoration of his tomb. Some fortunate individuals received from the king not only the tomb site but also the labor to build the tomb. The official Debehen claimed that "he [the king] arranged for fifty craftsmen to do the work on it daily and they were assigned the completion of the *wabet*" (the place of embalming). He boasted that his tomb was "100 cubits long and fifty cubits in breadth and five cubits high [?] [about 45 by 23 by 2.5 meters] ... larger than that which my father [could have] made when he was alive." He also claimed that the king forbade anyone to disrupt the men who worked on the tomb: "His majesty commanded that they [the workmen] not be taken for any work duty other than carrying out work on [my tomb]."[10] An official named Tetiseneb (Dynasty 6) also claimed to have received his tomb's plot at Saqqara from the king, but he adopted a more hands-on approach: "I paid the stonemason who made it for me so that he was satisfied with it [the payment]. I did the work within it with my own hand together with my children and my siblings."[11] Other Old Kingdom texts refer to artisans' being paid with bread, beer, linen, copper, oil, clothing, and grain, and one tomb owner commented on the satisfaction of his crew: "With regard to any person who worked therein for me, they worked on it thanking the god for me very greatly."[12]

Work on a tomb started as soon as the owner had resources to devote to the project, probably as soon as he had steady employment. In some, or perhaps most, cases, work progressed throughout the tomb owner's lifetime. A not uncommon claim was "I made this tomb while I was alive."[13] But many, perhaps the majority, of tombs were not complete at the time of the owner's death. In such cases, the eldest son, who was responsible for the burial, hastily finished decorating the tomb in paint rather in relief carving, or left entire walls blank, for by that time, the son was probably also working on his own tomb. Those owners whose tombs were completed during their lifetimes could stand back and marvel at their work. Debehen (Dynasty 4) described all the finished details of his tomb, including its false door, limestone walls, and statues, giving the impression that his tomb was complete.[14] Once finished, a tomb would stand open, ready to receive the burial. For the rest of his or her life, the owner would come to admire the tomb and would no doubt bring visitors as well to be impressed by its splendor.

Most tombs were composed of two parts – the subterranean burial chamber and the offering chapel above ground (Fig. 48). Both sections were targets for robbers and vandals, and thus security was a major consideration in tomb design. Although the offering chapel was semipublic and was intended to be visited by the living, it had doors to control access. The most vulnerable part of the tomb, the burial chamber, was protected by various mechanical and magical means. After the funeral, the entrance to the burial chamber was blocked with a mud-brick or stone wall making it inaccessible to all but the most determined robbers. Magic bricks, usually in sets of four (symbolizing the protection of the four cardinal points), were placed at the corners of the burial chamber, sealed into the walls of the chamber, or placed in the walls of the burial shaft. The brick for the east usually had the Anubis jackal (Fig. 49); the west, a *djed* pillar; the south, a torch; and the north, a mummiform figure. There was great variation in the quality and appearance of these guardians. Those from the tomb of Tutankhamun are topped with wooden statues, while other, lesser tombs were protected by crudely made

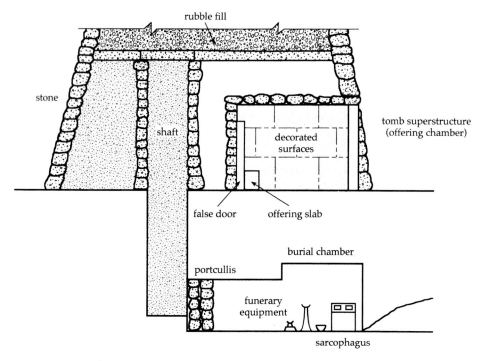

Figure 48. Diagram of a tomb with above-ground offering chamber (or chapel) and subterranean burial chamber. The burial chamber was sealed after the deposition of the coffin and the grave goods. The chapel served as an area where people could leave offerings and admire the wall decorations.

magic bricks with hastily drawn or incised hieratic inscriptions. These bricks are known from the New Kingdom into Dynasty 21, and then for unknown reasons, after disappearing for a time, they reappear in the Late Period.

Tombs were also protected by curses against anyone who might vandalize them or dismantle them in order to use the materials for their own tomb (Fig. 50). Although the form of curses changed over time, the most common threats promised physical suffering, loss of inheritance, lack of funerary offerings, and being "hated by god." These curses are very common, especially in the Third Intermediate Period when they include very detailed gruesome details of the physical suffering the offender shall endure, such as being roasted over a fire, or an ass violating the offender and his entire family.[15] A common formula is "in regard to ... [anyone] who shall do evil to the tomb of mine for eternity, by removing bricks or stone from it, no voice shall be given to him in the sight of any god, or any man."[16] This threat seems to take away the potential vandal's ability to appeal for mercy or to defend himself at the judgment. Other curse texts try to reason with

Figure 49. Magic brick made of mud with remains of the figure of a recumbent jackal. It bears the cartouche of Menkhepere (Thutmose III) and a passage from Book of the Dead Spell 151g. The notation in white ink indicates that the brick was on the eastern wall of the tomb, facing west. Thebes. Dynasty 18. OIM 10544. Photo Anna Ressman. Courtesy of the Oriental Institute of the University of Chicago.

the potential vandal: "O every man who would commit sacrilege in this pure place. Do not reach out your arms against me! [Instead] perform the rites ... which are here for the deceased."[17] Whether defacing tombs was seen as a serious and real problem, or only as a vague threatening possibility, the curses indicate that tomb owners did worry about it happening.

Other curses are specifically directed against those who might enter a tomb in a state of impurity: "All people who may enter into this my tomb in their impurity, after having eaten the abomination that an *akh*-spirit abominates, and while they are not clean for me as they should be clean ... I will seize him by the neck like a bird."[18] A similar curse in the tomb of Hezi at Saqqara (Dynasty 6) bars from entering "any man who shall enter this tomb ... after he has had sexual intercourse with women."[19] On a more positive note, blessings were also inscribed in tombs, promising to protect those who made the proper offerings to the tomb: "Anyone who shall make

Figure 50. Fragment of a curse threatening that the neck of anyone who damages the tomb or offerings will be wrung like that of a bird. Dynasty 6. OIM 10814. Courtesy of the Oriental Institute of the University of Chicago.

invocation offerings or shall pour water," one tomb owner wrote, "I shall protect him in the necropolis."[20]

Another major expense of preparing for death was the coffin(s) or sarcophagus. An elite person's tomb of the Old Kingdom might be equipped with a huge granite sarcophagus, the stone for which was laboriously brought from Aswan. These were very expensive and time consuming to produce. In his autobiographic text, the official Senedjemib-Mehi (Dynasty 5) claims to have spent a year and three months preparing his father's sarcophagus.

Figure 51. Interior of the wood coffin of Ipi-ha-ishutef painted with images of clothing, food, and objects of daily life that were wanted by the deceased in the afterlife. In the middle register are two cylindrical vessels and two *ankh*-shaped amulets. Below are a pair of sandals and a bag of natron. Saqqara. Dynasty 11. OIM 12072. Courtesy of the Oriental Institute of the University of Chicago.

In the meantime, the father's mummy was left in the embalmer's workshop awaiting the sarcophagus's completion.[21] Another burial option was a rectangular wood box that could be painted with representations of food and other objects needed in the afterlife (Fig. 51). By the New Kingdom, the fashion was to have sets of anthropoid coffins (Plate XIII), one inside another, with the outermost often nested within a rectangular wood sarcophagus. Economic records from about 1200 BC indicate that a decorated wooden coffin cost an average of 25 *deben* of copper (the most expensive in the records being 200 *deben*), a considerable expense, as compared to the 1 or 3 *deben* required to buy a sheep.[22]

Decorating the walls of the tomb was another major expense. The false door was usually a large slab that needed to be carved, inscribed, and painted before it was installed near the tomb shaft. If an official caught the eye of the king, this feature of the tomb might also be given as a royal favor. The physician Ny-ankh-Sekhmet (Dynasty 5) claimed that his wish for a false door was granted by the king. The pharaoh enthusiastically donated two false doors and personally supervised their construction in the royal audience hall, where he could come see their progress.[23] Ankh-Khufu (probably late Dynasty 5) too claimed that the king supervised the construction of the false door for his tomb, recording that "his majesty saw what was done daily."[24]

Wall paintings and reliefs were executed by professional draftsmen who consulted with the tomb owner about what scenes to create and how to arrange them. The repetition of scenes, such as the collection of taxes typical of the Old Kingdom, or New Kingdom depictions of Hathor receiving the deceased into the West, suggest that draftsmen shared standard pattern books of scenes from which a tomb owner could select. Further resources were devoted to the production of statues of the deceased that would receive offerings in the tomb.

Provisioning the Dead

The food offerings that were left for the soul of the deceased were yet another major funerary expense. Because the deceased lived forever in the afterlife, these offerings had to be provided in perpetuity, although the Egyptians were practical enough to recognize that, at some point, the arrangements for leaving food would break down as the family resources were directed elsewhere, the memory of the particular individual became dim, or the family moved away.

The cult of an important or wealthy person required huge amounts of food and supplies. The concern shown for providing for the offering cult is reflected in economic records from all periods that established funds to pay for the offerings after the death of the tomb owner. Little was left to chance. One of the longer and most explicit lists is preserved in the tomb of Ankhmeryre at Saqqara (Dynasty 6); it enumerates specific amounts of eye paints, oils, a wide variety of types of cakes and bread, meats, beers and wines, and fruit and vegetables.[25] Texts indicate that there was a sophisticated network for producing the offerings for private mortuary cults. The texts of Metjen (Dynasty 4) show that his food offerings were raised in different locations all over Lower Egypt and then conveyed to his tomb at Saqqara. He also received food from the funerary estate of the king's mother.[26] There are many economic records that deal with the buying and selling of plots of land that were used to raise food offerings. The official Tjenti even stated that "he begged them (the lands) from the king."[27]

Alongside the lists of what was desired for the offering cults are legal texts that sought to protect the sources of those offerings. Transfer of the fields that produced the grain to make funerary loaves might be prohibited, and the labor of the personnel who produced and presented the offerings was also carefully sheltered from being diverted to another cult.[28] Decrees that exempted (or protected) the workers on the royal funerary estates from being drafted for other state service are known as early as the Old Kingdom.[29]

An individual could set up a funerary endowment that would pay for priests to come to the tomb, leave food, and recite prayers. There were several different classes of priests involved (see Chapter 2). The lector (*khery hebet*) who read the spells is frequently mentioned. For example, an Old Kingdom text relates, "Beloved is the lector priest who shall come to my tomb and carry out rites in accordance with [those writings] of the lector. May the acts be carried out for me in accordance with what is on his papyrus roll."[30] Another category of priest frequently mentioned in the Old Kingdom tomb cults is the *ka* priest: "That *ka* priest who carries out the activity on my behalf under his [the son of the deceased] supervision, it is he who shall organize them [the offerings] daily." These priests worked in teams, often large groups of them as indicated by a text from Coptos that reads, in part, "My majesty has commanded that there be raised for you twelve inspectors of *ka*-priests … to do priestly duties … and who shall carry out the monthly festivals for her in her *ka* chapels."[31]

There were apparently conflicts over the control of the priests who served in the private mortuary cults. The tomb of Nyankhkhnum and Khnumhotep at Saqqara includes the directions that neither the children nor wives of the deceased should be allowed to "have power over" the staff of priests who have been assigned the duty of making offerings for the deceased. The text suggests that priests in private mortuary service could potentially be reassigned to another funerary establishment, for it comments that "with regard to any [*ka*] priest who shall be reassigned to another priestly duty: everything which

Figure 52. Group of statues that represent the deceased's family and the house workers who will prepare food for the deceased for eternity. The group also includes musicians and a set of six conical silos for grain. Giza (?). Dynasty 5. Courtesy of the Oriental Institute of the University of Chicago.

has been given to him shall be taken from him and given instead to the [*ka*] priests of his phyle" (i.e., a priest who still works for the family cult).[32]

Food for an individual's tomb could also come from offerings that were presented daily in a local temple of a god. A text in the tomb of Nykaiankh (Dynasty 5) records that his mortuary cult was to receive one-tenth of everything that entered the local temple, and that offering at his tomb was to be performed daily, at the first day of each month, at the "half months," and "at every festival throughout the year."[33] There were many festivals, so his tomb received a lot of attention.

Another means of providing food offerings was by covering the walls of the tomb or the coffin with images of food. Through the principle of substitution, the images were thought to be able to serve as actual food. Food could also be supplied by three-dimensional models, such as loaves of bread made of stone. To ensure that the symbolic food offerings would be ever present and fresh, stone statues of men and women making food could be included in the tomb. Some of these, such as the group of statues from the tomb of Nykauinpu, even include small silos to ensure that the workers never ran out of supplies (Fig. 52). In the Middle Kingdom, wooden models of entire workshops showing the household staff grinding grain, making beer, and slaughtering cattle were included among the burial goods (Plate XIV). In the New Kingdom, tombs were stocked with mummiform statues called shabtis who were ready to perform agricultural labor for the deceased (Fig. 53).

Food offerings could also be supplied by merely saying prayers that referred to provisions. The offerings were actualized by the recitation that magically produced or consecrated the "bread, beer, oxen, alabaster, incense and every good and pure thing" for the deceased. These offerings were originally referred to as "voice offerings" (*peret kherw*), literally, "what goes forth at the voice," because the act of pronouncing the names of the offerings along with the name of the deceased brought them into being in the afterlife – another example of the efficiency and economy of Egyptian rituals.

Individuals could actively participate in supplying food for the deceased by visiting tombs and speaking the name for food desired by the deceased. A standard element of wall inscriptions was the "appeal to the living" that encouraged visitors to participate in the cult by reciting, "Oh you who live on earth and who shall pass by this tomb of mine, pour water and beer for me which you possess. If you have nothing, then you shall speak with your mouth and offer with your hand, bread, beer, oxen, fowl, incense and pure things."[34] Graffiti by visitors to tombs suggest that some of them were not related to the tomb owner. They were probably drawn to the site by the reliefs and the architecture. This is an interesting phenomenon, for most necropolises are at some distance from villages, suggesting that the necropolis was a definite destination and that a walk among the tombs must have been a common recreation. The strength of the belief in the efficacy of the "appeal to the living" type texts is especially striking, for the literacy rate was very low – perhaps two to three percent in the dynastic period – and so it was unlikely that a random visitor to the tomb could actually read the invocation.

These same texts called on the living to also recite the name of the deceased. One text implored the living to say the name of the deceased "so that you shall cause me to be remembered without my being forgotten."[35] The same sentiment is more concisely recorded in the Late Period tomb of Petosiris: "A man is revived when his name is pronounced."[36] This association of the repetition of the name with the eternal life of the deceased is already stressed in the Pyramid Texts, some two thousand years earlier. The tomb and its decoration, with their many references to the tomb owner, were vital parts of the deceased's link with immortality.

Preparing the Mummy

Most of what we know about the embalming process comes from the mummies themselves and from the lengthy account of Herodotus (II:86.89). Following a death, the family members contracted with professional embalmers to take the body to a temporary reed and mat structure called the *ibu*, or "tent of purification." There the body was washed and then taken to another workshop, called the *wabet*, literally, the "pure place." A Dynasty 6 inscription relates that the official Mekhu heard that his father had died in Elephantine. When he arrived, he "found him there in the *wabet*, laid out in the manner of the dead,"[37] giving the impression that the *wabet* functioned as a local morgue. Some texts refer to the *wabet* as a temporary structure, although inscriptions from the tombs of Nefer and Kai refer to a *wabet*'s brick walls and rock-cut basins and drains.[38]

Oddly, there are few economic texts or references to embalmers or the organization of their profession. The most explicit is a demotic archive from a workshop in the town of Hawara.[39] That institution was headed by the *hery-seshta*, "he who is over the secrets." Herodotus (ca. 450 BC) referred to embalmers respectfully, as professionals who practiced the craft of mummification. Diodorus (1st c. BC) gave mixed reports of the repute of embalmers. On the one hand, he recorded a curious ritual in which the chief embalmer (according to him, called the "ripper-up" of the body) ran from the workshop in a hail of curses and stones from his fellow workers as ritual punishment for cutting into the body. Yet, he also commented that embalmers were "considered worthy of every honor and consideration." An Old Kingdom inscription from Saqqara relates that the deceased promised to be the "champion" of the embalmer, acknowledging his gratitude to the practitioner.[40]

Embalmers worked in teams. At Hawara, the chief embalmer was aided by another class of priests called *khetemu-netcher*, as well as by lower-ranking *weyt*, or embalmer technicians. The much earlier (Dynasty 6) autobiographical texts of the official Sebni at Aswan offers a glimpse of the variety of people that were involved in the embalming process. When Sebni traveled to Nubia to recover the body of his father and bring it back to Egypt for burial, he was accompanied by

> two embalmers, a senior lector priest, one who is on annual duty [i.e., full time], the
> inspector of the *wabet*, mourners, and the whole equipment from the *per-nefer* [a type

Figure 53. Mummiform statute (shabti) of Hedj-renpet that was thought to be able to perform services for the deceased. The shabti holds hoes in each hand for doing agricultural work and it wears a heart-shaped pendant. Dynasties 18–19. OIM 10580. Photo: Jean Grant. Courtesy of the Oriental Institute of the University of Chicago.

of embalming workshop], he brought *seti-heb* oil from the *per-nefer* the secrets of the *wabet* [i.e., the embalming techniques] ... from the house of weapons [referring to tools?], linens from the treasury, and all the needs of burial which come from the Residence.[41]

Demotic texts from Siut refer to specific duties in the first three days after death: collecting the body from the family and performing ceremonies in the embalmer's workshop (*per-nefer*). The next notation, for the fourth day, deals with the collection of linen wrappings. It continues with the supplies for the man who does the anointing and then for the man who "has to go and collect the people outside the town."[42] Presumably, this is a reference to professional mourners who were a standard feature of Egyptian funerals.

Texts indicate that the embalming process usually took forty days. The seventy days that are mentioned in many texts ("A good burial comes in peace. Your seventy days have been completed in your *wabet*") was considered an ideal interval for allowing the body to be wrapped and prepared for delivery to the family. The number of days was based on the astronomical phenomenon of decans, stars that remained below the horizon for seventy days before rising above the horizon, an allusion to the rising of the deceased from the afterlife. There was, however, much variation in the actual timing. Old Kingdom texts refer to the body of Senedjemib-Inti that stayed in the *wabet* for almost 500 days, and to Queen Meresankh (Dynasty 4) who was buried 273 (or 274) days after her death.[43] In contrast, a text at Deir el Medina (Dynasty 20) relates that a woman was buried only two days after her death, leaving virtually no time for ritual preparation of the body.[44]

Additional documentation of the mortuary process includes references to embalmers' activities in letters and economic texts, such as receipts. The only pictorial evidence consists of the highly simplified scenes of bodies on embalming beds that appear on some coffins (Plate XV). The most complete account of mummification is given by Herodotus, who related that the embalmers offered three different styles of preparation for burial, which they demonstrated to their clients by wooden models.

Embalming tools supply considerable, but incomplete, information about the way that embalmers worked. It has been suggested that a wood table discovered in the tomb of Ipy at Thebes (Dynasty 11) is an embalmer's table, and examples of stone tables with drains at the end have also been interpreted as embalmers' tables. While some scholars consider these to be offering tables, their rectangular shape and their slant toward the drain and basin suggest their association with embalming.

Items such as knives for slitting the body are known, as are the rectangular stone tablets with small depressions for storing the seven oils used in the mummification process. Several larger groups of materials have been identified as materials from embalmers' workshops. Typically, these caches contain flat saucers with the remains of resins, scraps of linen that seem to have been rags, whisk brooms, and linen tubes and bags filled with a salty substance that are assumed to have be used in drying out the body. One such cache, purchased in Luxor in 1932–3, contained fabric tubes and packets of what is assumed to be natron, and saucers and jars, but also mysterious objects made of rolls of linen (and reeds?) about two centimeters thick that were further wrapped in strips of linen and then twisted into circles and loops with tails (Fig. 54). They are heavily soiled with resin (?), perhaps indicating that they were in contact with the body. Their function is unknown, but they may have been used to position the limbs during the wrapping process.

Another embalmers' cache, associated with the burial of King Tutankhamun, was discovered in the Valley of the Kings in 1907. It contained about fifteen large whitewashed jars that held linen, small brooms and sticks, and dishes of resin.[45] A very similar cache of materials was discovered in the Valley of the Kings in 2005.[46]

Other remains from embalmers' workshops consist of identification tags that bear the name and often the filiation and age of the deceased (Fig. 55). Examples from Roman burials at Medinet Habu were hung around the neck of the mummy.

According to Herodotus, the process of mummification began with washing the body. An incision was then made in the left side of the abdomen to allow for the removal of the major organs. This opening was short, which made it difficult for the embalmers to remove the contents of the abdomen, much less to pierce the diaphragm and remove the lungs. The limited visibility of the body's interior may account for why the kidneys, which are separated from the organs in the abdomen by the smooth wall of the peritoneum, were often left in the body.

Some corpses were subjected to very invasive procedures, such as slitting the desiccated flesh along the legs and arms in order to introduce subcutaneous packing to make the limbs look more lifelike. A few examples of bodies from the Old Kingdom and First Intermediate Period were entirely defleshed and the bones coated in plaster. This was probably an effort to make the mummy more like a statue, which the Egyptians regarded as an imperishable image of the deceased.[47]

Although the ideal was to be mummified, not everyone could afford this luxury. One of the major expenses of the mummification process was the linen. The more lavish the mummy, the more linen that was used. Linen was so expensive that some burial shrouds and bandages were made of recycled garments. Even some royal mummies were found to have been wrapped (or at least rewrapped) in reused linen sheets rather than in bandages woven specially for the purpose. In contrast, some of the linen used to wrap the mummy of King Tutankhamun had notations on the corners indicating it was woven specifically for his funeral.

There is evidence that, for unknown reasons, some individuals who certainly could afford to be mummified were not. An ostracon from Deir el

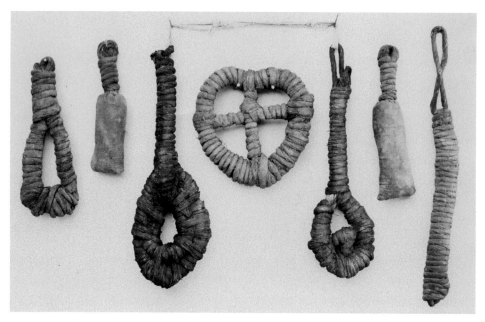

Figure 54. Materials from an embalmer's workshop including two tubes of natron and a group of resin-stained fabric objects whose function is unknown. Thebes. New Kingdom? Courtesy of the Oriental Institute of the University of Chicago.

Medina refers to a woman, Ta-hanu, who died and was buried only two days later. This is confirmed by archaeological evidence from the village, for other residents of the village were simply wrapped in linen without being mummified. However, Hatnofer, the father of Senenmut, a high official of Hatshepsut, who could certainly have afforded to be mummified, was not.

Overseeing the mummification and burial of a parent was the greatest obligation children had toward their parents. The child designated for this role bore the title "eldest son." In cases where there were no sons, a daughter, or even the widowed wife would assume the role and title of "eldest son."[48] This individual was granted a larger portion of the deceased's estate to help defray the cost of the burial. Funerary stelae frequently include the claim that "it is his son who makes his name live," a reference to the proper commemoration of the deceased and therefore to ensure a proper afterlife. This of course was the ideal, but letters reflect the complicated reality of family obligations. In one letter, a man petulantly complained that he dutifully buried his brother even though the deceased owed him linen and thirty measures of grain.[49]

Plate I. Stela of the nobleman Uha with an inscription calling for bread, beer, oxen, fowl, and "every good and pure thing" for eternity. Naga ed Deir (?). Dynasties 7–11. OIM 16956. Courtesy of the Oriental Institute of the University of Chicago.

Plate II. Scene of craftsmen as depicted in the tomb of the noblemen Nebamun and Ipuky. A man (*upper left*) weighs gold rings against an ox-head weight. *To the right,* woodworkers carve *djed* columns and *tayet* knots, perhaps ornaments for furniture. *Below,* men put finishing touches on a sphinx, engrave a text on a jar, and make jewelry and fancy boxes. Such scenes of everyday activities preserved those actions for the afterlife. Tomb of Nebamun and Ipuky at Thebes (TT 181). Dynasty 18. Facsimile by Norman de Garis Davies. Courtesy of the Oriental Institute of the University of Chicago.

Plate III (left). Mery, a temple singer of Amun, with her *menat* (beaded necklace) and her sistrum (rattle), which made sounds thought to be pleasing to the gods. Singers with these ritual instruments would accompany the priest as he made offerings to the god. Tomb of Sennefer at Thebes (TT 96). Dynasty 18. Photo: C. F. Nims. Courtesy of the Oriental Institute of the University of Chicago.

Plate IV (below). Reconstruction of the façade of the Temple of Ramesses III at Medinet Habu, with its brightly painted façade and cedar masts topped with flags. The pylons are carved with scenes of the king smiting enemies before the god. These compositions affirmed the power of the king to his subjects. Dynasty 20. Courtesy of the Oriental Institute of the University of Chicago.

Plate V. Reconstruction of the sanctuary of the Luxor Temple with the naos that sheltered the statue of the god. The double doors of the naos are opened, revealing the divine statue. Courtesy of Jean-Claude Golvin.

Plate VI. Silver statue of a falcon-headed god, possibly a cult statue for the god
Horus or Re. Dynasty 19 (?). SF04.070. Courtesy of the Miho Museum, Shumei
Culture Foundation Collection.

Plate VII. Nakhtamun and his wife pray to Hathor who appears in the form of a cow emerging from the western hills of Thebes. The west, as the direction of the setting or dying sun, was considered to be the land of the dead. Tomb of Nakhtamun at Thebes (TT 341). Dynasty 19. Photo: C. F. Nims. Courtesy of the Oriental Institute of the University of Chicago.

Plate VIII. Procession during the Beautiful Feast of the Valley showing statues of the deceased Amunhotep III and Queen Tiye. The large fans held over the statues proclaim their divinity. Tomb of Amuneminet at Thebes (TT 277). Dynasties 19–20. Photo: C. F. Nims. Courtesy of the Oriental Institute of the University of Chicago.

Plate IX. Men, wearing floral *weseh* collars, celebrating the Beautiful Feast of the Valley. Tomb of Haremheb at Thebes (TT 78). Dynasty 18. Photo courtesy of Melinda Hartwig.

Plate X. The presentation of a floral *ankh* bouquet to the nose of the deceased Pairy and his wife by their son during the celebration of the Feast of the Valley. Pairy inhales the scent of the flowers that are imbued with the power of Amun. The text above Pairy encourages him to forget his cares and see the beauty of his tomb. Tomb of Pairy at Thebes (TT 139). Dynasty 18. Photo courtesy of Melinda Hartwig.

Plate XI. Reconstruction of the front of a votive bed decorated with a scene of a woman in a boat in a marsh. She plucks papyrus from the marsh, a ritual that was associated with the goddess Hathor. Figures of Bes stand at either side. Votive beds were probably used in rituals that invoked fertility and rebirth. Medinet Habu. Dynasties 22–24. Watercolor by Angela Altenhofen.

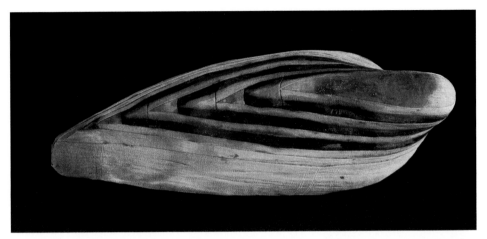

Plate XII. Mummy of an ibis in geometric linen wrappings. The ibis was considered to be the *ba* or spirit of the god Thoth. Ibises were raised in temple precincts, mummified, and sold to people who visited the temple. In the later periods of Egyptian history, animal mummy cults became widespread. Abydos. Roman Period. OIM 9238. Photo: Jean Grant. Courtesy of the Oriental Institute of the University of Chicago.

Plate XIII. Set of coffins consisting of a cartonnage inner coffin (*right*) and two nested wood anthropoid coffins for the Lady Shepetenkhonsu. Thebes. Dynasty 22. Courtesy of the Oriental Institute of the University of Chicago.

Plate XIV. Model workshop showing butchers (*right*) and bakers at work. A group of tall beer jars stand in a basket in the center of the model. Sedment el Gebel. Dynasties 9–10. OIM 11495. Photo: Jean Grant. Courtesy of the Oriental Institute of the University of Chicago.

Plate XV. Stages in the mummification process as shown on a coffin. *Lowest register*, the body (shown as a black silhouette) is purified. *Next register*, the body is laid on a funerary bed as the jackal-headed god Anubis officiates. *Above*, Anubis stands over the wrapped mummy, which is shown with the four canopic jars (*left*) and with oars to navigate the way to the afterlife (*right*). *Uppermost register*, priests perform the Opening of the Mouth that revived the deceased. Ptolemaic Period. Hildesheim, Pelizaeus-Museum 1954. Photo © Roemer-Pelizaeus-Museum, Hildesheim.

Plate XVI. Scene of a funeral procession showing the ornate shrine containing the sarcophagus and coffin being dragged to the tomb by a team of oxen. A priest dressed in a panther skin offers incense and pours a purification. Men and women mourners to the left and right raise their arms in a gesture of grief. Tomb of Roy at Thebes (TT 255). Dynasty 18. Photo: C. F. Nims. Courtesy of the Oriental Institute of the University of Chicago.

Plate XVII. A *tekenu* bundle flanked by two statues being drawn to the burial. The *tekenu* contained materials from the mummification process that were not placed in the coffin or the canopic jars. Tomb of Nebamun at Thebes (TT 17). Dynasty 18. Photo: C. F. Nims. Courtesy of the Oriental Institute of the University of Chicago.

Plate XVIII. Akhenaten as a sphinx in the rays of the Aten, which is shown as the globe of the sun. The rays of the sun end in human hands that reach out to the king and bestow an *ankh* (life) sign to the nose of the king. 1964.003. Dynasty 18. Photo: Christian Tepper. Courtesy of the August Kestner Museum.

Figure 55. Limestone label used to identify a mummy in an embalmer's workshop. The demotic inscription identifies the deceased as a woman named Esoeris, daughter of Pachois. Roman Period, late first century BC–early first century AD. OIM 25285. Photo: Anna Ressman. Courtesy of the Oriental Institute of the University of Chicago.

The Funeral

One of the most moving descriptions of an ancient funeral is recorded in a text in the tomb of Dheuty at Thebes:

> The beautiful burial, may it come in peace after your seventy days are completed in your embalming hall. May you be laid out on a bier in the house of rest and be drawn by white oxen. May the ways [i.e., the road] be opened with milk until your arrival at the entrance to your tomb. May the children of your children all be assembled and wail with loving heart. May your mouth be opened by the chief lector priest, may you be purified by the *sem*-priest, may Horus weigh your heart for you after he has opened your eyes and ears. May your limbs and bones be present for you. May the transfiguration spells be read for you, and may the mortuary offerings be performed for you. May your heart be with you in the right way ... you being restored to your previous form as on the day when you were born. May the *sa-mer*-priest be brought to you, and may the Friends sing the litany.[50]

There must have been great variation in the scale and complexity of funerals, both across time and across economic and social standing. Our most explicit source of information comes from tomb paintings that show idealized elaborate funerals that may not have been particularly common.

After the ceremonial seventy days required to prepare the corpse, the body was released from the workshop. It was placed in a coffin, or set of coffins, which in turn was enclosed in a large shrine. Tomb scenes depict the production of these shrines, and some examples have survived. The funerary shrine was mounted on a sledge (Plate XVI) to make it easier to transport over sand. The coffin was accompanied by a smaller shrine that contained a compartmented box for the canopic jars that held the desiccated lungs, liver, stomach, and intestines that had been removed during mummification. A third element was the *tekenu*, a shapeless bundle (or a bundle with a human head) on a sledge (Plate XVII). It is thought that the *tekenu* contained material left from the embalming process that was not, or could not be, enclosed in the canopic jars, which were usually so small that they contained only a symbolic sample of the four major organs.[51] No actual examples of *tekenu* have been recovered. Once mounted on sledges, the shrines were drawn by cattle or oxen in the funerary procession. Tomb scenes show participants sprinkling milk in the procession's path to lubricate and symbolically purify the way.

In the New Kingdom, the period for which we have the most explicit information, the funerary procession recreated a ritual drama alluding to the passage to the West and the deceased's union with the gods. The procession included different ranks of priests, the embalmer, craftsmen, and the family and friends of the deceased. In the tomb of Tjay at Thebes, the participants shown are various ranks of priests (chief lector, *sem*, *imy-s*-priest, *sa-mer*, and *imy-khent*) and the "Nine Friends" who represent the Followers and Sons of Horus and who drag the coffin and sing liturgies. Following this group was a sculptor, a carver, craftsmen (?), a carpenter, "the two mourning birds" (two women who represent Isis and Nephthys), a group of professional mourners, and the family of the deceased. High officials would be accompanied to their tomb by their colleagues in government service; the funerary entourage of the official Amenemope included both viziers. Such an entourage would have been a very loud and dramatic presence as it traveled through the west bank necropolis to the tomb site.

The procession set off from the embalmers' workshop in the morning. The first act in the ritual drama of burial was the crossing of the Nile from East – the land of the living – to the West – the abode of the dead. New Kingdom texts refer to the ferry as the *neshmet* barque, the sacred boat of Osiris, an allusion to the deceased's association with the god of the afterlife.

The association with Osiris was furthered by statues (or priestesses) that represented Isis and Nepythys, the sisters of Osiris, who were the archetypical mourners in Egyptian mythology (Fig. 56).

In some texts, the Nine Friends appear, pulling the sarcophagus, as they sing the litany "beware O earth!" In the painting on the east wall of Tutankhamun's burial chamber (Fig. 57), they are followed by two priests with white bands on their shaved heads and an additional official. The Friends are exhorted by the lector priest who calls them to put "your arms on the ropes!"[52]

The funerary procession was also accompanied by porters who carried the grave goods and by professional mourners, most often groups of women, who wailed, bared their breasts, and threw dust in their hair as a sign of grief (Fig. 58). In the New Kingdom, the period from which we have our most explicit liturgies and stage directions for the funerary rituals, the tombs of the necropolis had become perfectly adapted for these rituals, having developed into a combination of tomb and temple. A tomb's forecourt was often walled, creating a semiprivate space for the performance of the rites.

Once the procession arrived at the tomb, the mummy was stood upright, its face to the south to be "bathed in light," and absorb the life-restoring power of the sun. Texts relate, "May your mummy be set up in the sight of Re in the court of your tomb, you being given over to the scale of the necropolis. May you emerge vindicated!"[53] Assmann has suggested that at this moment a priest recited Chapter 125 of Book of the Dead, which records the judgment of the dead before the gods.

In scenes depicting funerals, the mummy is usually shown in the embrace of Anubis (Fig. 59), while the widow collapses in grief at the foot of the coffin. It is unclear whether these are mythological scenes of the god Anubis himself, or realistic portrayals of a priest wearing a jackal mask. Although a single helmet-style Anubis mask has survived from the Late Period (Fig. 60), it seems more likely that these scenes showing an animal-headed human are symbolic portrayals of the deity.[54]

Once the procession reached the entrance to the tomb, the priests performed the Opening of the Mouth to restore the deceased's ability to see, speak, hear, and taste. This mortuary ritual was derived from the Old Kingdom ceremony that activated funerary statues, enabling them to serve as the recipient of offerings for the deceased. The Opening of the Mouth

Figure 56. Nepythys (*left*) and Isis (*right*), the sisters of Osiris, in the form of winged goddesses, guarding the mummy of their brother. Dendera. Greco-Roman Period. Photo: Emily Teeter.

was divided into a series of individual rituals. The first was primarily for the purification of the body. A *sem* priest and two lectors circled the mummy four times as they intoned, "Be pure! Be pure!" In the next sequence, the *sem* fell into a trance in order to assume the role of the son of the deceased. The other priests then "woke" him saying, "Waking the sleeping one, the *sem*-priest." The *sem* responded, "I have seen my father in all his forms," thus beginning a ritual dialogue between the priests that calls on the *sem* to protect his "father," symbolically placing the priest in the role of Horus and the deceased in that of Osiris. One very detailed account of the Opening of the Mouth from the Ramesside Period (ca. 1100 BC) continued with a sequence in which the *sem* having seen all forms of his "father" described them to the craftsmen who accompanied the funeral. This may be a reference to

Figure 57. The ceremonial Nine Friends dragging the sarcophagus to the tomb. The Friends are followed by two bald priests and another official. Tomb of Tutankhamun. Dynasty 18. Photo: Harry Burton. Copyright: Griffith Institute, University of Oxford.

the statues of the deceased that had been brought to the tomb. The purpose of this part of the ritual was to activate them as recipients of offerings, just as the mobility of the mummy was restored by the ceremony. The dialogue with the craftsmen continued: "Make it [the funerary statue] like my father! ... Make my father for me! Make it like my father! Who is it who makes it for me?" In the next sequence, the violence visited on the statue by the act of its creation – the carving, hacking, and sawing – was neutralized by more invocations: "Who are they who wish to approach my father? Do not smite my father! Do not touch his head!" The *sem* then traced his finger along the mouth of the statue, allowing it to speak and to eat.

The following sequence of the ritual involved the grisly slaughtering of a calf in the presence of its mother. The lector priest was instructed to "run quickly with it" (the foreleg of the calf) to the mummy as it still streamed blood and twitched,[55] a sign of its continued power. The bellowing of the mother of the calf, who witnessed the slaughter of her offspring, was equated with the sound of mourning for the deceased.[56] The sequence of the ritual in which the leg was held up to the mummy and the statue was

Figure 58. A group of female professional mourners weep and throw dirt on their heads at a funeral. Tomb of Ramose at Thebes (TT 55). Dynasty 18. Photo C. F. Nims. Courtesy of the Oriental Institute of the University of Chicago.

called "opening the eyes and mouth." The importance of this sequence is confirmed by a text in the tomb of Rekhmire (Dynasty 18): "A foreleg will be cut off for your mummy. May your *ba* go above and may your corpse go below," indicating that the ritual enabled the separation of the physical remains from the energy of the soul. The foreleg was a particularly appropriate symbolic offering because it has the same form as the hieroglyph for "power" and because it also resembles the adze that the *sem* priest used in the ritual.

In the next sequence of the Opening of the Mouth, the *sem* continued "carrying out the opening of the mouth and eyes, first with the *djedft-* implement and the finger of electrum," as he touched the face of the statue and the mummy with his own finger, in imitation of cleaning out the mouth of a newborn. Other objects, including grain, a flint knife (*pesshef-kef*) that was possibly associated with birth rituals, and water were offered.[57] The statue and mummy were then further purified, and according to some sources, were wrapped in a linen shroud. At the conclusion of the ritual, the priests recited a summary of the rituals and their efficacy for the deceased:

Figure 59. Anubis, the guardian of the necropolis, embracing the coffin of the priest Ramose on the day of his burial. Ramose's wife, Henuttawy, has collapsed in grief at the feet of her husband's coffin. A priest (*far left*) recites the spells of the Opening of the Mouth ceremony (note the tools on the table before him), while two other priests purify the mummy with incense and liquids. Dynasties 18–19. Art Institute of Chicago 1920.264, Museum Purchase Fund. Photo © The Art Institute of Chicago.

> I have given breath to those who are in hiding, I have enabled those who are in the netherworld to breathe ... I have caused them to rest in their chapels and their offerings to endure ... The breath of life, it comes and creates his image, his mouth is opened ... His name endures forever, because he is an excellent *akh* in the netherworld. He hears the call of those among his relatives. He protects the body of the one who pours water for him ... He emerges as a living *ba*, he assumes its form according to the wish of his heart, wherever his *ka* wishes to tarry![58]

This completed the cycle of life, death, and rebirth. The priests brought the dead back to life and enabled the deceased to respond to the pleas of the living. The deceased was now fully mobile and responsive in the netherworld.

Other funerary rituals were performed after the Opening of the Mouth. Some involved dance. One type of dancer performing at funerary rituals was

Figure 60. Clay mask in the form of the head of Anubis, the guardian of the necropolis, which may have been worn by priests during funerary ceremonies. This is a rare example of such a mask, and not all scholars agree that they were worn during rituals. Dynasties 21–24. Hildesheim, Pelizaeus-Museum 1585. Photo © Roemer-Pelizaeus-Museum, Hildesheim.

the *muu*, who wore tall basketwork headdresses in imitation of archaic marsh dwellers (Fig. 61). Near the tomb, the *muu* erected a temporary reed shelter that replicated the precincts of the holy cities that the deceased would visit after death. The *muu* dance was thought to help ferry the deceased across waters to the afterlife.[59] New Kingdom representations show that sometimes a troupe of dwarves was also hired to dance at the mouth of the tomb. Dwarves were considered to be evocative of eternal youth because of their short stature, and their presence at the funeral stressed the idea of the rebirth and rejuvenation of the deceased.[60]

In the New Kingdom, some tombs show the ritual breaking of red pots (Fig. 62). Red was a color that, in some contexts, was associated with the evil gods Seth and Apophis. Smashing the pots, an act of sympathetic

Figure 61. *Muu* dancers who impersonated the people of the marshes who wore tall basketwork crowns at funerals. The *muu* performed a dance at the entrance of the tomb. Tomb of Antefoker at Thebes (TT 60). Dynasty 12. Photo: C. F. Nims. Courtesy of the Oriental Institute of the University of Chicago.

magic, neutralized danger for the deceased in the afterlife and was thought to frighten away enemies.[61]

Upon the conclusion of the rituals, the mummy, its funerary furnishings, the statues, and chests of clothing, food, and drink were deposited in the tomb. The Nine Friends were charged with dragging the coffin. Scenes of this sequence of the funeral bear captions such as "Carrying by the [Nine] Friends. Oh Friends! Carry him on your arms! Oh Sons of Horus, hurry with your father, carry him!" An Old Kingdom text recounts the difficulties of completing a burial that, at that time, required lowering a huge stone sarcophagus down a deep vertical shaft. The deceased promises that he will give special favors to the "lector priest, embalmer, and all eighty men who shall lower the lid of his sarcophagus into its place."[62]

Once the coffin and funerary goods were in the burial chamber, the Nine Friends may have had a brief last meal with the deceased.[63] There is archaeological evidence that such a wake was held for King Tutankhamun. The

Figure 62. The ceremony of breaking red pots (*left of center*) on the day of burial, a ceremony that was thought to dispel evil. Saqqara. Tomb of Horemheb. Dynasty 18. Photo: Emily Teeter.

remains of the feast were discovered in 1907 not far from his tomb. The find consisted of perhaps fifteen huge pottery jars (the deposit was damaged by its excavator, and so exact counts are not known), jammed with other dishes. The dishes included small token offering bowls that are inscribed with the food that was offered (incense, grapes, cakes, and some sort of drink). Four beakers for wine were supplied. Leftovers packed in the jars indicate that the menu included cow, sheep, or goat ribs and a variety of birds (ducks and geese). The guests were supplied with festive floral collars, simplified versions of the great floral ornaments that have been discovered on coffins. Some scholars believe that the meal was held in the burial chamber, but the evidence is not clear.[64] To cite only one specific example to the contrary, the burial chamber of King Tutankhamun was far too small and too packed with shrines and burial goods to accommodate the participants of a ritual meal. When the meal was over, the floral collars and all the dishes and leftovers were packed inside the large pottery vessels. Materials that were used during the mummification of the king (ends of bandages, wiping cloths, kerchiefs to keep the embalmers' wigs or hair clean), and bags of natron, were added to the jars, and the ensemble was buried either in the tomb itself, or outside near the tomb. In a final act of purification, the footprints of the living were swept from the floor of the burial chamber.[65]

After the many rituals, the dancing, the recitation of prayers and the offering of food, the weary funerary party watched as the burial chamber was bricked up and sealed, and the shaft was filled with rubble. The party retraced their steps to the Nile and crossed to the land of the living. They might return forty days or a year later for a brief commemoration of the death.[66] Then, every year, during the Beautiful Feast of the Valley (see Chapter 4), the living would return to visit the blessed dead.

In summary, death in ancient Egypt was a highly regulated affair that involved the entire society, from the craftsmen who made the coffins and grave goods to the architect who designed the tomb, from the different ranks of priests who enacted rites of protection and rejuvenation to even the king himself, who might grant land for the tomb. The elaborate rituals that accompanied death and burial involved the living and the realm of the dead, bringing the two spheres together. They formalized the celebration of death and rebirth, creating a sense of optimism that life in the hereafter would be positive, thereby lessening one of the humanity's greatest uncertainties – what happens at the end of life.

8

Communicating with the Dead

The sense that the world of the living was so similar to the land of the dead is shown by the ease of communication that existed in ancient Egypt between the two realms. The dead could communicate with the living, and the living had access to the land beyond. Contact could be initiated by either side. The messages from the living to the dead were usually practical rather than philosophical. The living did not seek omens or advice from the beyond, but instead hoped to enlist the support of the dead with everyday matters – resolving disputes, gaining power over rivals, or securing the favor of the gods or protection from divine or human enemies.

Less controlled, and hence more dangerous, were the messages initiated by the dead. When satisfied with offerings, the dead spirits were benign. But when dissatisfied for any reason, they were capable of creating all sorts of mayhem on earth. Their displeasure could be manifested as haunting, evil omens, or illness. In some cases, the cause of unexpected, and according to the sources, unwarranted evil, was "any dead man or woman."[1] Other texts refer to the "eye of the dead person" that could bring misfortune.[2]

Akh Spirits

Most beyond-the-grave communications were between a living person and an *akh*, or "transfigured spirit," an aspect of a person's energy and personality that was manifested after death. The *akh* lived in the world of the gods and the dead, but it was able to communicate with and to aid, or hinder, the living. The *akh* was thought to have a special relationship with Osiris, Amun, and especially Re. In the Book of the Dead, *akhs* tow the barque of Re, and travel in the sun barque, where they sit as judges of the recently deceased who clamor to join the gods.[3] Book of the Dead Spell 64 records that the *akh* retained the appearance of the individual as he or she was before death: "I have entered [the transition to the afterworld] as an ignorant one. I have come forth as an able *akh*. I shall be seen in my human form forever." There is no tradition of the *akh*'s physically appearing to the living like a ghost, but *akhs* were considered to be omnipresent, and the living could see them when they slept and entered the liminal zone that separated the living and the dead.

Although potentially everyone had an *akh*, texts suggest that upon death, there was a transition in which the *akh* was activated through the knowledge of certain ritual texts or as the result of the performance of proper spells and rites by priests upon the mummy: "going forth … having been transfigured [literally made an *akh*] by the lector priest … for whom everything has been done by the embalmer."[4] One text suggests that the transition to being an *akh* was not automatic: "I am an able *akh* and I know everything by means of which one may become an *akh* in the necropolis."[5]

The idea that the *akh* was a powerful force is vividly illustrated by the cult of the *akh iker n Re* ("able spirit of Re"), a category of transfigured spirits that was thought to have a special relationship to and communication with the gods, especially Re. Most documents about the *akh iker n Re* come from Deir el Medina in western Thebes, but a few examples have been found elsewhere in Egypt. Our best evidence for these *akhs* is stelae, most of which date to the New Kingdom. Most of these stelae have been recovered from the ruins of houses or from village shrines, suggesting that they were part of a localized ancestor cult. The majority of them are modest round-topped stone monuments that show the *akh* seated, usually before a table of offerings (Fig. 63). Many show the *akh* sniffing a water lily, probably a reference to rebirth. While the majority of the stelae are dedicated to men, a significant number commemorate female *akhs*. The person who dedicated the stela may be shown offering to the spirit or adoring it. In other cases, only the *akh* is shown. Genealogical studies of the individuals depicted or referred to on the stelae indicate that the *akhs* were recently deceased members of the dedicator's family – fathers, sons or daughters, brothers or sisters, or husbands – rather than members of long-past generations or legendary peo-ple. This suggests that the potency of the power of the person's *akh* was recognized soon after death, when the stela was commissioned.[6] It is not known why particular individuals were singled out for this special status.

Akhs could also be represented by busts showing only the head and shoulders of the person (Fig. 64), a form of statuary that is very unusual in Egyptian art. Like the *akh* stelae, most of these busts are from the Theban area, although some have been recovered from as far away as Memphis and Aniba in Nubia. Unlike stelae, the busts are genderless, and only a few have inscriptions to identify them. Their precise function is not known. It has been suggested that they were carried through the village of Deir el Medina during processions; given their modest size, this is plausible. One stela that shows a woman pouring a liquid offering before one of the busts suggests that they were set up in homes and perhaps in chapels (Fig. 65).[7] The fact that most of these busts lack inscriptions is particularly puzzling. In ancient Egypt, artistic and religious traditions dictated that without a name, statues or depictions could not effectively represent their subjects. This anomaly has raised the suggestion that the busts were anonymous so that they could be reused and associated with different *akhs* at different times.[8]

Akhs were thought to be able to intercede with the gods on behalf of the living. In order to win favor with the *akh*, members of the family left food offerings to provision the *akh* in the afterlife. Some texts detail what was required to maintain good relations with a local *akh*. One advises, "One makes invocation offerings to an *akh* in return for interceding for the sake of the survivor,"[9] indicting that a satisfied *akh* could be a source of help to the living. Another notes that the *akh* "protects the body of one who pours water for him."[10] And a third complains, "He [the *akh*] has not given any-thing to my daughter who makes funerary offerings to the *akh*."[11] The Cairo Calendar (Dynasty 19) has numerous notations of days on which the living should make offerings to the *akhs* in order to appease and satisfy them. One specifically says that the offerings should be made "in your house," referring to a household cult.[12]

If sufficient offerings were not left, there was danger that the *akh* would become a haunting spirit, much like a ghost. In a New Kingdom text now in Turin, a dissatisfied *akh* is blamed for all sorts of misfortune: "Any misfortune is due to him; the game seized in the field; it is he who does a thing like that. As for the loss on the threshing floor; that is the *akh*!" *Akhs* were credited with further mischief:

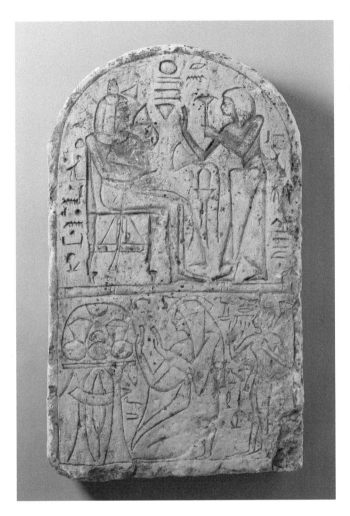

Figure 63. An *akh iker n Re* stela showing the *akh*, a man named Nakht, seated in the upper register. His brother is shown presenting incense to him. In the lower register, his sister and another relative raise their hands in adoration. Such stelae were probably kept in houses, where they were the focus of a household cult. Medinet Habu. Dynasties 19–20. OIM 14287. Photo: Anna Ressman. Courtesy of the Oriental Institute of the University of Chicago.

You [the *akh*] enter heaven and eat the stars that are in it. You sit down on the soil, and then you dislodge the seed that people have sown in it. You stretch your hand toward the desert, and kill all the game that is in it. You are put on the border of the sea and you make all the fishes die that are in it.[13]

Akh spirits were even blamed for creating dangers that caused members of the community to die.[14] A magical text relates the ways that an *akh* might cause death: "death of the eyes" (blindness?), by falling, by a bird's bone (choking on a bird bone?), and the more mysterious "death of a man who acts as a woman."[15] The Instructions of Ani (Dynasty 20) contain a slightly more sinister allusion to the activities of the spirits: "Appease the *akh*, do what he likes and abstain from what he detests. May you be spared from his many evil deeds. From him comes all misfortune."[16] Considering the

Figure 64. Limestone bust representing an *akh iker n Re*, a deified member of the community. Such sculptures were kept in homes where they were the focus of an offering cult. Dynasty 19. Brooklyn Museum of Art 54.1, Charles Edwin Wilbour Fund.

potential evil that *akhs* could cause among the living, it is not surprising that the term *akh* is translated in Coptic, the late form of the ancient Egyptian language, as "demon."

One could protect oneself from an evil-minded *akh* by wearing a charm in the form of a spell written on a strip of papyrus and then enclosed in a wood or metal cylinder. These protective charms were worn on a cord around the neck. The magical spell on the papyrus stated that a certain god had promised to protect the wearer (see Fig. 46). These "oracular amulet decrees" date to Dynasties 22–23, but they echo an earlier tradition of prayers to the god Osiris who, as the god of the dead, was considered to be the supervisor of the *akhs*. The text provided a defense not only against evil spirits but also against dangers such as the "the eye of the dead person," that is, apparently, the evil eye.[17] Another text purported to repel "every dead man, every dead

Figure 65. Line drawing of a stela showing a woman holding a smoking incense burner and pouring an offering before an *akh* bust (see Fig. 64). Such rituals were thought to keep an *akh* spirit happy and prevent it from doing harm to the family or community. Drawing by Mary Winkes. Courtesy of Florence Friedman.

woman, every male enemy, every female enemy, who would do evil to" a person. If charms could not protect the living from evil spirits, one could go to a third party – the god(s) – for protection. A decree of Amun stipulated that a dead woman, Princess Neskhons, was not to harm her husband and relatives from the beyond.[18]

Letters to the Dead

There were a variety of methods for contacting the spirits of the dead, but letters were the most common form of communication. Because the realm of the dead was considered to be so close to the world of the living, the Egyptians thought little of writing letters to the dead as if the recipient were simply away for a while. This was true even though the vast majority of the living – and presumably of the dead – were illiterate. Only a few letters to the dead are known. Most are written on pottery vessels or jar stands that, in all probability, were left at the tomb (only a few have been found in situ) with offerings that would attract the soul of the deceased to the message (Fig. 66). The texts follow a standard format. A letter opens with a formal greeting to the dead person. Then, the writer appeals to the good will of the spirit by reminding it of good deeds that were done on its behalf; in some cases, the appeal is made so stridently that the writer seems

Figure 66. A letter to the dead written on a jar stand. The text is from a man asking his deceased father and grandmother for their protection and for their help in having a child. Dynasty 11. OIM 13945. Photo: Anna Ressman. Courtesy of the Oriental Institute of the University of Chicago.

to be attempting to give the spirit a guilty conscience. The letter closes with the matter at hand – a request for the spirit to keep the writer or his or her family from harm, or to desist from harming the living from the afterlife, or, often, to intercede on behalf of the living with other spirits who are blamed for misfortunes.

In one instance, the coffin of the Lady Ikhtay served as an intermediary between the living and dead. The lady's husband, the scribe Butehamun, wrote a letter to her coffin, expressing his disappointment that she would not communicate with him and assist him with some unstated matter of daily life. He addressed the coffin in the most polite terms:

> Oh you noble chest of the Osiris, the Singer of Amun, Ikhtay who lies at rest beneath you, hearken to me, and transmit my message. Say to her since you are

near to her: "What is your condition? How are you?" It is you who shall say to her "… If I can be heard where you are, tell the lords of eternity to let your brother (i.e., husband) come to [you] that you may be his support …" It is you who should speak well within the necropolis since I committed no abomination against you while you were on earth. So then may you grasp my situation. Swear to god in every manner saying, "It is according to what I have said that things shall be done."[19]

The content and specific complaints in many of the letters, like Butehamun's letter to the coffin, are difficult for an outside reader to understand, because the writer, and presumably the deceased, knew all the details of the issue and therefore did not feel compelled to fully explain the situation. However, most of the letters to the dead seem to concern themselves with minor matters for which the living required some assistance from the deceased. Most letters are supplications to the *akh* of the deceased to intercede on the behalf of the living, to arbitrate between rivals in inheritance, or perhaps to overcome sickness. All can be classified as domestic complaints. Most letters blame the recipient or some other being in the afterlife for creating difficulties for the living. Many of these letters are so practical in nature and conversational and heartfelt in tone that it is a shock to remember that they were written to a dead person.

One such communication, written on a stele of the First Intermediate Period, records the following exchange:

A communication by Merirtyfy to Nebetiotef. How are you? Is the West [the land of the dead] taking care of you as you desire? Now since I am your beloved upon earth, fight on my behalf and intercede on behalf of my name. I did not [garbled] a [funerary spell] in your presence when I perpetuated your name upon earth. Remove the infirmity of my body! Please become a spirit for me [before] my eyes so that I might see you in a dream fighting on my behalf. I will then deposit offerings for you [as soon as] the sun has risen and outfit your offering slab for you.[20]

This letter has all the crispness of a business transaction – the writer trades the promise of offerings for the *akh* in exchange for the promise of health, a quid pro quo between the living and the dead. The writer even wants confirmation from the spirit by having it appear to him in a dream "fighting on [his] behalf."

Another letter, written on papyrus, contains a message from a man to his deceased wife expressing his exasperation at the way she is treating him. He was apparently in some sort of trouble or was experiencing a string of bad luck that he ascribed to his wife. He complained that she was treating him poorly despite the care that he had lavished on her throughout her life and during her final illness:

> To the able spirit Ankhiry: What have I done against you wrongfully for you to get into this evil disposition in which you are? What have I done against you? As for what you have done, it is your laying hands upon me though I committed no wrong against you. From the time that I was living with you as a husband until today, what have I done against you that I should have to conceal it?

He then related how well he had cared for her during her lifetime by marrying her, remaining faithful to her, and providing for her. When she became ill he brought the master physician to attend to her, but she subsequently died. He reminded her that he took a leave of absence from pharaoh's service when she died and that he paid his respects to her mummy:

> I and my people wept sorely for [you] in my quarter [?]. I donated clothing of fine linen to wrap you up in and had many clothes made. I overlooked nothing good so as not to have it done for you. Now look, I've spent these last three years without entering [another] house [i.e., not having taken another wife], although it is not proper that one who is in the same situation as I be made to do this. Now look, I've done this out of consideration for you. Now look, you don't differentiate good from evil.[21]

The pained widower expressed his frustration that some sort of unspecified illness had befallen him; his only explanation was that his wife was to blame, despite his exemplary behavior toward her. He complained that he has been loyal to his wife by not remarrying after her death and that he did not deserve to be bothered by her *akh*.[22] This comment is telling, suggesting that some men feared that their deceased spouses might resent a subsequent marriage and take revenge for the husband's lack of fidelity, even though they were separated by death.

In another letter one can sense sibling rivalry. A son wrote to his dead father complaining that he was being "injured" by his deceased brother "even though there is nothing that I, your son, did or said." He stated that he had been dutiful in burying his brother, even bringing his body home so that it could be buried in a tomb "among his necropolis companions." Moreover, he had fulfilled this duty although his brother still owed him thirty measures of Upper Egyptian barley and other carefully enumerated items.[23]

In many of the letters, the writer contacted the dead to try to determine the source of personal misfortune and to find a means of relief. In one example, written from a man to his deceased wife, he reminded her that he was in no way responsible for her death. He asked her, "If it is the case that [these injuries] are being inflicted against your will ... your deceased father remains influential [in] the necropolis," suggesting that his father-in-law could find the source of the malevolence.[24]

Although most of the appeals to the dead are general complaints about their evil influence, others contain specific requests. In a text written on a jar stand, a man addressed his dead father and grandmother asking them to assist his wife, Seny, in having a son. He blamed her infertility on two dead servants who were interfering from the afterlife. The son reminded his father of the power of akhs: "This is a reminder of the fact that I told you regarding myself. You know what Idu [a man whose relationship to the family is unclear] said regarding his son. As for what may be in store in the beyond, I won't let him suffer from any affliction." He then comes to the point:

> Moreover let a healthy son be born to me for you are an able spirit [akh]. Now as for those two maidservants, Nefertjentet and Itjai who have caused Seny to be afflicted, confound them! And banish for me whatever afflictions are directed against my wife, whom you know I have need of. Banish them completely!

In closing, the writer changed his tone, assuring the spirit of a reward for interceding: "As you live for me, may the Great One [Hathor?] favor you and the face of the Great God be kindly disposed toward you and he will give you pure bread from his two hands."[25]

Some letters took a scolding tone. In one, a woman complained to her deceased husband that a woman named Wabut and her son had seized her furniture and servants. She sarcastically wrote,

> Will you remain calm about this? I had rather that you should fetch [me] away to yourself so that I could be there beside you than to see your son dependent upon Izezi's son [one of the group who took the property]. Awaken your [deceased] father Iy against Behezti [another man who threatened the family]! Rouse yourself and make haste against him![26]

The deceased apparently kept abreast of the events of the living. One letter that made a request and promised water offerings in exchange reads, in part,

> What about the maidservant Imiu who is ill? Aren't you [the deceased] fighting on her behalf day and night with whoever, male or female, is acting against her? ... Fight on her behalf anew this day that her household may be maintained and water poured out for you [as a funerary offering]. If there is [no help] from you, your

house [i.e., household of his living family] shall be destroyed. Can it be that you are unaware that it is this maidservant who keeps your house going among people?[27]

Here the deceased was asked to intercede on behalf of a third party, a maid in the household of the deceased. The letter hints at deeper problem within, or between, families.

Dreams and Nightmares

Dreams were another way of communicating with the dead. To the Egyptians, sleep was a transitional state, a state of heightened awareness that allowed the sleeper access to places that were far away in terms of space and perception, including the realm of the transfigured *akhs*. The word for dream, *reswt*, is derived from the word for "awake," reflecting the idea that in a dream, the sleeper was considered to be awake in another realm. The sleeper could see and communicate with the dead but in a physically passive way. He or she could see, and be seen, but the sleeper was powerless to act or to affect the actions of the *akhs*.

As noted in Merirtyfy's letter to the dead, one could request that a spirit appear in a dream in order to communicate. But this could have its downside. Another letter from Naga ed Deir complains that a spirit intruded into a man's dreams and was "looking at me" in a manner malevolent enough to motivate a letter of complaint. The dreamer could also see things and people that were far off or that were usually invisible. A Ramesside dream book refers to the dreamer who declared, "Behold, I see something far away from me, as something that touches me."[28] A Late New Kingdom dream book (P. Chester Beatty III) and earlier letters to the dead refer to a "city of the dead," the *niwet wat* (literally, the "one city") where dreamers could see the spirits of the dead and rejoin, at least in their dreams, their deceased families. One letter mentions the community of the deceased in the "one city." In that text, the writer appeals to his dead father to intercede on his behalf because "you have witnesses with you in the one city."[29]

Another letter to the dead from Naga ed Deir illustrates how dreams could be a portal to communication between the living and the dead. In that letter, a man named Heni wrote to his dead father complaining that he was being bothered by their servant Seni who had died some time in the past. He claimed to know that Seni was the cause of his problems because he saw the servant's bad behavior in a dream. Because the father appeared

Figure 67. Wood figurine of an enemy, his arms bound behind him. "Dead Henui, son of Intef" is written on its chest thereby identifying the figurine as Henui. The destruction of the figurine, perhaps by burning, would ensure Henui's death. First Intermediate Period. Louvre E 27204. © Musée du Louvre.

in that dream as well, Heni beseeched his father to keep Seni from harming him: "Indeed, let his lord take heed so that he [Seni] no longer creates disturbance. He should be guarded until he has ceased to visit me … once and for all."[30]

Dangers presented in dreams, especially nightmares, or night terrors (for which there was a separate and specific term), were taken so seriously that there were spells and rituals for preventing them. A magical spell on Papyrus Leiden I 348 (v.2) specifies who was to blame for bad dreams – male and female *akhs*, as well as more generic male and female dead and "adversaries in the sky and in the earth." Amulets to promote good dreams were inscribed with spells such as "I shall make every dream she has seen good, I shall make every dream that someone else has seen for her good."[31] This last reference suggests that the amulet was so potent that it could protect the wearer from dreams that other people had about her, in which she might still be vulnerable to attack.

The earliest tools for preventing nightmares were execration figures, small figurines (Fig. 67) that were commonly made of pottery or stone, or bowls that were inscribed with the names of enemies or of evils that the individual wished to overcome. The owners of the figurines would smash them, destroying the danger through an act of substitution. A figurine from the Middle Kingdom is inscribed with names of enemies of Egypt and ends with a list of more general evils, such as bad speech, plots, "and all bad dreams and all bad sleep."[32] The Chester Beatty Dream Book instructs worried dreamers to recite an invocation to Isis. A mixture of bread and herbs marinated in beer and incense could then be rubbed on the dreamer's face with the result that "all the bad dreams that he has seen will be driven out." Another spell for preventing nightmares, from Dynasty 18, appears as part of a prescription reputed to drive out every kind of bleeding and malevolent influence and "to prevent the seeing of dreams."[33]

Surveying the ways in which the living could communicate with the dead provides insight into the workings of the mind of the ancient Egyptians. There was little separation between the realms of the living and the dead, and the living and dead relied on each other. The *akhs* were appealed to for solutions to a myriad of problems of daily life – illnesses, fertility, and feuds between households. *Akhs* were even called as witnesses in lawsuits. But the nature of the ancient society was not one of an overly superstitious community that blamed every ill on capricious and inherently evil spirits. In Egypt, there was a more measured and reasoned association of cause and result. If a family did not leave funerary offerings, then the dead had justification to cause harm. Letters to the dead were almost Victorian in their formal and formulaic structure. The writer greeted the deceased, reminded the dead person of the good that was done on his or her behalf, and then made a request. This is a not a reflection of a society that cringed in fear of the dead. Rather, the dead, if treated with respect and care, were allies whose ability to intercede in so many features of daily life gave support and hope to those who were left behind.

9

Magic to Charm
and to Kill

Popular imagination has long painted the Egyptians as masters of magical arts. In the Book of Exodus, the king was attended by "wise men" but also by "sorcerers." This reputation continued in Classical literature. Lucian (2nd c. AD) related that Pancrates was trained in magic by the goddess Isis and that he was able to bring inanimate objects to life – a tale made famous by Goethe in the *Sorcerer's Apprentice* (1797). Another magician, Harnuphis, created a miraculous rainfall that was commemorated on coins struck by Emperor Marcus Aurelius.[1] For centuries, much of the world agreed with Clement of Alexandria (3rd c. AD) who called Egypt "the mother of magicians."[2]

Toward a Definition of Magic in Ancient Egypt

Despite the Egyptians' reputation for sorcery, scholars disagree about what constituted magic in ancient Egypt, and especially where the division between magic and religion lies. In James Frazer's classic definition from *The Golden Bough* (1906–15), magic is a means of manipulating and controlling supernatural forces for one's own purpose whereas religion involves worshipping and appeasing those forces. Applying this definition to Egypt is problematic – communication with the gods in order to influence personal affairs was an established part of mainstream Egyptian cults. Indeed, most Egyptian rituals involved making offerings to the god in the effort to produce a specific outcome. Does that mean that there was no magic in Egypt, or does it mean that the bulk of Egyptian religious rituals are in fact better thought of as magic?

Recent definitions have attempted to provide more specific guidelines for distinguishing magic from religion. Joris Borghouts has suggested that magical texts "belong[ed] to the sphere of private, non-institutional everyday magic used for the living and against the dangers of various natures crossing the borderland between life and death."[3] Jan Assmann has proposed a similar solution – that magic was a ritual for home use, in contrast to the religious practices that made up the formal ritual enacted in the temples.[4] Robert Ritner has found a distinction in the role of the magician versus the role of the priest – the magician assumed the being of the god, whereas the priest simply called upon the god.[5]

The close ties between magic and religion continue to puzzle scholars, perhaps because of the assumption that magic is a more primitive practice that is eventually replaced by "religion." However, it is clear not only from ancient Egypt but from other societies as well that the progression is not linear and that magic and religion existed, and exist, side by side.[6]

In Egypt, the force of magic itself was personified by a god named Heka, who was depicted as a man with upraised arms on his head. In the New Kingdom, Heka was believed to be the source of knowledge that imbued magicians with transformative power. One text warned, "Guard against these magicians who know their spells, since the god Heka is in them himself … cause the hearts of their elders there to forget their magical power, they who act as they desire against the entire land using their magic which is in their bodies."[7] Furthermore, most magical texts centered on stories of the gods, placing the conjurer in the role of a deity in order to re-create a situation or an event referred to in myth. For example, to ward off evil, a magician may liken himself to "the Horror that has come forth from Dep" or the "Birth goddess that has come forth from Heliopolis."[8] The temporary transformation or role-playing of the magician immersed him in a dense network of established mythological beliefs. Magicians were not calling upon an alternate and deviant theology, but were participating in the realm of established religious practices.

Given this close relationship, it is helpful to refer to the Egyptians' own definitions of magic. The Instructions for Merikare (Dynasty 10), states that "god made for them [mankind] magic as weapons to ward off what might happen," indicating that magic was one of many weapons that could be used to secure the well-being of humans – or could be used for ill, for magic itself was considered to be morally neutral. Magic could be used as a tool to destroy enemies of the state, but it could also be turned against the king himself. The close ties between the state and magic gave the latter an unusual legitimacy. Books of magical spells were found in the libraries of kings, and some spells were composed for the use of the ruler.

It is best, then, to consider magic in ancient Egypt as a valid and accepted – although a clearly distinguishable – part of religious belief. In a culture in which regular communication with the gods was natural, what we view as magic was just another means through which humans could effectively communicate with deities to seek protection from illness or from enemies. The aims of magic were often modest. Most evidence for magic from the dynastic era describes protective spells, especially against ill health (the bite of snakes and sting of scorpions) and for the destruction of enemies, through the substitution of images and figurines. By the Late Period, magical spells are increasingly concerned with medical cures, minor curses, and love charms.[9]

Who Were the Magicians?

Egyptians used several terms to identify those who used magical spells, but none translates exclusively as "magician." Again, this is an indication of the integration of magic into the overall religious system. A group of titles include priests of Sekhmet (*hem netcher Sekhmet*); "scorpion charmer" (*kherep Serqet*, one who casts spells to heal those stung by scorpions); priest of Heka (*hem netcher Heka*), which is known from the Old Kingdom; and amulet maker (*sau*). Egyptians were not the only practitioners of magic in their time – a text refers to "the magic of a Syrian" and "the magic of a Nubian."[10]

The survival of written magical spells suggests that one of the most important aspects of being a magician, indeed a prerequisite, was the ability to read, or at a minimum, a knowledge of the content of spells. In texts from the Old Kingdom, a worker of magic is called "one who knows things." Many references are made to magicians who are lector priests because they recited temple liturgy and thus had to be able to read. In his autobiography, a man named Iyenhor claims, "I am an [excellent] *akh* who knows magic. Men know that I am an excellent lector priest."[11] Another magical spell of the Old Kingdom refers to "every lector priest who shall make for me transfigurations and offering."[12] In the Middle Kingdom tales of wonder related in Papyrus Westcar, the three magicians all bear the title "chief lector priest." In one of the most famous uses of magical arts, the conspiracy against the life of Ramesses III, the accused men include three scribes who were from "the House of Life," another who was a lector priest, and a fifth who was a priest of Sekhmet.

The association between magic, literacy, and the ability to acquire knowledge was well established throughout Egyptian religion. Knowledge of things and of the names of individuals gave power over them. In funerary texts, the deceased claims power over the demons of the underworld stating: "I know you, I know your name." In another text Horus proclaims, "One is able to work magic for a person by means of their name."[13] For a charm to be effective it was an absolute requirement that the victim's real name had to be known and worked into it. For example, figurines, which through sympathetic magic could kill one's enemies, had to be personalized, thereby "activated" with the names of those foes (see Fig. 67).

If the ability to work magic was based on knowledge, how widely known were magical practices? Was such knowledge restricted to an elite circle? The texts are ambiguous. One cautions "every lector priest who shall make for me transfigurations and offerings in accordance with the secret writings of the skills of the lector priest. Recite those transfigurations … for I am an excellent *akh* and I know all the magic spells which should be known by every excellent *akh*."[14] Here the texts are referred to as "secret writings," yet they are ascribed to the domain of a lector priest, which was a title held by a great number of men. Another text warns, "Do not reveal it [a spell against crocodiles] to the common man. It is a mystery of the House of Life."[15] A box of tools belonging to a magician discovered at the Ramesseum bore an image of Anubis on its lid labeled with the god's epithet *hery seshta*, "he who is over the secrets." Do these texts refer to a body of specialized knowledge that was accessible only after initiation into a secret society made up of magician-priests? This issue is still debated. With the exception of brief references to something that may have been a ceremony at Karnak in the Third Intermediate Period in which priests were formally introduced to the god,[16] there is no evidence for a specific initiation ceremony or ritual that created a closed body of magic practitioners. Perhaps the reference to "secret" was a more general reference to the knowledge accessible through writing – which, in a society estimated to have had a literacy rate of about three percent, would have been considered inaccessible to or "secret" from most of the population.

Evidence for Magical Practices

There is both written and material evidence for magic. The textual evidence falls into two groups. The first comprises the literary texts that include Middle Egyptian stories (many of them set in the Old Kingdom), such as the account of the magicians Webaoner, Djadja-em-ankh, and Djedi in the Westcar papyrus. In that tale, each magician bears the title "chief lector priest" and their utterances are called "sayings of magic" (*heka*). In the first section of the story, set in the reign of King Nebka, Webaoner manufactured a crocodile of wax seven fingers in length. After reading his "magic words," he threw it into the pool. The small wax crocodile grew to seven cubits long (about three and a half meters), and it ate a townsman who was having an affair with the magician's wife. After seven days, Webaoner brought the king to the pool to show him "a marvel which has taken place in your majesty's time." The magician called on the crocodile to return the townsman. Once upon the bank, the crocodile opened its mouth so that the king could see the adulterer. When the king exclaimed about the fearfulness of the creature, Webaoner bent down and grasped it, and, in an echo of the biblical story of the rod and snake, the crocodile again took on its shape as a wax figurine. The story ends with the king condemning the adulterer and the crocodile reassuming its living form and diving to the bottom of the pool with the townsman. In another story on the papyrus, Djadja-em-ankh's powers enable him to fold over the waters of the king's pleasure pool in order to retrieve an amulet that had fallen from the hair of one of the king's favorites. And, in yet another part of the story, Djedi, who is described as being 110 years old, was able to rejoin the head and body of a decapitated goose and make it walk across the room. He also made a lion so docile that it would walk behind him unleashed.

From the New Kingdom come stories of the power of Prince Khamwaset, the son of Ramesses II, and from the Late Period, we learn of Naneferkaptah in the demotic Setna story. By the Ptolemaic and Roman eras, such references increase considerably. They include the story of Nectanebo, who wrecked an enemy's fleet by making wax images of the ships and invoking the gods to destroy the vessels they represented.[17] A significant feature of these literary references is that the magic was conducted in the palace, by priests, with the approval of and often in the presence of the king, underscoring the perceived legitimacy that magic had.

The second type of textual evidence for magic is the corpus of magical spells. The earliest surviving examples date to the Middle Kingdom, but it is reasonable to assume that there were earlier examples that have not survived. Most magical spells from the dynastic period have a distinctive three-part formula. The first part is a title that announces the purpose of the spell: "A means to save a man from the plague of the year [a reference to the five days at the end of the year which were perceived as unlucky]; an enemy will have no power over him." This is followed by the incantation, in which the individual invokes and assumes the role of one god, or even of many gods, in a mythological setting that has some relevance to the desired result. In this example, after a great number of gods are called on, the spell continues:

> Hail to you gods there! Murderers who stand in waiting upon Sekhmet [a particu-
> larly unpredictable and therefore dangerous goddess] who have come forth from
> the eye of Re ... who brings slaughtering about, who create uproar, who hurry
> through the land, who shoot their arrows through their mouths, who see from afar!
> Be on your way, [be distant] from me! Go on, you, I shall not go along with you!
> You shall have no power over me ... for I am Re who appears in his eye! I have
> arisen as Sekhmet, I have arisen as Wedjyet ... I will not fall for your slaughtering.

This part is followed by the practical directions for the performance of the spell: "Words to be said over a piece of fine linen. These gods are to be drawn on it and it is fitted with twelve knots. To offer them bread and beer and burning incense. To be applied to a man's throat."[18] Other spells include instructions such as that the spell "be said over clay in which a knife is enclosed, a bundle [?] of *dbit* or *anb* plants," or that it "be said over a lion of faience, threaded to red linen. To be applied to a man's hand."[19]

The archaeological record is a rich source of evidence for magical practice. Among the earliest are the simple figurines, inscribed with the names of enemies, that were broken to "kill" the foe (see Fig. 67). Among the most intriguing remains of magical practice is the magician's equipment recovered from the shaft of a Dynasty 13 tomb at the Ramesseum in western Thebes. It consisted of a wooden box containing papyri inscribed with magical-medical texts. Near it was a wood figurine of a woman wearing a mask of the deity Beset or Bes (Fig. 68) and holding serpent figurines in her hands, a bronze wand in the form of a snake, a square rod incised with scenes of animals, an ivory clapper in the form of a human hand, and figurines of baboons and a lion that in other contexts are referred to as *abas* (literally, "fighters"), who acted as gods of protection.

This is an extraordinary collection of items. A few objects similar to those found in the magician's kit have been recovered from other places, but the

Ramesseum assemblage as a whole has contributed to a greater understanding of the relationship of the items to each other and to their function in magical practices. Another example of the snake wand, in bronze, one and a half meters long, was recovered from the Theban tomb of Mentuhotep dating to the early Eighteenth Dynasty (Fig. 69). Although how such rods were used is not recorded in extant ancient Egyptian sources, their potency and association with magic is recorded in the Bible. In Exodus 4:2–7, they are regarded as proof of God's power. When Moses was told to cast his rod on the ground, it became a serpent. When Moses took it back into his hand, it was again transformed into a rod. In a later passage (Exodus 7:10–13), Aaron's serpent rod consumed the serpents conjured by the magicians of the Egyptian court.

The square rod with animals from the Ramesseum is also known from other sources.[20] Other examples, all from the Middle Kingdom, are made of short, rectangular pieces of steatite that were threaded on a rod. Opposing sides of the steatite pieces are decorated with files of animals (Fig. 70), and some have a protective *wedjet* eye or the hieroglyph for "protection." Small figurines of animals, such as turtles, were affixed to the top of the steatite elements, and a leopard head decorated the end cap. These animals were known as "fighters" (*ahas*) who avert evil.[21] It is not known how these rods were used, but the presence of the *aha* gods identifies them as tools of a magician.

The mask that the Ramesseum figurine wears is also known from the Middle Kingdom site of Kahun, where a similar example made of canvas was recovered (Fig. 71).[22] It shows signs of repair and repainting, indicating that it was well used, perhaps worn for the performance of some ritual. The mask may represent either Bes or his female counterpart, Beset, both of whom are associated with the protection of women and children.

Spells of Protection

Many examples of Egyptian magic are for defensive purposes, intended to ward off sickness or evil. One group of spells gives general magical protection against the spirits (*akhs*, see Chapter 7) who cause sickness. One text advises the magician to invoke a series of gods by name:

> Come to me, ascend to me, unite yourselves for me after [you] have brought up for me anything bad, any bad revolting matter [?], any bad sickness that is in this body [of mine] … It is to make an end of the sickness that is cleaving to you, oh gods

Figure 68. Wood statue from the "magician's box" from the Ramesseum. This figure of a woman wears a mask representing the god Bes (see Figs. 71 and 73), and she holds a snake wand (see Fig. 69). Dynasties 12–13. Photo courtesy of the Manchester Museum, University of Manchester.

there that I have fetched a herb … Make an end to any bad sickness that is cleaving itself to me![23]

This was to be said over an object made of tamarisk wood. Another "spell for conjuring the *akh* from the belly" advises the practitioner to recite a spell invoking Isis, Horus, and Nephthys "[over a series of signs] drawn in fresh ink on the belly of a man, on the sore spot on him."[24] Other spells were invoked specifically against nightmares: "This spell is to be said by a man who has a nightmare in his own place. Bread should be given to him as well as some fresh herbs which should be soaked in beer and myrrh. A man's face should be rubbed with it. A means to dispel any nightmares he has seen."[25]

Magic was thought to be especially useful for the protection of the most vulnerable members of society: a mother and her newborn child. Because they

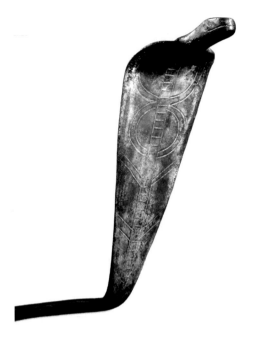

Figure 69. Section of a bronze snake wand. Such wands are associated with Egyptian magical practice, and they are referred to in the Bible, where both Moses and Aaron used snake wands to demonstrate their power. From the tomb of Mentuhotep (TT 37). EA 52831. Dynasty 18. Photo © The Trustees of the British Museum.

were considered to be defenseless, the *abas* (fighter gods) were called on to protect them. These gods, as already mentioned, were depicted in the form of hippopotamuses, tortoises, and composite animals, many of which hold long knives or lean on the hieroglyph for "protection," tools that they use to ward off evil. These images were carved on curved ivory wands (Fig. 72) that were probably used to draw a circle of protection around the mother and child. The ends of some of the wands are scuffed and worn where they have been dragged along the ground, and another example has been mended, suggesting repeated use. These can be dated from the Old Kingdom into the Second Intermediate Period (1900–1650 BC). Most are without any provenience, but some have been found in context – one in the magician's kit from the Ramesseum – and others have been excavated from the private cemetery at Lisht. Their presence in tombs suggests that they functioned to protect both the living and the dead. A few examples bear inscriptions that confirm their magical function. One is inscribed: "Words spoken by the multitude of amuletic figures [the *aba* gods]. 'We have come in order to protect the lady Meriseneb.'" Another is inscribed: "Cut off the head of the enemy when he enters the chamber of the children whom the lady has born!" A third example has the straightforward dedication: "Protection for the lady of the house Seneb."[26]

Children could be protected by other forms of magic. One "spell of the dwarf" was to be said four times over a dwarf of clay placed on a woman who

Figure 70. Section of a magic wand decorated with a striding lion and winged griffin topped with a human head. A series of these steatite blocks were threaded onto a wooden or metal shaft. Dynasty 12. 1949.350. Photo: Christian Tepper. Courtesy of the August Kestner Museum.

was suffering in birth.[27] The dwarf, the god Bes (Fig. 73), was supposed to help the placenta descend.

In the Third Intermediate Period, children were protected by amuletic decrees (see Fig. 46 and Chapter 6) in which a god promised to protect the child from all sort of evils, such as gods who make a demon against someone, or dangers such as drowning, being struck by thunder, or being crushed by a collapsing wall. Other decrees cast a wider spell of protection promising, "I [the god] shall enable him to grow up. I shall enable him to develop."

A very common means of obtaining magical protection was by wearing amulets – essentially, good-luck charms made in a wide variety of shapes. Amulet makers (*sau*) were associated with the magic arts. Amulets were worn by the living, and they were also supplied to mummies for protection in the afterlife. The Book of the Dead and other texts give specific instructions for the manufacture of amulets, including their materials, their forms, and their placement on the body (Fig. 74).

The shape of the amulet was often related to its function or to myths that referred to protection. Most common were amulets in the form of protective gods (Isis, Horus, Thoth, Bes) or in the shape of hieroglyphs that refer to specific attributes such as rejuvenation or balance. Among the most common amulet was the scarab beetle, the hieroglyph for "to come into being," which conferred life and health. Another exceedingly common amulet was the *wedjet*

Figure 71. Painted fabric mask of Bes or his female counterpart, Beset, which may have been worn by a magician. Kahun. Dynasty 12. Photo courtesy of the Manchester Museum, University of Manchester.

eye, the eye of Horus that denoted health and rejuvenation. Some amulets were charged with magical power by means of spells. One instructs: "spell to be said over gold and garnet beads and sealed with an image of a hand and a crocodile."[28] Here, the intent was that the hand and the crocodile would drive evil away from a child. Coffin Text Spell 83 refers to the protection offered by an amulet in the shape of the forepart of a lion:

> Words to be said over the forepart of a lion made of carnelian and set at the neck of a man when he descends into the world of the dead ... Thus he will have power over the four winds of heaven and become an excellent *akh* as king of all the winds of heaven. As for every man who knows this spell, he shall not die a second time; his enemies shall not prevail over him; magic will never restrain him on earth. It means coming forth at his desire from the realm of the dead; it means becoming an excellent *akh* in the presence of Osiris.[29]

Another spell was intended to close the mouth of any male or female snake. It was to be said over a lion of faience threaded on red linen. "To be applied to a man's hand. It is to be given as a protection of the bedroom."[30]

Magic to Cure

In the dynastic period, magic was more commonly used to cure than to kill. The medico-magical spells emphasize the close association of religion and medicine and how, in a prescientific culture, religion was a potent and legitimate tool for affecting medical cures. These spells again refer to mythological events. One such spell, to cure a burn, recalls how Isis

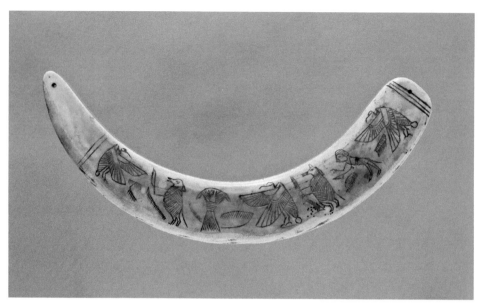

Figure 72. Ivory wand that was probably used to draw a protective circle around a mother and her child. It is decorated with gods called *abas* ("fighters"), who are armed with knives to repel evil. Dynasty 12. OIM 10788. Photo: Anna Ressman. Courtesy of the Oriental Institute of the University of Chicago.

rescues her son, Horus. The recitation was accompanied by the instructions, "Words to be said over the milk of a woman who has given birth to a male child, gum and hairs of a cat. To be applied to the burn." Another spell equated the magician with Horus: "I am Horus, hurrying over the desert to the place that is aflame." Isis is told of the condition of her son: "His upper part is afire, his lower part is afire; there is no place where he can escape from it!" The goddess extinguishes the flame with the water of her mouth. This spell was to be said three times, as the magician made a mass of grass, coriander, fruit, fat, oil, and wax that was to be put on a bandage over the burn.[31]

Among the most common injuries against which magical spells were directed were being stung by a scorpion, bitten by a snake, or snatched by a crocodile, all vivid reminders of the Egyptians' natural surroundings and the dangers that their environment posed. The emphasis on snakebites also alludes to the mythological tales of Apophis, the snake god who threatened the sun god Re. Like spells against heat and thirst, many of the spells against these injuries consist of invocations to Isis and Horus because of the cycle of myths in which Isis saves her son. One spell touts the power of Isis as a healer: "Now

Figure 73. Clay statue of Bes, a god who was especially associated with the protection of women and children. One spell calls for a dwarf of clay to be placed on the mother to lessen the pain of giving birth. Roman Period. Courtesy of W. Benson Harer, Jr.

Isis was a wise woman. Her heart was more rebellious than an infinite number of men, more smart than an infinite number of gods."[32] As with other types of magical spells, these are accompanied by ritual actions, such as

> Words to be said over an image of Atum-Horus-Heknu ... To be drawn on the hand of the sufferer. To be licked off by the man. To be done in the same manner on a piece of fine linen to be applied to the sufferer's throat. The herb is "scorpion's herb." To be ground with beer or wine. To be drunk by the one who suffers from a scorpion's sting.[33]

Another spell to protect against crocodiles instructs, "This spell is to be said [over] a clay egg. To be given into the hand of a man at the bow of the boat. If something on the water surfaces, [it] should be thrown upon the water."[34]

Figure 74. Section of a Book of the Dead with instructions about the appropriate forms and materials for amulets. Among the amulets pictured are (*top register*) a papyrus column of feldspar, a vulture of gold, and a *djed* column of gold, and (*below*) another papyrus column, a collar of gold, and a *tayet* knot of jasper. Ptolemaic Period. OIM 9798j. Courtesy of the Oriental Institute of the University of Chicago.

Another way of harnessing magical protection against illness was through the use of a cippus, a type of stela carved with a representation of Horus the Child, identified as such by his nudity and sidelock, standing on, and immobilizing, crocodiles (Fig. 75). He grasps other symbols of evil: the

Figure 75. Cippus (healing statue) showing a young Horus immobilizing dangerous animals (crocodiles, scorpions, lions, oryx, and vipers). The back of the cippus is covered with texts that call on deities for protection. Water was poured over the text and drunk as a remedy for illness. This cippus is only fourteen centimeters tall and could easily be moved from place to place with a traveler. Ptolemaic Period. OIM 16881. Photo: Anna Ressman. Courtesy of the Oriental Institute of the University of Chicago.

wild oryx of the desert, scorpions, and a lion. The sides and back of cippi are covered with hieroglyphic texts that call on deities, primarily Isis, the mother of Horus, to cure the sting of scorpions, the bite of snakes, and other less specific ills. These texts are derived from myths in which Isis hid Horus in the marshes of Khemmis to protect him from the wrath of Seth, and in which Isis and Thoth cured Horus after he was bitten by a poisonous creature. Cippi texts emphasize granting breath, a reference to shortness of breath, a symptom of snake or scorpion bites. Cippi come in a range of sizes, from small portable examples to very large ones that were probably set up in a local shrine. The most famous example of a cippus is the Metternich Stela in the Metropolitan Museum (Fig. 76) that is entirely covered with finely cut detailed hieroglyphs. The introductory text of Isis states, "Recitation by

Figure 76. The Metternich
Stela, one of the most elaborate
examples of a cippus. As with
smaller examples (see Fig. 75),
Horus on the Crocodiles
appears on the front. This very
large example (83.5 cm) stood
in the Temple of the Mnevis
Bull in Heliopolis, where
the afflicted could come and
be cured by drinking water
that had been poured over it.
Dynasty 30. The Metropolitan
Museum of Art, Fletcher Fund,
1950 (50.85). Image © The
Metropolitan Museum of Art.

Isis, the great, the god's mother: 'Don't fear, my son Horus! I will be around
you as your protection and drive away all evil from you and [from] any man
who is suffering as well.'"[35]

The protective power of a cippus was realized by pouring water over
it (or immersing small examples), and then drinking the liquid. It was
believed that the water became magically activated by its contact with the

inscriptions and the image of Horus on the Crocodiles. Most cippi are made of stone to withstand their repeated contact with water. Some were associated with legendary healers, the most famous being Djed-Hor of Athribis, a city in the Delta. For unknown reasons, Djed-Hor became an intermediary, an approachable contact between sufferers and the gods Isis and Horus. Several cippi of Djed-Hor are known. His cult was so popular, and thought to be so efficacious, that one of his cippi was equipped with a basin into which the magically activated water could flow for his adherents to scoop out and drink, much like a receptacle for holy water in a Catholic church.

Spells to Maim and Kill

Magical spells that seek to destroy or kill are relatively rare in the dynastic period, although they become more common in the Greco-Roman era. In the earlier period, they were more commonly aimed at enemies of the state than against personal foes.

Most examples involve a sort of role playing in which the conjurer and the intended victim symbolically reenact a myth. In one example, the magician evoked a fight between the gods and a bull. The magician assumed the roles of, and called upon Montu (a god of power), Osiris (the god of the afterlife), and other deities, while his opponent was likened to a "young bull whose horns have tasted (the effect of) a fight," but who was eventually vanquished by the gods. The text instructs the magician to recite:

> Montu has come that he may take hold of your horn. Seth has come that he might strike you. In case you seize my feet – I am Montu! In case you kill [me] – I am Osiris! ... Come to me Montu ... Come that you may put [the enemy's name] into my hand like a fluttering bird ... I will sever [the enemy's] bones and devour [his] flesh.[36]

In another spell, the magician assumed the identity of Horus to completely confound and physically confuse the enemy:

> You will stand still, you who are coming! I am somebody ... who acts as fighter [aha] ... I will enter your belly as a fly and then I will see your belly from its inside. I will turn your face into the back of your head, the front of your feet into your heels! Your speech is no use, it will not be heard. Your body becomes limp, your knee becomes feeble ... I am Horus, the son of Isis, [I] will leave on my [own] feet.[37]

This spell makes an allusion to inversions – the unnatural and terrifying transformation of the known and usual into the unnatural and perverse, and hence the face on the back of the head and the heels in place of toes.

Most spells that were aimed at a specific enemy involved the manufacture of a figurine of the adversary that was then ritually killed by the act of breaking or smashing, transferring the destruction from the figure to the real enemy. As with other aspects of magic (and religion overall), it was essential that the enemy be identified and specified by name. There are about a thousand examples of such figurines from the dynastic period. The earliest examples of these so-called execration (cursing) figurines date to the reign of Pepi II at the end of the Old Kingdom. A group excavated at Giza, intended to represent Nubians, was identified as "every rebel of this land, all people, all patricians, all commoners, all males, all eunuchs, all women, every chieftain, [every Nubian, every strongman, every messenger] who shall rebel in [followed by a series of place names], who will rebel or who will plot or who will plot by saying plots or by speaking anything evil against Upper Egypt or Lower Egypt forever."[38] Although these represented generic enemies from specific places, later examples were often labeled with specific personal names.

Two other large deposits of execration figurines were found at the Middle Kingdom fort at Mirgissa in Nubia. One consisted of inscribed potsherds and 350 figurines. The other was made up of about 200 fragments of broken red vases bearing inscriptions, ostraca, 346 mud figurines, and three limestone prisoner figurines of bound enemies (and the head of another). The malicious intent of the deposit was made clear by the presence of a human sacrifice and by four crucibles supplied to burn and destroy the four prisoner figurines. These vessels are known from religious texts as the "furnace of the coppersmiths" that consumed enemies.[39] This group, and the Giza deposit, show the extent to which magic was legitimate and accepted, for these deposits were intended to kill enemies of the state.

From the early Middle Kingdom comes another group of magical items intended to maim. In this case, it may have been officials of the state who were the objects of ill intent. This cache consisted of five alabaster plaques; a clay figurine inscribed with a long, unfortunately illegible text; and six crude human figurines made of folded sheets of wax. The alabaster plaques were inscribed with the name "Intefoker the son of Intefoker and Satsisobek." All three names are followed by the hieroglyphic determinative that denotes an enemy. Although these are common Middle Kingdom names, the two generations of names match the genealogy of the Intefoker who was the vizier (akin to prime minister) to King Senwosert I.[40] It is unfortunate that the long text on the figurine cannot be read to clarify the function of this deposit, but its similarity to other groups of materials inscribed with names suggests that the objects were to be destroyed in order to kill the high official. From the end of Dynasty 12 comes yet another deposit of red pots, these inscribed with the names of members of the royal family.[41] Although nothing more is known about this group, it is tempting to see these too as magical efforts to harm individuals, in this case, members of the court.

The best-known and best-documented example of magic figurines used with the intent to kill are recorded in Papyrus Harris, which recounts the attempt by courtiers to kill King Ramesses III. The plot was discovered and foiled.[42] Two other papyri (Rollin and Lee) document the trial of the accused and give more information about the plot. This is the only account of a trial for sorcery in ancient Egyptian records. The case was especially prominent not because it concerned an attempt to kill with magic, but because the object of the attempt was the king himself.

The documents give a picture of deep-seated palace intrigue. Tiye, one of the lesser queens of Ramesses III, was desperate to ensure that her son Pentaweret ascend the throne in place of Ramesses (the future Ramesses IV), the son of the chief queen. According to Papyrus Lee, the conspirators obtained a "secret book of magic from the royal library ... to plan their evil deed." This book of magic is further described as "a writing of the scrolls of User-Maat-Re-Mery-Amun [Ramesses III]"; in other words, it came from the king's own library, not from the secret trove of a sorcerer. The trial described in the papyri was not about the use of magic per se, for magic was considered to be a legitimate tool of the state, but about the use of the spells against the king rather than against enemies of Egypt.[43]

The papyri record that Queen Tiye assembled a group of co-conspirators led by a man with a political grudge, Pabakikamen, a court official whom "Pre did not allow to become majordomo," probably a reference to his promotion to a higher post not being confirmed by an oracle of the god Pre. The text relates, "He began to make writings of magic for exorcising [and] for disturbing." Papyrus Lee elaborates that Pabakikamen stated, "Give to me a papyrus for giving to me terror and respect ... and he began to petition the god for the derangement [?] of people." He then made "some gods of wax and some potions for laming the limbs of people. They were placed in the hand of Pabakikamen ... and the other great enemies, saying: 'Let them approach.' Now after he allowed the ones who did evil to enter – which they did, but which [the god] Pre did not allow them to be successful." Papyrus Lee supplies further details: "He began to make inscribed people of wax in order to cause that they be taken inside by the hand of the agent Idrimi for the exorcising of the one crew and the enchanting of the others."[44]

Apparently, the investigators had found another conspirator who was charged with taking the wax figurines into the private chambers. Although the rest of the details of the plot are unknown, once discovered, the conspirators were put to trial. The text continues, "He [Pabakikamen] was examined, and truth was found in every crime and every evil which his heart had found fit to do [namely] that truth was in them, and that he did them with all the other great enemies like him, and that great crimes worthy of death ... were what had been done. Now when he realized the great crimes worthy of death that he had done, he killed himself."[45] In the end, twenty-eight men and six women were indicted. All but five were executed or allowed to kill themselves.

The wax figurines central to the plot against Ramesses III are known from other sources, and wax itself was considered to be a substance especially suited to magical practices. Chapter 175 of the Book of the Dead refers to wax figurines of the enemies of the king, inscribed with the names of the intended victims, which were to be bound with black string. In the late Middle Kingdom story recorded on Papyrus Westcar, mentioned previously, the lector priest Webaoner opened his chest of ebony and electrum (similar in function to the box found in the Ramesseum?) and took wax from it with which to manufacture a crocodile seven fingers long. After the magician said his magic words, it became a fearful creature seven cubits in length. After other magical utterances, Webaoner was able to turn it back into a wax figure. As seen in the conspiracy against Ramesses III, the potency of wax as a magical substance was considered to be real, not just a trope of the literary tradition. One papyrus of the Greco-Roman Period explicitly states, "Now as for wax, it is made into enemies specifically to slaughter his name and to prevent his *ba* from leaving the place of execution. As for wax, one makes [execration] figures with it to destroy his name."[46] Spell 147 of the Book of the Dead (among others) refers to the potency of wax: "[Words] to be said over an image of the enemy, made of wax, with the name of the enemy written on its breast with the abomination of the *weba*-fish, put into the ground in the place of Osiris,"[47] counseling the conjurer to bury the figurine just as Osiris was buried.

Other texts from the Late Period, but which may be rooted in Middle Kingdom traditions, relate how figurines of wax could be used to kill enemies of the state.[48] One text advises that a coffin of wax be used to "bury" symbolic enemies:

> This spell is said over Apep [a snake god, also known as Apophis, who was the embodiment of evil] drawn on a new papyrus with fresh ink and placed within a coffin ... Then inscribe for yourself these names of all male and female enemies whom your heart fears as every enemy of pharaoh whether dead or alive, the name of their fathers, the name of their mothers, the name of [their] children; [to be placed] within a coffin to be made (also) in wax, to be placed on the fire after the name of Apep.[49]

However, wax figurines were not always used for evil. A New Kingdom text relates that the sting of a scorpion could be cured by making a cat of wax. In imitation of real life, the "cat" would attack the scorpion. In the Third Intermediate Period, protective wax figurines of the Four Sons of Horus (deities who protected the embalmed viscera) were attached to the wrappings of mummies.

Reviewing the many ways that the Egyptians could use magical means to promote a certain outcome, whether to kill an enemy or to cure or to protect oneself from evil gods or influences, it is clear that magic was a well-established part of Egyptian religious practice. Egyptians would have hardly recognized magic as a separate part of their beliefs. Magic was used by kings and the state, as well as by specially trained lector priests, and perhaps by others who have not left a record of their deeds. In the form of water charged with healing power through contact with cippi, magic was also available to a much wider audience. In the dynastic era, magic was used primarily for defensive and protective purposes, and spells to kill were usually aimed at perceived enemies of the state. Yet, the majority of Egyptian magical spells fall into the category of medical practices that are the forerunners of more scientific medical procedures. As with so many other aspects of Egyptian religion, magic developed as a means of alleviating problems, both large and small, and of coping with an unpredictable and sometimes dangerous world.

The Amarna Period

Practical Aspects of "Monotheism"

Egyptian religion provided believers with comfort through the many assurances that it provided. It helped to explain the unexplainable – the great mysteries of death and birth. The gods were approachable. Their human, or partially human, form and their behavior made them familiar. Faith supported the structure of Egyptian society by providing a paternal king who was both godlike and – in theory at least – accessible and protective. It is not difficult to see how so many features of Egyptian religion stayed generally static for hundreds of centuries, reinforcing a conservative society in a potentially threatening world. Yet, there was one brief historical moment – the Amarna Period – in which the Egyptians' beliefs were challenged and disrupted, a moment when religious philosophy and practice were altered to introduce an apparently far less appealing and less functional set of beliefs. This negative appraisal of ancient Egypt's religious "revolution" is not just a modern opinion, for the new religion did not outlive its promulgator by more than a few years. The Amarna religion, its precepts, and its actual impact on Egyptian society are still among the most debated topics in Egyptology.

The "Amarna Period" (roughly 1350–1325 BC) refers to the reigns of Amunhotep IV (who changed his name to Akhenaten) (Fig. 77) and his two successors, Smenkhkare and Tutankhamun. During his reign, Amunhotep IV initiated a new theology that was nothing less than a complete reconsideration of the nature of the world and the relationship of the king and his

Figure 77.
Akhenaten.
Dynasty 18.
Louvre N 831/
AF 109. ©
2006 Musée du
Louvre/Christian
Décamps.

subjects to the divine. Dominating this theology was the god of Akhenaten, the Aten, the incarnation of the sun. The precepts of Atenism were not set down in a clear fashion as a set of commandments or laws. Rather, they came directly from the king, who received them from the god itself in the form of divine revelations. This origin marks the Amarna religion as the world's first in the series of received theologies. The relationship between the god and king is reflected in texts that claim that "there is none that know him [the Aten] except your son [Akhenaten] ... for you make him aware of your plans and strength."[1] This new theology, or philosophy, which was spelled out most explicitly in the Hymn to the Aten that appears in six private tombs at Tell el Amarna, was centered on the role of light, incarnate as the god Aten, as the only giver and renewer of life. As the theology matured under Amunhotep IV/Akhenaten, Egyptian art and architecture underwent dramatic changes to accommodate it.

By the fifth year of his reign, in a dramatic move that cemented his break with the past, Akhenaten moved the court to Tell el Amarna (hence the name Amarna Period), a desolate site in Middle Egypt. There, an entirely new capital city was built in honor of the Aten. The royal policy was to discourage the worship of other gods. Although the temples of other gods were not officially closed, state financial support for the other cults was transferred to the cult of the Aten. The most direct action was taken against the gods who dwelled in the great temples of Karnak and Luxor in ancient Thebes, perhaps because the rituals enacted in them were so closely linked with the traditional idea of kingship. The names of the Theban gods, especially Amun's, were physically hacked from the temple walls and even from the tops of obelisks that were nearly thirty meters tall. The written reference to other gods was attacked in private monuments too, even when the personal name of an individual happened to include the name of another god. Never before had this sort of intolerance been seen in Egypt.

Although some of the historical details at the end of his reign are sketchy, Akhenaten apparently died after seventeen years on the throne. The new religion barely outlived him. His successor, Smenkhkare (there is great uncertainty about the identity of Akhenaten's immediate successors), ruled for no more than two years. Smenkhkare was probably followed by Tutankhaten ("Living Image of the Aten"), who, early in his reign, restored the old religion, changed his name to Tutankhamun ("Living Image of Amun"), and returned the court to Thebes and Memphis.

The Nature of the Aten and the Rise of the God

The Aten was not an invention of Akhenaten. Middle Kingdom texts refer to the Aten, and there are numerous references to the deity from the

Figure 78. The Temple to the Aten at East Karnak. The portico was decorated with colossal statues of the king, his arms crossed, holding the royal scepters. The statues portrayed the king with an elongated face and heavy hips and thighs, perhaps an allusion to the androgyny of the creator god. Dynasty 18. Photo © CNRS-CFEETK.

Eighteenth Dynasty. One text from the time of Hatshepsut refers to the Aten as "the disk that created all being." By the reign of Amunhotep III, the father of Akhenaten, there was intense interest in solar deities, and especially in the Aten, as the givers of life and renewers of life.

Amunhotep IV began to formulate the new theology early in his reign. He singled out the Aten for special veneration in temples built at East Karnak. Unlike earlier kings, who built temples dedicated to one god but included a wide variety of deities in that same complex, Amunhotep's temples at East Karnak were dedicated exclusively to the Aten (Fig. 78). This construction was the culmination of his new conception of the gods. In the early Amarna Period, deities, especially creator gods (Khepri and Ptah) or solar gods (Re, Horakhty, and Atum), were combined with the Aten. Unlike in earlier periods, when the combined gods kept their own identities, in these new formulations each god's identity was merged into that of the Aten. In texts on the stelae of the architects Suty and Hor, who lived in the formative period late in the reign of Amunhotep III, the gods Re and Khepri are associated with creation, but the Aten is referred to as the one "who has created all and made them live ... who brought himself into being, who has no fashioner."[2]

The Amarna theology focused on the sunlight of the Aten as the sole source of life: "Oh living Aten who initiates life." The theology attempted to simplify the complicated world of the many gods and the complex explanations of life and life after death contained in the Book of the Dead and other compendiums of mortuary theology into a simple message: all life comes from the sunlight that is the Aten. This new philosophy banished Osiris, Isis, Horus, and Amun, as well as their complicated cults and the statues, processions, and offerings that came with them. What was left was the simple message that the sun was life and that all life comes from light. At first glance, this message might have had great popular appeal. The traditional theology was, on the one hand, a cumbersome mix of deities, beliefs, and concepts. But, on the other, its complexity created a sense of safety and comfort. There were seemingly infinite ways in which the god(s) could be approached, and many and variant road maps to explain the many terrors and uncertainties of what happened after death.

The Aten's status as the sole god is repeatedly stressed in references to the "uniqueness" of the sun disk. Texts in the tomb of the nobleman Aye at Amarna relate that "there is no other than him [the god]" and "being unique and risen in your aspects of being as the living Aten-manifest, far [yet] near,"[3] indicating that the god was omnipresent, yet beyond the realm of approach or human experience.

The form of the god also underscored its uniqueness and its inaccessibility to humans. The Aten was represented as the orb or globe of the sun (Plate XVIII). In contrast, traditional gods had always appeared in forms that were recognizable, most commonly in wholly human form or as a hybrid in which the head of an animal was fused to a human body. Hands and feet allowed the traditional deities to move, to give and receive, and to interact with humans. The deities had eyes and mouths that enabled them to observe and to speak with human beings. The abstract form of the Aten was the antithesis of this accessibility. As the personification of an abstract concept – light – the Aten could not speak or interact with humans.

The abstraction of the Aten was further emphasized by the absence of myths to explain its origins. The humanity of most other gods was stressed by the way in which they were grouped into families – Osiris, Isis, and their son Horus, or the Theban triad of Amun, his wife Mut, and their son

Khonsu. In contrast, the Aten had no consort, although it did have one son, the king Akhenaten, "the one whom the Aten had begotten," "Waenre [the prenomen of Akhenaten], your beautiful son," "your [the Aten's] beloved son ... who issued from Aten."[4] The god itself was said to have come from nothingness: "who made himself," and "O god ... it is you who were made when there was no one who made any of this."[5]

Another major difference between the Aten and the traditional gods was its relationship to humans. In contrast to earlier texts that stated that one could "know the god," in the Amarna theology it was stated that "one cannot know" the Aten, for that relationship was reserved exclusively for the king. This aspect of the theology is emphasized repeatedly through such phrases as "no one knows him [the Aten] except your son" (i.e., the king) and in the many scenes that show the rays of the Aten raining down on the king and his family, but not on his subjects. The rays of the sun end in small human hands that hold an *ankh*, the hieroglyph for "life," to the noses of the king and the queen (Fig. 79). Texts refer to the rays "embracing" the king and giving him "continuity." All non-royal individuals stand outside the range of the Aten's rays, which in a sun-filled land like Egypt is truly extraordinary. This religion and its iconography were clearly formulated to stress the power of the king and the king's superiority in relation to his subjects.

The constant reminders that the king was "unique" in his solo communication with the Aten are among the most striking and troubling aspects of this new theology. The king was able to determine "what was in his [the Aten's] heart," and he and the god shared an unspoken, private, and privileged communication: "There is none who knows you [the god] except your son [Akhenaten] for you make him aware of your plans and your strength."[6]

With the fervor of new converts, courtiers recorded how the king expressed the new theology and inspired their devotion in disseminating it. The fan bearer May wrote,

> He [the king] has doubled my favors for me like grains of sand, for I was the first of officials in front of the subjects, and my lord advanced me so that I might execute his teachings as I listened to his voice without cease. My eyes are seeing your beauty in the course of every day ... How fortunate is the one who listens to your teaching of life.[7]

And the courtier Aye recorded, "My lord instructed me just so that I might practice his teaching. I live by adoring his Ka, and I am fulfilled by following

Figure 79. Akhenaten, Nefertiti, and their daughters under the rays of the Aten. The king and queen's special relationship with the Aten is symbolized by the tiny *ankh* (life) signs that the god's rays hold before the noses of the royal couple, giving them the divine "breath of life." Dynasty 18. Egyptian Museum, Berlin 14145. Bildarchiv Preussischer Kulturbesitz/Art Resource, NY.

him."[8] The chief builder Maanakhtef described himself as "a disciple whom his [majesty] instructed,"[9] and Meryre claimed that "I live at hearing what you say," and "How fortunate is the one who stands in your presence and turns his heart to [your] instructions."[10] The chamberlain Tutu claimed that "every day he [the king] rises early to instruct me, insomuch as I execute his teaching."[11] These passages all give the impression that the king was surrounded by a select group of courtiers to whom he gave personal instruction in the new theology so that they could become the new faith's devotees and messengers.

Impact of the New Theology

What was this new religion about, and what did it mean to the people who lived at the time? Did the developments in Thebes and Tell el Amarna mean anything to them? It is clear that this new theology fundamentally changed the religious practices of Egyptians. In the traditional religion, people worshipped a wide variety of deities. Offerings were to be left for the gods at shrines or in temple courtyards, and the deities could be accessed through prayers. The gods were close to the people who regularly took shelter under their protection. In the Amarna Period, people had no immediate contact with the deity because the pathway of communication with the Aten ran through – and ended with – the king. People were expected to worship the Aten through the intermediary of the king who would transmit their piety to the god. Under the new religion, piety for the gods was transformed into loyalty to the king, for he was the sole conduit and interpreter of the Aten who, in turn, was the sole source of life. Numerous texts attest to the single-minded devotion expressed by the king's courtiers as they sought the king's favor in an effort to reach the god: "How fortunate is he who follows you, for you cause all he has made to keep on existing," and "How fortunate is one who stands in your presence and turns his heart to [your] instructions, for you then grant him the old age that is yours to give."[12] "Praise the Lord of the Two Lands, effective form of the disk [in Egyptian *akh n Itn*, the name of the king]; fate who gives life, lord of commands, [who gives] light for every land ... through whose Ka one is sated, the god who makes the great and builds the lowly; air for every nose, through whom all breathe." The courtier Aye proclaimed,

> I was one true to the king, the great companion to be confided in ... one whom he fostered ... I was in front of the officials and companions of the king, [being] the first of his lord's followers. He has set Maat [truth] in my inner being, and my abomination is lying. I live only by worshipping his Ka, and I am fulfilled only by seeing him. My lord, who makes a good fate for his favorite ... the god who gives life.[13]

The phraseology of the adoration of the king verges on fanatical. The king is called "my breath by whom I live, my north wind, my millions of Niles flowing daily."[14]

Such passages reflect a major change in theology. Previously, one's desired fate – to pass to a happy afterlife – was determined by an individual's moral behavior while alive. Under the new theology, people's actions ceased to determine their fate, for adoration of the king and obedience to him replaced good deeds and behavior. As related by the courtier Aye, "I was excellent, a possessor of character ... I followed his [the king's] voice [i.e., commands] without cease, and the result of this is the reward of an old age in peace ... May you [the king] grant me a good old age like a favorite of yours."[15] He further proclaimed, "[May] adoration be given to you when you rise in the horizon [and] until your setting from life comes to pass; and may my favor be lasting every day [in the presence of] Waenre [Akhenaten] until the old age which is his to give comes about, in favor and tranquility."[16] The worship of god had been replaced by adoration of his sole messenger, the king.

The Conception of the Afterlife in the Amarna Period

Unlike the traditional theology that had evolved gradually over a millennium and a half, the Amarna doctrine emerged rapidly over several years, which may account for the incomplete way in which it addressed many aspects of life and death. One of the most obvious shortcomings of the theology, and a striking one in comparison to the traditional religion, was its conception of the afterlife. In the traditional theology, the dark frightening hours of the night were inhabited by thousands of genies and gods. The horrors of this realm were carefully detailed in mortuary literature such as the Amduat, the Book of Gates, and the Book of the Dead. The richness of mortuary beliefs in the pre-Amarna age gave tremendous comfort by assuring that those who lived their lives morally would traverse the night to be reborn at dawn into a perfectly recognizable replica of the world in the hereafter. Further comfort was provided by the belief that, to a great extent, individuals controlled their own fates, for rebirth was dependent on the way in which one conducted oneself during life. Each individual spirit was judged before the gods, and each had to recite the negative confession in which the deceased proclaimed that he or she had not lied, stolen, committed adultery, or profaned the king or the gods.

In contrast to this busy conception of the hereafter, the realm of the dead in the Amarna Period was simply a place without the light of the Aten, an empty void. In the Amarna Period, the afterlife revolved around the king, for he dispensed life after death:

> May your corpse be firm, may your name last … May you inhale the breezes of the north wind. May you be given offerings and provisions, and may you receive sacrificial food which is the king's to give [with] bread, beer, and food in every place of yours … May you occupy your place which is the king's to give in the necropolis of Akhet-Aten [Tell el Amarna].[17]

In the tomb of Aye at Amarna it is related, "May you [the king] grant me a good old age like a favorite of yours. May you give me a good funeral by the decree of your Ka in my tomb within which you ordained for me to rest in the mountain of Akhet-Aten, the place of the favored ones."[18] "I am like any favorite of yours who follows your Ka. May I depart [i.e., die], laden with your favor, following old age ... lifetime is in your [Akhenaten's] hand and you grant it to whomever you wish."[19]

Accessibility to the afterlife through worshipping the king was a frequent theme of the mortuary texts at Amarna: "Worship the king, unique like Aten, without another who is great except for him, and he will give you a lifetime of tranquility with food and provisions which are his to give." "How prosperous is one who carries out his teachings, for he shall reach the district of the favored ones [i.e., the necropolis]."[20]

In contrast to the complicated mortuary beliefs of other periods, those of the Amarna era were much simpler. The texts already cited indicate that the transition to the afterlife was the king's to give in exchange for his subjects' loyalty. This is also expressed in the decoration of private tombs at Tell el Amarna. The composition of the reliefs there changed from scenes that showed the deceased before the gods to scenes of people adoring the king. No longer, with a rare exception, was the tomb owner the focus of scenes depicting him banqueting or supervising his estate. The new iconography dwelled on the king's palace and details of activities within. The processions of gods were replaced by scenes of the king and queen in their chariots, processing along the main streets of the city. In the main chamber of private tombs, the king and queen were shown presenting offerings to the Aten. In contrast, the owner of the tomb was shown in small scale, making the owner difficult to differentiate from other courtiers who have gathered to adore the king. Some reliefs show the tomb owner before the king being rewarded with gold collars (Fig. 80), but even these scenes emphasize the role of the king in the official's life. These tomb scenes show that an individual was no longer the focus of his or her own afterlife – eternal existence was focused on the royal family, who were the dispensers of eternity.

In earlier (and later) periods it was believed that after death the *ba*, the energy of the individual represented as a human-headed bird, left the tomb at daybreak and rejoined the living, sitting in trees and drinking cool water from the canals. In the Amarna Period, the *ba*'s activity was limited to visiting the Temple of the Aten to receive the "breath of life" and offerings (referred to as "the unused offerings of your father Aten")[21] from the divine altars: "As for my *ba*, may it come forth to see your rays and receive nourishment from

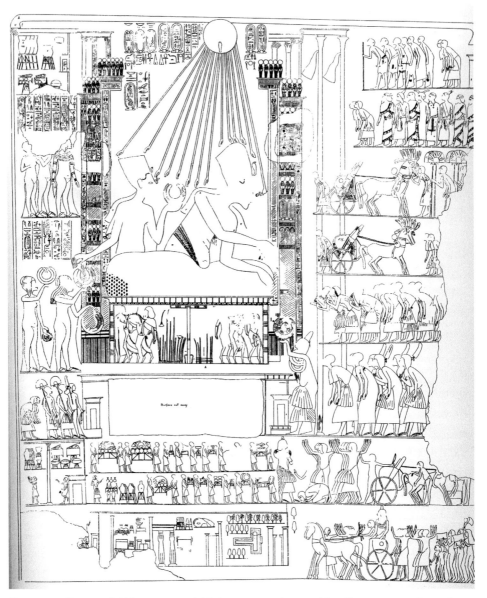

Figure 80. Scene of Akhenaten and Nefertiti awarding gold collars, a sign of royal favor, to Meryra, the Royal Scribe and Overseer of the Household of the Queen. Meryra, his neck laden with collars, stands to the bottom right of the "window of appearances" where the royal family displayed themselves to their subjects. Two princesses (*left*) hand the collars to their mother. Dynasty 18. Tomb of Meryra II at Amarna. Courtesy of the Egypt Exploration Society.

its offerings ... may I partake of everything which issues from [the temple of the Aten]"[22] This must have had an impact on how people viewed death. The freedom of the *ba* was a liberating idea because it assured the deceased that they would mingle with the living, enjoy the warmth of the sun, and have mobility.

Impact of the New Religion on Society

In pre-Amarna society, a significant percentage of the elite population held priestly ranks (see Chapter 2) as well as posts of responsibility in the civil service. The types of priests were differentiated by titles whose status and duties were clearly demarcated, from the First Priest down though the ranks of lectors, God's Fathers, and simple *wabs*. The incorporation of so many people into the priesthood in very orderly ways and with stated duties may have had the effect of more fully involving people in society and creating another web of social support through their interrelated duties.

At Amarna, the situation was dramatically different. The fifty-odd tombs of courtiers cut into the northern and southern cliffs record the titles of the highest officials at the new capital. What is striking is the near absence of priestly titles – gone are the *wabs* and lectors and the various ranks of *hem netcher* priests. Most of the high nobility at Amarna hold titles that focus on the king (Chamberlain, Cup Bearer, Fan Bearer at the Right Hand of the King), or administrative titles such as scribe, steward, Overseer of the Storehouse of the Aten, Master of the Horse or Chariotry, Overseer of Building Projects, and Chief of the Medjay (police). The few priestly titles are scribe of the offering table of the Aten, First Priest of the Aten (*bak tepy*) in the Temple of the Aten, steward of pacifying the Aten, and God's Father. But even these titles are rare, and some are oddly constructed. The title "First Priest" uses the word *bak* ("servant") rather than the *hem netcher* (literally, "servant" [of the god]) of the old First Priest of the traditional gods, signaling a break with tradition. The highest priest bears the title Greatest of Seers, which was held by two men (Meryre and Re-Pawah). This title was formerly held by the High Priest of Heliopolis, the city associated with the sun god Re (and it was also known from Thebes and Hermonthis). The choice of this title was probably thought to be appropriate because of the solar nature of the Aten. There are fewer types of priests attested at Amarna, perhaps because the god communicated only with the king, so there was no need for a hierarchy of priests, especially since the elaborate daily offering service (see Chapter 3) had been replaced by the simple offering of flowers and food on the offering tables of the Aten temples.

What Did the Amarna Theology Offer the People?

From the perspective of the people, it is hard to imagine what appeal the Amarna theology could have offered. Clearly, it had an impact on not only how people approached the god and the king but also on how they conducted their lives. When Akhenaten moved Egypt's administrative center to Tell el Amarna, members of the vast civil service bureaucracy had to move with him or lose their government positions. They had to leave one of the most sophisticated cities in the world, a town so famous that it was called simply "The City" because it had no peer, for a settlement that was deliberately built in an isolated and undeveloped place. They left behind their homes, their familiar surroundings, and most important of all, the tombs of their families. This must have been wrenching, for one of their primary obligations was to bury their parents and to maintain their funerary cults. The move cut people off from direct contact with their gods and disrupted the familiar cult rituals of offering and giving prayer. It replaced a sense of pride in moral behavior with a mindless loyalty to the king as the sole dispenser of one's old age and afterlife.

The focus of the movement was entirely on the king – he was the sole communicant with the Aten, and it was he who granted health and an afterlife. This was a great change from previous periods when people were more broadly focused on their own lives as individuals within the greater society. In the pre-Amarna Period, they had a variety of deities to whom they could appeal. In theory, each person determined his or her own fate through righteous or corrupt actions. The Amarna experience veered close to totalitarianism – to a world in which people are compelled to serve the ego and will of a single powerful individual who holds all within his grasp.

Within all religious systems there are skeptics, and one can see some deviations from the official line, even at Amarna. Amulets and small objects depicting gods Bes and Taweret, parts of necklaces sacred to Hathor, and representations of the king and queen in the guise of Shu and Tefnut have been found. A prayer calling on Amun was recovered from the workmen's village at Amarna, providing clear evidence of the veneration of the traditional gods.[23] Attempts were made to retain some of the familiar trappings of belief even in the face of a state-mandated theology. In the tomb of the courtier

Huya a rare funeral scene is shown. The coffin of Huya stands beside offerings as a leopard-clad priest officiates and a mourner laments the death.[24]
This is a wholly traditional scene except for the omission of references to
the god Osiris and of the image of the god Anubis who normally attends the
coffin. Shabtis (mummiform figurines that represent the deceased as Osiris)
have also been recovered from Amarna, some inscribed for Akhenaten himself. Some of them have traditional texts referring to Osiris, while others
substitute the name Aten. These suggest that the people of Amarna, and
even the king, were attempting to find a safe middle ground between the
new and old theologies and that there was not universal adherence to the
new religion.

Yet was there ever active opposition? There are only a few hints, some
from the reign of Akhenaten and other, more direct indications of dissent
after his death. One of the earliest signs of opposition to Akhenaten's new
theology is recorded on official boundary stelae that were set up to delin-
eate the perimeters of the new city:

> Now, as for my father Hor Aten who lives! As for the [break in text] in Akhet-Aten
> it was worse than those which I heard in regnal year 4; it was worse than those
> which I heard in regnal year 3; it was worse than those which I heard in regnal year
> 2; it was worse than those which I heard in regnal year 1; it was worse than those
> which king Nebmaatre [Amunhotep III, father of Akhenaten] heard; it was worse
> than those which king Menkheperre [Thutmose III] heard and it was worse than
> those heard by any kings who had [ever] assumed the White Crown.[25]

Although this tantalizing text is sketchy, it apparently refers to active opposition to the king or to his program in Thebes, opposition that might have
motivated Akhenaten's move to Tell el Amarna.

Other brief references relate to efforts to enforce the new theology.
Punishments were inflicted on those who turned away from the Aten indicating that there were individuals at Amarna whose faith in the Aten and the
king were not assured. In the tomb of the chamberlain Tutu there are references to the dangers of speaking against the regime: "All of you who follow
him, may you hearken to his teaching ... [As for the opponent of] this [god?
theology?], he descends to the slaughter and fire devours his limbs ... [As
for someone about whom one] hears a report ... while it is in the mouth of
other ... so that he sets it here ... he becomes an enemy among you and
hides."[26] And in the tomb of Ramose there is another comment concerning those who apparently did not embrace the new theology: "[As for any
dissidents] fear of him [the king] is in their hearts."[27] Although there is no

contemporary documentation of active resistance by those who refused to abandon their traditional beliefs, a letter written a century later stated that a man died in "regnal year 9 of the rebellion," suggesting that there was some sort of revolt a few years after the move to Amarna. A court proceeding in which the event under investigation happened was "in the time of the enemy of Akhet-Aten [i.e., Akhenaten]."[28]

Conclusion

The bits of evidence that we have concerning the impact of the Amarna Period are tantalizing, yet so fragmentary that it is difficult to assess what this era actually meant. Did people go to Amarna out of devotion to the king and genuine endorsement of the new religion? Or, did certain members of the nobility follow the king in order to keep their positions and to hope for advancement in a smaller court setting? In contrast to the opaqueness of the public reaction, the lack of regard for the governmental, political, and religious changes of Amarna by the successors of Akhenaten is quite clear. Within the first few years of his reign, Tutankhamun (who came to the throne as Tutankhaten) abandoned Amarna and returned the court to Thebes and Memphis. His lengthy restoration inscription described the appalling condition of the temples, whose buildings had become "foot-paths," and whose shrines were overgrown with grass. Even if it is hyper-bole, the text summarized the preceding era as causing the land to fall into "wrack and ruin," stating that the "gods were ignoring the land." The resto-ration's impact on the people is evident, for the king installed new priests, restored the familiar positions, and reinstituted the offering rituals that employed so many priests and consumed such quantities of incense, fabric, unguents, and food, which must have stimulated the local economy. It is perhaps a mark of the greater utility and the appeal of traditional beliefs that they reemerged so rapidly after the death of Akhenaten.

Afterword

An Appraisal of Egyptian Religion

The preceding chapters have attempted to show how ancient Egyptian religious beliefs and practices functioned in the community and how those beliefs formed patterns of human behavior. The influence of religion was everywhere. The most prominent features of the built landscape – temples and tombs – served as sacred space, and so much of the immense material legacy of the culture – coffins and mummies, statues, figurines, amulets, and papyri – are manifestations of religious beliefs. These physical traces of Egyptian religion and cult practices are uniquely and distinctively products of Egypt – they cannot be mistaken for the material legacy of any other culture. This distinctiveness may be due to the close relationship of the material culture to the environment. Their myths, religious beliefs, and resulting cult actions are all reflections of the natural world of the Egyptians, who were keen observers of their physical surroundings. Just as the environment of the Nile Valley is unique, the culture that it stimulated is unlike any encountered elsewhere.

However, it is not just the religion's creativity and uniqueness that are so striking but also its longevity. It is safe to suggest that the beliefs and practices that comprised Egyptian religion must have benefited individuals and the society itself, and must have provided what people wanted and needed. If not, the beliefs surely would have been abandoned rather than embraced as they were for three millennia.

Perhaps the key to understanding the long-term survival of Egyptian cult practices was that they seem to have offered people a tremendous amount of comfort and support. Offering rituals assured the people that their gods would continue to heed their pleas and to help them. Religious beliefs empowered people and allowed them to improve their personal situations. Magical spells and actions, such as substituting for their enemies inscribed images that could be burned, smashed, or broken, allowed for the elimination of a foe from a safe distance and avoided direct conflict. Even if the ritual was not effective, the action gave the conjurer a sense of satisfaction and relief. Individuals could battle the forces of sickness through spells and potions, or could drink water charged with curative power by the inscriptions carved on a cippus. The idea that one could communicate with the dead through writing is a simple and compassionate solution to the grief that follows death. One was not separated forever from loved ones who were lost – they were simply away and could continue to communicate with the living.

The comforting aspect of religious beliefs must have been widespread because most cult practices were easily accessible. Chapels to deities dotted the Egyptian landscape, and Chapels of the Hearing Ears were located on the exterior walls of temples, where they could be approached by anyone. Portable stelae decorated with the ears of the god and intercessory statues gave petitioners immediate contact with gods who were regarded as being sympathetic and helpful. Access to the deities was aided by the potential low cost of worshiping them. Although one could lavish immense resources on commissioning a stone statue for dedication in the temple, a statue of inferior materials and workmanship was deemed to be as effective. In a society where there were enormous disparities between the elite and the non-elite, the equal effectiveness of prayer, without regard to a person's wealth, must have appealed to and reassured the non-elite that they had the same chance as the elite to be helped by the gods. This equality before the gods is reinforced by texts that stated that it was proper behavior, not worldly goods, that determined a person's fate before the gods.

The accessibility of religion can also be related to the level of personal involvement religion afforded Egyptians and the opportunities it gave for the less well connected to serve the gods. The structure of the priesthood reflected this inclusive rather than exclusive structure of worship. For much of the duration of Egyptian civilization, priests, priestesses, and temple musicians (especially the lower ranks) worked part-time, enabling a larger number of people to participate in the formal temple cult. There is no evidence that the lower ranks of priests were literate, making those posts available to a much wider and diverse circle of the lesser elite. It is likely that working in the temple was seen as a community undertaking and that the temple served as a node of social activity.

Part of the longevity of cult practices and their evident success in meeting the needs of the society may be due to the practicality and pragmatism of the underlying religious beliefs. They were not derived from an abstract philosophy that was available only to the literate elite. The beliefs and their resulting cult activities were especially suited for a population with a high percentage of illiterate individuals who could observe the fundamental aspects of religion all around them. For example, the concept of life after death was based on nothing more complicated than recognizing what life was like and then extending that beyond death, or than observing the undying cycle of the birth, death, and rebirth of the sun. Certainly, more detailed knowledge about the transit from life to the hereafter was provided by spells from the Book of the Dead or other texts that were the domain of the high elite, but they were embellishments, not essential parts of the belief.

Another aspect of Egyptian cult practices that may have contributed to their longevity was their flexibility and variability. It was not a religion built on dogma. One could worship the god or gods in a temple, a wayside chapel, or at home. The idea of rebirth too reflects variability. It was framed in terms of the solar cycle or in union with the god Osiris. Service to the deceased in the afterlife could be provided by paintings or by statues of servants or by written reference to them. There was always a multiplicity of ways, each as effective as the other, to achieve the same result.

The economic aspect of Egyptian cults also contributed to their longevity. The whole society benefited economically from religious customs, including the men who built tombs and temples; the craftsmen who made funerary offerings of wood, stone, or faience; the people who wove textiles for clothing or for mummification; and the thousands of men and women who worked in the temples as priests, singers, porters, and guards, as well as the farmers and herdsmen whose crops and livestock were presented as temple offerings and then reverted to the temple staff as wages. The products that religious cults demanded were the economic underpinnings of the society.

Many of the religious practices discussed in these pages were effective social modulators. Oracles of the god were an ideal way of ensuring community harmony. Rather than directly accuse an individual of wrong-doing, the god, in the form of an oracle, could make the judgment. Correct behavior could be ensured by traditions such as the sense of the *bau* (spirit) of the god lingering over the wrongdoer. And as already touched on, the lavish offerings of the rich and the meager ones of the poor were equal before the god, at least in theory, perhaps lessening a sense of antagonism between the rich and the poor.

Finally, the evidence suggests that Egyptian religion was embraced by the society because of the excitement and joy that it gave. The thrill of seeing the great Theban processions of the gods accompanied by musi-cians, troops of soldiers, acrobatic dancers, and white-clad priests must have been a welcome diversion from daily life and tasks. Rituals and festi-vals, such as the Beautiful Feast of the Valley, that involved the ritualized and hence socially acceptable excessive consumption of alcohol to create an ecstatic mood of singing and dance must have been a welcome release for members of a society that otherwise celebrated and encouraged quiet and meek behavior.

Although so many aspects and practices of ancient Egyptian religion seem exotic and arcane to us today, they were, in the context of the ancient society, reasonable and functional manifestations of a belief system that created a complex and enduring network of support for individuals and the society.

Notes

Chapter 1: The Egyptian Mind

1. As pointed out by Oldridge (2007, 4–5) in the context of medieval belief in witches and demons, quoting David Stannard: "We do well to remember that the [premodern] world ... was a rational world, in many ways more rational than our own. It is true that it was a world of witches and demons, and of a just and terrible God who made his presence known in the slightest act of nature. But this was the given reality about which most of the decisions and actions of the age, throughout the entire western world, revolved."
2. Oldridge 2007, 3.
3. This is "mythopoeic thought" outlined by Henri Frankfort. See Frankfort, Wilson, Jacobsen, and Irwin 1946.

Chapter 2: Priests

1. Haring 1997, 4.
2. Sauneron 1980, 56.
3. Sauneron 1980, 39.
4. Lichtheim 1980, 23.
5. Frood 2007, 108.
6. Kruchten 1989, 257.
7. Lichtheim 1980, 25.
8. Haring 1997, 6.
9. Strudwick 2005, 220.
10. Kruchten 1989, 254.
11. Haring 1997, 224.
12. Strudwick 2005, 195.
13. Strudwick 2005, 194.
14. Strudwick 2005, 201; Russo 2007, 207.
15. Assmann 2005, 210.
16. Strudwick 2005, 288.
17. Breasted 1905, vol. 2, 99 (§ 239).
18. Papyrus British Museum 10383 in Haring 1997, 222.
19. Kruchten 1989, 256.
20. Lichtheim 1980, 31, 33, n. 1.
21. Lichtheim 1980, 19.
22. Pinch 1994, 51.
23. Breasted 1905, vol. 3, 232 (§ 553).

24. Haring 1997, 219–20.
25. Lichtheim 1980, 14.
26. Lichtheim 1980, 19.
27. After Sauneron 1980, 47.
28. Frood 2007, 41.
29. Nims 1965, 96.
30. Frood 2007, 36.
31. Sauneron 1980, 46–7.
32. Lichtheim 1980, 19.
33. Frood 2007, 97.
34. After Lichtheim 1980, 42.
35. Strudwick 2005, 288.
36. Strudwick 2005, 289.
37. Frood 2007, 131.
38. At Karnak, Kruchten 1989, 175–86, 259.
39. Kruchten 1989, 259, 261.
40. Strudwick 2005, 289.
41. Strudwick 2005, 232.
42. Taylor 2001, 177.
43. Sauneron 1980, 47, 50.
44. Lichtheim 1980, 15–16.
45. Sauneron 1980, 39.
46. After Strudwick 2005, 236, 277.
47. Strudwick 2005, 264.
48. Allen 1936, 151.
49. Strudwick 2005, 277.
50. Sauneron 1980, 39.
51. After Haring 1997, 5.
52. Haring 1997, 4.
53. Haring 1997, 4, 5, 12.
54. Strudwick 2005, 196–8; Lichtheim 1980, 14.
55. Strudwick 2005, 166–7.
56. Reymond 1973, 9.
57. Strudwick, 2005, 108.
58. Kemp 1989, 195.
59. Haring 1997, 92.
60. Haring 1997, 11.
61. Haring 1997, 11.

Chapter 3: Inside the Temple

1. Lichtheim 1973, 124.
2. Yamamoto 2002.
3. After McDowell 1999, 95.
4. Hatshepsut (CG 7001a); Shabako (CG 70007); Nectanebo (CG 70019) in Roeder 1914.
5. Frood 2007, 184 (Amenmose, Dynasty 20).
6. Lichtheim 1980, 34.
7. Morenz 1973, 152.
8. Žabkar 1968, 39.
9. Lichtheim 1980, 90–6.
10. After Morenz 1973, 151.
11. Lorton 1999, 193.
12. Lorton 1999, 198.
13. Morenz 1973, 88.
14. Lorton 1999, 179.

15. Lorton 1999, 179–80.
16. Collins 2005, 30, 34.
17. As opposed to the many funerary texts that attract a person's *ba* to the corpse.
18. After Žabkar 1968, 40.
19. After Lichtheim 1980, 105.
20. Among the examples, Murnane 1995, 213.
21. McDowell 1999, 95.
22. Haring 1997, 47.
23. Blackman 1918.
24. For a similar tradition of clothing statues in Ugaritic texts, see Lewis 2005, 92, 95.
25. Haring 1997, 394.
26. Haring 1997, 418.
27. Kitchen 1999.
28. Teeter 2007, 312; Haring 1997, 118.
29. Lorton 1999, 127–8.
30. Cogan 1974, 28–9.
31. El-Saghir 1991, 20.
32. Dunand and Zivie-Coche 2004, 281.

Chapter 4: Festivals

1. Murnane 1995, 237.
2. Watterson 1998, 106.
3. Simpson 2003, 341.
4. Lichtheim 1988, 71.
5. Lavier 1985.
6. Lichtheim 1988, 122.
7. Tooley 1996,175.
8. Raven 1982, 29.
9. Coulon 1995, 1996.
10. Raven 1982,16–17.
11. Raven 1982, 20.
12. Tooley 1996, 167.
13. Tooley 1996, 178.
14. Traunecker, Le Saout, and Masson 1981, 136.
15. Nims 1965, 94.
16. Bell 1997, 101.
17. After Haeny 1997, 115.
18. Winlock 1947, 84, pl. 40.1; Schott 1953, 94.
19. Winlock 1947, 85;Winlock 1942, 217.
20. After Pinch 1993.
21. After Schott 1953, 95.
22. For these texts, see Schott 1953.
23. Schott 1953, 94.
24. Schott 1953, 114.
25. After Schott 1957, 14.
26. Davies 1944, 78.
27. After Schott 1953, 112, 83.
28. Sadek 1987, 132.
29. After Sadek 1979, 52.
30. After Černý 1927, 183; Kitchen 1983, 104, 370.
31. Wente 1963, 34.
32. Nims 1965, 93.
33. McDowell 1999, 178–80.
34. Andreu 2002, 253.

Chapter 5: Contacting the Gods

1. Wente 1990, 219.
2. Nims 1971, 108.
3. Nims 1955, 116–17; Nims 1971.
4. Nims 1971.
5. Nims 1954, 78–9.
6. Nims 1954, 80.
7. Sadek 1987, 248–9.
8. Pinch 1993, 344.
9. Gardiner 1930, 21 pl. X.4.
10. Kessler and Nur el Din 2005, 157.
11. Kessler and Nur el Din 2005, 134.
12. Kessler and Nur el Din 2005, 151.
13. Kessler and Nur el Din 2005, 155.
14. Bothmer 1960, 151.
15. Strudwick 2005, 106.
16. Robins 2001, 40.
17. Simpson 1974, 13.
18. Simpson 1974, 11–12.
19. Simpson 1974, 5 n. 30, pl. 43.
20. Frood 2007, 169.
21. Roehrig 2005, 300.
22. Lichtheim 1980, 31.
23. After Lichtheim 1980, 26.
24. Rizzo 2004, 516.
25. Rizzo 2004, 517.
26. After Lichtheim 1980, 22.
27. After Rizzo 2004; Jansen-Winkeln 1998, 3–5.
28. Pinch 1993, 334.
29. Wildung 1977, 87.
30. Wildung 1977, 92.
31. McDowell 1999, 115.
32. Borghouts 1982, 24–5.
33. After Ray 2002, 142.
34. Szpakowska 2003, 195.
35. Vernus 1978; Frood 2007, 85–9.
36. Thompson 1940, 71; Dunand and Zivie-Coche 2004, 306.
37. After Thompson 1940, 70.

Chapter 6: In the Presence of the Gods

1. Lichtheim 1976, 106.
2. Kruchten 2001a, 282.
3. Kruchten 2001a, 281.
4. Dunand and Zivie-Coche 2004, 314; Frankfurter 1998, 146.
5. Dunand and Zivie-Coche 2004, 315.
6. After McDowell 1990, 223–4.
7. Lichtheim 1976, 141.
8. Wente 1990, 219.
9. Wente 1990, 184.
10. Frankfurter 1998, 147.
11. Kruchten 2001b, 610.
12. Frankfurter 1998, 150.
13. Dunand and Zivie-Coche 2004, 315; Frankfurter 1998, 146.

14. Kruchten 2001b, 609.
15. Wente 1990, 191.
16. Blackman 1925, 251–3.
17. Ritner 1993, 218–19.
18. Borghouts 1982, 13–14.
19. After Borghouts 1982, 6.
20. Borghouts 1982, 4.
21. Borghouts 1994, 129.
22. After Borghouts 1982, 7.
23. Borghouts 1982, 30.
24. Assmann 2005, 199.
25. After Lichtheim 1980, 42–3.
26. Edwards 1960, 71, 31, xxi, 15.
27. After Edwards 1960, 10, 45, 71.
28. Edwards 1960, 66–7.
29. Borghouts 1982, 15.
30. Szpakowska 2003, 178 n.75.

Chapter 7: Death and Funeral Rites

1. Wente 1990, 218.
2. After Lichtheim 1980, 63.
3. Wente 1990, 216–17.
4. After Lichtheim 1980, 46.
5. Lichtheim 1980, 140.
6. Strudwick 2005, 297.
7. Strudwick 2005, 271.
8. Strudwick 2005, 274.
9. After Strudwick 2005, 365; Assmann 2005, 112.
10. After Strudwick 2005, 272.
11. After Strudwick 2005, 258.
12. Strudwick 2005, 252, 273, 299.
13. Strudwick 2005, 224, 272.
14. Strudwick 2005, 272.
15. Morschauser 1991.
16. Strudwick 2005, 218.
17. Tomb of Petosiris, in Morschauser 1991, 267.
18. Demarée 1983, 207.
19. Strudwick 2005, 277.
20. Strudwick 2005, 220.
21. Brovarski 2001, 102; Strudwick 2005, 314–15.
22. Janssen 1975, 525.
23. Wilson 1947, 241–2; Strudwick 2005, 303. The false door is exhibited in the Cairo Museum (no. CG 1482).
24. Strudwick 2005, 263.
25. Strudwick 2005, 432–3.
26. Strudwick 2005, 193.
27. Strudwick 2005, 202.
28. Strudwick 2005, 271.
29. Strudwick 2005, 103–8; for the New Kingdom, Frood 2007, 179.
30. Strudwick 2005, 229 (Dynasties 5–6).
31. Strudwick 2005, 119.
32. Strudwick 2005, 194.
33. Strudwick 2005, 195–6.
34. Strudwick 2005, 229.

35. Gardiner and Sethe 1928, 10.
36. Lichtheim 1980, 46.
37. Strudwick 2005, 338.
38. Brovarski 1977, 113.
39. Reymond 1973.
40. Gardiner and Sethe 1928, 10.
41. After Strudwick 2005, 337.
42. Reymond 1973, 27 n. 6.
43. Brovarski 2001, 102; Strudwick 2005, 314.
44. Toivari-Viitala 2001, 223.
45. Winlock 1941.
46. Schaden 2007, 2010.
47. After Assmann 2005, 105.
48. Wente 1990, 216 (no. 351); Strudwick 2005, 202 (no. 115).
49. Wente 1990, 212.
50. Assmann 2005, 301.
51. Reeder 1994; Assmann 2005, 308.
52. After Assmann 2005, 308.
53. Assmann 2005, 319.
54. See Leprohon 2007, 270–2.
55. Lorton 1999, 165.
56. Assmann 2005, 324.
57. Roth 1992.
58. Assmann 2005, 327.
59. Settgast 1963, 43; Meeks 2001, 358; Reeder 1995.
60. Assmann 2005, 301.
61. Ritner 1993, 144–7.
62. Gardiner and Sethe, 1928, 10 (Teti cemetery at Saqqara); Strudwick 2005, 424.
63. Assmann, 2005, 329; Settgast 1963.
64. Winlock and Arnold 2010.
65. Strudwick 2005, 433.
66. Toivari-Viitala 2001, 225.

Chapter 8: Communicating with the Dead

1. Gardiner and Sethe 1928, 5, 11.
2. Szpakowska 2003, 26; Borghouts 1973, 114.
3. Friedman 1994, 113–14.
4. Strudwick 2005, 216.
5. After Demarée 1983, 211.
6. Friedman 1994, 113; Demarée 1983, 282.
7. Friedman 1994, 109.
8. Friedman 1994, 116.
9. Demarée 1983, 214.
10. Assmann 2005, 327.
11. After Gardiner and Sethe 1928, 5.
12. Bakir 1966, 20, 30, 31, 33.
13. After Borghouts 1994, 126.
14. Borghouts 1994, 126.
15. Borghouts 1974, 4.
16. Demarée 1983, 270.
17. Edwards 1960, 16, 104.
18. Dunand and Zivie-Coche 2004, 165.
19. After Wente 1990, 217–18; Frandsen 1992, 33.
20. After Wente 1990, 215.

21. After Wente 1990, 216–17; Gardiner and Sethe 1928, 8–9.
22. Wente 1990, 217.
23. Wente 1990, 212.
24. Wente 1990, 214.
25. After Wente 1990, 213; pictured in Teeter 2003, 37.
26. After Wente 1990, 211.
27. After Wente 1990, 215–16.
28. Szpakowska 2003, 163.
29. Szpakowska 2003, 27.
30. After Wente 1990, 213.
31. Edwards 1960, 21.
32. Szpakowska 2003, 163.
33. Szpakowska 2003, 163, 189.

Chapter 9: Magic to Charm and to Kill

1. Hornung 2001, 59.
2. Pinch 1994, 47.
3. Borghouts 1974, 2.
4. Assmann 2002, 310.
5. Ritner 1993, 5.
6. See Oldridge (2007, 13) for his comments how Christian texts such as John 1:1 have been used as magical texts, and how candles from Christian churches are used to protect from demons. As he succinctly states, "Magical ideas were remarkably vital and adaptable, and were at least as enduring as official theology."
7. In the Book of the Heavenly Cow, see Ritner 1993, 202–3.
8. Borghouts, 1978, 15, no. 16.
9. Hornung 2001, 57, has suggested that magic gained popularity in the Late Period because people were forced to rely on it as the support of the state and its judicial system faltered.
10. Edwards 1960, 10.
11. Strudwick 2005, 280.
12. Strudwick 2005, 221–2.
13. Pinch 1994, 31.
14. Strudwick 2005, 221–2.
15. After Borghouts 1978, 87, no. 126.
16. Kruchten 1989, 259, 261.
17. In the Alexander Romance, cited in Pinch 1994, 91.
18. After Borghouts 1978, 12–14, no. 13.
19. After Bourhouts 1978, 91, no. 137; 94, no. 142.
20. Loeben 2008.
21. Pinch 1994, 79.
22. Pinch 1994, 44, 132. See also Leprohon 2007, 265, 270–2, for masks in cult.
23. After Borghouts 1978, 21, no. 25.
24. Borghouts 1978, 22, no. 26.
25. Borghouts 1978, 4, no. 7.
26. After Bourriau 1988, 114–15; Pinch 1994, 20.
27. Borghouts 1978, no. 61.
28. Pinch 1994, 115.
29. After Andrews 1994, 79.
30. Borghouts 1994, 142.
31. Borghouts 1978, 25–6, nos. 35, 36.
32. Borghouts 1978, 51, no. 84.
33. Borghouts 1978, 55, no. 84.
34. Borghouts 1978, 87, no. 126.
35. Allen 2005, 49.

36. After Borghouts 1978, 1, no. 2.
37. After Borghouts 1978, 1–2, no. 3.
38. Ritner 1993, 139.
39. Ritner 1993, 143, 159.
40. Ritner 1993, 199–200.
41. Ritner 1993, 201.
42. For this series of events, see Vernus 2003, 108–20.
43. As noted by Ritner 1993, 199.
44. Ritner 1993, 197.
45. Translation after Ritner 1993, 193–4.
46. Papyrus Salt 825 noted by Ritner 1993, 185; Raven 1983, 10.
47. Allen 1936, 147.
48. The Book of Overthrowing Apep (P. Bremner Rhind) and P. British Museum 10252; see Ritner 1993, 211, and Raven 1983, 14.
49. After Ritner 1993, 184; Faulkner, 1937, 174–5.

Chapter 10: The Amarna Period

 1. Murnane 1995, 115.
 2. Murnane 1995, 27–8.
 3. Murnane 1995, 118, Allen 1988, 90–1.
 4. After Murnane 1995, 110, 144.
 5. Murnane 1995, 111.
 6. After Murnane 1995, 115.
 7. Murnane 1995, 144.
 8. Murnane 1995, 111.
 9. Murnane 1995, 142.
10. After Murnane 1995, 156, 155.
11. Murnane 1995, 192.
12. After Murnane 1995, 155.
13. After Murnane 1995, 112.
14. Murnane 1995, 111.
15. Murnane 1995, 118, 112.
16. After Murnane 1995, 117.
17. After Murnane 1995, 119.
18. Murnane 1995, 112.
19. After Murnane 1995, 112, 117.
20. After Murnane 1995, 119.
21. Murnane 1995, 112.
22. Murnane 1995, 131.
23. Freed, Markowitz, and D'Auria 1999, 257.
24. Davies 1905, pl. 22.
25. After Murnane 1995, 78.
26. Murnane 1995, 198.
27. Murnane 1995, 183.
28. Murnane 1995, 241.

Bibliography

Allen, James P. 1989. "The Natural Philosophy of Akhenaten." In *Religion and Philosophy in Ancient Egypt*, edited by W. K. Simpson, pp. 89–101. Yale Egyptological Studies 3. New Haven, CT: Yale University Press.

2005. *The Art of Medicine in Ancient Egypt*. New York: Metropolitan Museum of Art.

Allen, T. George. 1936. "Types of Rubrics in the Egyptian Book of the Dead." *Journal of the American Oriental Society* 56: 145–54.

Altenmuller, Hartwig. 1975. "Bestattungsritual." In *Lexikon der Ägyptologie I*, edited by Wolfgang Helck, pp. 745–65. Wiesbaden: Otto Harrassowitz.

Andreu, Guillemette (editor). 2002. *Les artistes de Pharaon: Deir el-Médineh et la Vallée des Rois*. Paris: Réunion des Musées Nationaux.

Andrews, Carol. 1994. *Amulets of Ancient Egypt*. Austin: University of Texas Press.

Assmann, Jan. 2002. *The Mind of Egypt*. New York: Henry Holt.

2005. *Death and Salvation in Ancient Egypt*. Ithaca, NY: Cornell University Press.

Bakir, Abd el Mohsen. 1966. *The Cairo Calendar no. 86637*. Cairo: General Organization of Government Printing Offices.

Bell, Lanny. 1997. "The New Kingdom 'Divine' Temple: The Example of Luxor." In *Temples of Ancient Egypt*, edited by Byron Shafer, pp. 127–84. Ithaca, NY: Cornell University Press.

Blackman, Aylward. 1918. "The House of the Morning." *Journal of Egyptian Archaeology* 5: 148–65.

1924. *The Rock Tombs of Meir. Part IV: The Tomb-Chapel of Pepi 'onkh the Middle Son of Sebkhotpe and Pekhernefert (D, No. 2)*. Archaeological Survey of Egypt, Twenty-fifth Memoir. London: Egypt Exploration Society.

1925. "Oracles in Ancient Egypt." *Journal of Egyptian Archaeology* 11: 249–55.

1926. "Oracles in Ancient Egypt II." *Journal of Egyptian Archaeology* 12: 176–85.

Bleeker, C. J. 1967. *Egyptian Festivals*. Leiden: E. J. Brill.

Bonnet, Hans. 1952. *Reallexikon der Ägyptischen Religionsgeschichte*. Berlin and New York: Walter de Gruyter.

Borghouts, Joris F. 1973. "The Evil Eye of Apopis." *Journal of Egyptian Archaeology* 59: 114–50.

    1974. "Magic Texts." In *Textes et Langages de L'Égypte Pharaonique (Hommage à Jean-François Champollion)*, vol. 3, edited by Serge Sauneron, pp. 2–19. *Bibliothèque d'Étude* 64/3. Cairo: Institut français d'Archéologie Orientale du Caire.

    1978. *Ancient Egyptian Magical Texts.* Religious Texts Translation Series: NISABA, vol. 9. Leiden: E. J. Brill.

    1980. "The 'Hot One' (*p3 šmw*) in Ostracon Deir el-Médineh 1265." *Göttinger Miszellen* 38: 21–8.

    1982. "Divine Intervention in Ancient Egypt and Its Manifestation (*b3w*)." In *Gleanings from Deir el Medîna*, edited by R. J. Demarée and Jac. J. Janssen, pp. 1–70. Egyptologische Uitgaven 1. Leiden: Nederlands Instituut voor Het Nabije Oosten.

    1994. "Magical Practices among the Villagers." In *Pharaoh's Workers: The Villagers of Deir el Medina*, edited by Leonard Lesko, pp. 119–30. Ithaca, NY: Cornell University Press.

Bothmer, Bernard (editor). 1960. *Egyptian Sculpture of the Late Period, 700 BC to AD 100.* Brooklyn: Brooklyn Museum.

Bourriau, Janine. 1988. *Pharaohs and Mortals: Egyptian Art in the Middle Kingdom.* Cambridge: Cambridge University Press.

Breasted, James H. 1905. *Ancient Records of Egypt.* 5 vols. Chicago: University of Chicago Press.

Brovarski, Edward. 1977. "The Doors of Heaven." *Orientalia* 46: 107–15.

    2001. *The Senedjemib Complex. Part I: The Mastabas of Senedjem Inti (G 2370), Khnumenti (G 2374), and Senedjemib Mehi (G 2378).* Giza Mastabas 7. Boston: Art of the Ancient World/Museum of Fine Arts.

Bruyère, Bernard. 1930. *Meret Seger à Deir el Médineh.* Mémoires publiés par les Membres de l'Institut français d'Archéologie orientale du Caire 58. Cairo: Institut français d'Archéologie Orientale du Caire.

Cauville, Sylvie. 1988. "Les mystères d'Osiris à Dendera." *Bulletin de la Sociéte Française d'Egyptologie*, no. 112 (Juin): 23–36.

Centrone, Maria. 2006. "Corn-Mummies, Amulets of Life." In *Through a Glass Darkly: Magic, Dreams and Prophecy in Ancient Egypt*, edited by Kasia Szpakowska, pp. 33–45. Swansea: Classical Press of Wales.

Černỳ, Jaroslav. 1927. "Le culte d'Amenophis Ier chez les ouvriers de la nécropole thébaine." *Bulletin de l'Institut Français d'Archéologie Orientale* 27: 159–203.

    1931. "Une Expression Désignant la Réponse Négative d'un Oracle." *Bulletin de l'Institut Français d'Archéologie Orientale* 30: 491–6.

Cogan, Mordechai. 1974. *Imperialism and Religion: Assyria, Judah, and Israel in the Eighth and Seventh Centuries B.C.E.* Society of Biblical Literature Monograph Series 18. Atlanta: Society of Biblical Literature.

Collins, Billie Jean. 2005. "Cult Images in Hittite Anatolia." In *Cult Images and Divine Representation in the Ancient Near East*, edited by N. Walls, pp. 13–42. Atlanta: American Schools of Oriental Research.

Cooney, Kathlyn. 2007. *The Cost of Death: The Social and Economic Value of Ancient Egyptian Funerary Art in the Ramesside Period.* Egyptologische Uitgaven 22. Leiden: Nederlands Instituut voor Het Nabije Oosten.

Coulon, Laurent, François Leclèrc, and Sylvie Marchand. 1995. "'Catacombes' osiriennes de Ptolémée IV à Karnak." *Karnak* 10: 205–38.

Curnow, Trevor. 2004. *Oracles of the Ancient World*. London: Duckworth.

Davies, Norman de Garis. 1905. *The Rock Tombs of El Amarna. Part III: The Tombs of Huya and Ahmes*. Archaeological Survey of Egypt, Fifteenth Memoir. London: Egypt Exploration Fund.

——— 1944. *The Tomb of Rekh-mi-re' at Thebes*. New York: Metropolitan Museum of Art.

Demarée, Robert J. 1982 "'Remove Your Stela' (O. Petrie 21 = Hier. Ostr. 16, 4)." In *Gleanings from Deir el-Medinah*, edited by R. J. Demarée and Jac. J. Janssen, pp. 101–8. Leiden: Nederlands Instituut voor Het Nabije Oosten.

——— 1983. *The 3h ikr n Rꜥ-Stelae: On Ancestor Worship in Ancient Egypt*. Egyptologische Uitgaven III. Leiden: Nederlands Instituut voor Het Nabije Oosten.

Dick, M. B., and C. Walker. 1999. "The Induction of the Cult Image in Mesopotamia: The Mesopotamian miš pi." In *Born in Heaven, Made on Earth: The Making of the Cult Image in the Ancient Near East*, edited by M. B. Dick, pp. 55–121. Winona Lake, IN: Eisenbrauns.

Doxey, Denise. 2001. "Priesthood." In *The Oxford Encyclopedia of Ancient Egypt*, vol. 2, edited by Donald Redford, pp. 69–73. Oxford: Oxford University Press.

Dunand, Françoise, and Christiane Zivie-Coche. 2004. *Gods and Men in Egypt, 3000 BCE to 395 CE*. Ithaca, NY: Cornell University Press.

Edwards, I. E. S. 1960. *Oracular Amuletic Decrees of the Late New Kingdom*. Hieratic Papyri in the British Museum, fourth series. London: Trustees of the British Museum.

Eggebrecht, Arne (editor). 1993. *Pelizaeus-Museum Hildesheim: Die Ägyptisches Sammlung*. Mainz: Verlag Philipp von Zabern.

Eigner, Diethelm. 1984. *Die monumental Grabbauten der Spätzeit in der thebanischen Nekropole*. Vienna: Verlag der Österreichischen Akademie der Wissenschaften.

Eyre, Chris. 1987. "Work and the Organization of Work in the New Kingdom." In *Labor in the Ancient Near East*, edited by Marvin Powell, pp. 167–221. New Haven, CT: American Oriental Society.

Faulkner, Raymond O. 1937. "The Bremner-Rhind Papyrus III." *Journal of Egyptian Archaeology* 23: 166–85.

Frandsen, Paul John. 1992. "The Letter to Ikhtay's Coffin: O. Louvre Inv. No. 698." In *Village Voices*, edited by R. J. Demarée and A. Egberts, pp. 31–49. Leiden: Nederlands Instituut voor Het Nabije Oosten.

Frankfort, Henri, John Wilson, Thorkild Jacobsen, and William Irwin. 1946. *Before Philosophy: The Intellectual Adventure of Ancient Man*. Chicago: University of Chicago Press.

Frankfurter, David. 1998. *Religion in Roman Egypt: Assimilation and Resistance*. Princeton, NJ: Princeton University Press.

Freed, Rita, Yvonne Markowitz, and Sue D'Auria (editors). 1999. *Pharaohs of the Sun: Akhenaten, Nefertiti, Tutankhamen*. Boston, New York, and London: Bulfinch Press/Little, Brown and Co. in association with the Museum of Fine Arts, Boston.

Friedman, Florence. 1994. "Aspects of Domestic Life and Religion." In *Pharaoh's Workers: The Villagers of Deir el Medina*, edited by Leonard Lesko, pp. 95–117. Ithaca, NY: Cornell University Press.

Frood, Elizabeth. 2007. *Biographical Texts from Ramessid Egypt*. Atlanta: Society of Biblical Literature.

Gardiner, Alan H. 1930. "A New Letter to the Dead." *Journal of Egyptian Archaeology* 16: 19–22.

Gardiner, Alan, and Kurt Sethe. 1928. *Egyptian Letters to the Dead*. London: Egypt Exploration Society.

Gaudard, François, and Janet Johnson. 2010. "Six Stone Mummy Labels in the Oriental Institute Museum." In *Honi Soit Qui Mal y Pense* (Festschrift for Heinz-Josef Thissen), edited by H. Knuf, C. Leitz, and D. von Recklinghausen, pp. 193–209. Leuven: Uitgeverij Peeters.

Goedicke, Hans. 1994. "A Cult Inventory of the Eighth Dynasty from Coptos (JE 43290)." *Mitteilungen des Deutschen Archäologischen Instituts, Abteilung Kairo* 59: 71–84.

Graefe, Erhart. 1986. "Talfest." In *Lexikon der Ägyptologie VI*, edited by Wolfgang Helck, pp. 187–9. Wiesbaden: Otto Harrassowitz.

Griffith, J. Gwyn. 1977. "Hakerfest." In *Lexikon der Ägyptologie II*, edited by Wolfgang Helck, pp. 929–31. Wiesbaden: Otto Harrassowitz.

——— 1988. "Intimations of Egyptian Non-Royal Biography of a Belief in Divine Impact on Human Affairs." In *Pyramid Studies and Other Essays Presented to I. E. S. Edwards*, edited by John Baines, T. G. H. James, et al., pp. 92–102. London: Egypt Exploration Society.

Grundlach, Rolf. 2001. "Temples." In *The Oxford Encyclopedia of Ancient Egypt*, vol. 2, edited by Donald Redford, pp. 363–79. Oxford: Oxford University Press.

Gunn, Battiscombe. 1916. "The Religion of the Poor in Ancient Egypt." *Journal of Egyptian Archaeology* 3: 81–94.

Habachi, Labib. 1977. "Gottesvater." In *Lexikon der Ägyptologie II*, edited by Wolfgang Helck, pp. 825–6. Wiesbaden: Otto Harrassowitz.

Haeny, Gerhard. 1997. "New Kingdom 'Mortuary Temples' and 'Mansions of Millions of Years.'" In *Temples of Ancient Egypt*, edited by Byron Shafer, pp. 86–126. Ithaca, NY: Cornell University Press.

Haring, B. J. J. 1997. *Divine Households: Administrative and Economic Aspects of the New Kingdom Royal Memorial Temples in Western Thebes*. Egyptologische Uitgaven 13. Leiden: Nederlands Instituut voor Het Nabije Oosten.

Hornung, Erik. 1982. *Conceptions of God in Ancient Egypt: The One and the Many*. Ithaca, NY: Cornell University Press.

——— 1992. *Idea into Image: Essays on Ancient Egyptian Thought*. New York: Timken.

——— 1994. "Black Holes Viewed from Within: Hell in Ancient Egyptian Thought." *Diogenes* 42/1, no. 165: 133–56.

——— 1999. *Akhenaten and the Religion of Light*. Ithaca, NY: Cornell University Press.

——— 2001. *The Secret Lore of Egypt: Its Impact on the West*. Ithaca, NY: Cornell University Press.

James, T. G. H. 1984. *Pharaoh's People: Scenes from Life in Imperial Egypt*. London: Bodley Head.

Jansen-Winkeln, Karl. 1998. "Beiträge zu den Privatinschriften der Spätzeit." *Zeitschrift für ägyptische Sprache und Altertumskunde* 125:1–13.

——— 2007. *Inschriften der Spatzeit, Teil II. Die 21–24. Dynastie*. Wiesbaden: Otto Harrassowitz.

Janssen, Jac. J. 1975. *Commodity Prices from the Ramessid Period*. Leiden: E. J. Brill.

Karl, Doris. 2000. "Funktion und Bedeutung einer *weisen Frau* im alten Ägypten." *Studien zur altägyptischen Kultur* 28: 131–60.

Kees, Hermann. 1964. *Die Hohenpriester des Amun von Karnak von Herihor bis zum Ende der Äthiopenzeit.* Leiden: E. J. Brill.

Kemp, Barry. 1989. *Ancient Egypt: Anatomy of a Civilization.* London: Routledge.

Kessler, Dieter, and Abd el Halim Nur el-Din. 2005. "Tuna al-Gebel: Millions of Ibises and Other Animals." In *Divine Creatures: Animal Mummies in Ancient Egypt,* edited by Salima Ikram, pp. 120–63. Cairo: American University in Cairo.

Kitchen, Kenneth. 1974. "Nakht-Thuty – Servitor of Sacred Barques and Golden Portals." *Journal of Egyptian Archaeology* 60: 168–74.

——— 1983. *Ramesside Inscriptions VI.* Oxford: Blackwell.

——— 1999. "The Wealth of Amun at Thebes under Ramesses II." In *Gold of Praise: Studies on Ancient Egypt in Honor of Edward F. Wente,* edited by Emily Teeter and John A. Larson, pp. 235–8. Studies in Ancient Oriental Civilizations no. 58. Chicago: Oriental Institute Press.

Koenig, Yvan. 2002. "Conclusion. La magie égyptienne: Pour une meilleure prise en compte de la magie." In *La magie en Égypte: À la recherche d'une définition,* edited by Yvan Koenig, pp. 399–413. Paris: Musée du Louvre.

Kruchten, Jean-Marie. 1989. *Les Annales des Prêtres de Karnak (XXI–XXIIImes Dynasties) et Autres Textes Contemporains Relatifs à l'Initiation des Prêtres d'Amon.* Orientalia Lovaniensia Analecta 32. Leuven: Departement Oriëntalistiek.

——— 2001a. "Law." In *The Oxford Encyclopedia of Ancient Egypt,* vol. 2, edited by Donald Redford, pp. 277–82. Oxford: Oxford University Press.

——— 2001b. "Oracles." In *The Oxford Encyclopedia of Ancient Egypt,* vol. 2, edited by Donald Redford, pp. 609–12. Oxford: Oxford University Press.

Kurth, Dieter. 1984. "Reinigungszelt." In *Lexikon der Ägyptologie V,* edited by Wolfgang Helck, pp. 220–2. Wiesbaden: Otto Harrassowitz.

Lavier, Marie-Christine. 1985. "Les Mystères d'Osiris à Abydos d'apres les Stèles du Moyen Empire et du Nouvel Empire." In *Akten des Vierten Internationalen Ägyptologen Kongresses München 1985,* edited by Sylvia Schoske, pp. 290–5. Studien zur Altägyptischen Kultur, Beihefte 3. Hamburg: Helmut Buske Verlag.

Leclère, François. 1996. "A Cemetery of Osiris Figurines at Karnak" *Egyptian Archaeology* 9: 9–12.

Leprohon, Ronald J. 2007. "Ritual Drama in Ancient Egypt." In *The Origins of Theater in Ancient Greece and Beyond: From Ritual to Drama,* edited by E. Csapo and Margaret Miller, pp. 259–92. Cambridge: Cambridge University Press.

Lewis, Theodore. 2005. "Syro-Palestinian Iconography and Divine Images." In *Cult Images and Divine Representation in the Ancient Near East,* edited by N. Walls, pp. 69–107. Atlanta: American Schools of Oriental Research.

Lichtheim, Miriam. 1973. *Ancient Egyptian Literature: A Book of Readings.* Vol. 1: *The Old and Middle Kingdoms.* Berkeley and Los Angeles: University of California Press.

——— 1976. *Ancient Egyptian Literature: A Book of Readings.* Vol. 2: *The New Kingdom.* Berkeley and Los Angeles: University of California Press.

1980. *Ancient Egyptian Literature: A Book of Readings*. Vol. 3: *The Late Period*. Berkeley and Los Angeles: University of California Press.

1988. *Ancient Egyptian Autobiographies Chiefly of the Middle Kingdom*. OrbisBiblicus et Orientalis 84. Freiburg: Unversitätsverlag; Göttingen: Vandenhoeck and Ruprecht.

Loeben, Christian. 2008. "Ein 'riesen-luxus-Zaubermesser' – vielleicht von Konigen Hatschepsut? Sowie Zwei weitere mit agyptischer Magie assoziierte Objekte im Kestner-Museum Hannover." *Bibliothèque d'Étude* 143: 275–84.

Lorton, David. 1999. "The Theology of Cult Statues in Ancient Egypt." In *Born in Heaven, Made on Earth: The Making of the Cult Image in the Ancient Near East*, edited by M. B. Dick, pp. 123–201. Winona Lake, IN: Eisenbrauns.

McDowell, Andrea G. 1990. *Jurisdiction in the Workmen's Community at Deir el-Medîna*. Egyptologische Uitgaven 5. Leiden: Nederlands Instituut voor Het Nabije.

1999. *Village Life in Ancient Egypt: Laundry Lists and Love Songs*. Oxford: Oxford University Press.

Meeks, Dimitri. 2001. "Dance." In *The Oxford Encyclopedia of Ancient Egypt*, vol. 1, edited by Donald Redford, pp. 356–60. Oxford: Oxford University Press.

Meeks, Dimitri, and Christine F. Meeks. 1996. *Daily Life of the Egyptian Gods*. Ithaca, NY: Cornell University Press.

Morenz, Siegfried. 1973. *Egyptian Religion*. Ithaca, NY: Cornell University Press.

Morschauser, Scott. 1991. *Threat-Formulae in Ancient Egypt*. Baltimore: Halgo.

Murnane, William J. 1995. *Texts from the Amarna Period in Egypt*. Atlanta: Scholars Press.

Nelson, Harold. 1949. "The Rite of 'Bringing the Foot' as Portrayed in Temple Reliefs." *Journal of Egyptian Archaeology* 35: 82–6.

Nims, Charles. 1954. "Popular Religion in Ancient Egyptian Temples." In *Proceedings of the 23rd International Congress of Orientalists*, edited by D. Sinor, pp. 79–80. London: Royal Asiatic Society.

1955. "Places About Thebes." *Journal of Near Eastern Studies* 14: 110–23.

1965. *Thebes of the Pharaohs*. London: Elek Books.

1971. "The Eastern Temple at Karnak." *Beiträge zur Ägyptischen Bauforschung und Altertumskunde (Fest. Ricke)*, Cairo 12: 107–11.

Oldridge, Darren. 2007. *Strange Histories*. London: Routledge.

Pinch, Geraldine. 1993. *Votive Offerings for Hathor*. Oxford: Griffith Institute.

1994. *Magic in Ancient Egypt*. Austin: University of Texas Press.

Quirke, Stephen. 1992. *Ancient Egyptian Religion*. London: British Museum.

Raven, Maarten. 1982. "Corn Mummies." *Oudheidkundige Mededelingen uit het Rijksmueum van Oudheden te Leiden* 63: 7–38.

1983. "Wax in Egyptian Magic and Symbolism." *Oudheidkundige Mededelingen uit het Rijksmueum van Oudheden te Leiden* 64: 7–47.

Raven, Maarten, and Wybren Taconis. 2005. *Egyptian Mummies: Radiological Atlas of the Collections in the National Museum of Antiquities at Leiden*. Leiden: Brepols.

Ray, John. 2002. *Reflections of Osiris: Lives from Ancient Egypt*. Oxford: Oxford University Press.

Redford, Donald B. 1981. "A Royal Speech from the Blocks of the 10th Pylon." *Bulletin of the Egyptological Seminar* 3: 87–102.

1984. *Akhenaten: The Heretic King*. Princeton, NJ: Princeton University Press.

Reeder, Greg. 1994. "A Rite of Passage: The Enigmatic Tekenu in Ancient Egyptian Funerary Ritual." *KMT: A Modern Journal of Egyptology* 15, no. 3: 53–7.

1995. "The Mysterious Muu and the Dance They Do." *KMT: A Modern Journal of Egyptology* 6, no. 3: 68–77.

Reymond, E. A. E. 1973. *Catalogue of Demotic Papyri in the Ashmolean Museum*. Vol. 1: *Embalmers' Archives from Hawara*. Oxford: Griffith Institute.

Ritner, Robert. 1993. *The Mechanics of Ancient Egyptian Magical Practice*. Studies in Ancient Oriental Civilizations no. 54. Chicago: Oriental Institute.

2006. "'And Each Staff Transformed into a Snake': The Serpent Wand in Ancient Egypt." In *Through a Glass Darkly: Magic, Dreams and Prophecy in Ancient Egypt*, edited by Kasia Szpakowska, pp. 205–25. Swansea: Classical Press of Wales.

Rizzo, Jérôme. 2004. "Une mesure d'hygiène relative à quelques statues-cubes déposées dans le temple d'Amon à Karnak." *Bulletin de l'Institut Français d'Archéologie Orientale* 104: 511–21.

Robins, Gay. 2001. *Egyptian Statues*. Princes Risborough, Buckinghamshire: Shire.

Roeder, Günter. 1914. *Catalogue Général des Antiquités Égyptiennes du Musée du Caire*. Vol. 85, nos. 70001–70050 *Naos*. Leipzig: Breitkopf and Härtel.

Roehrig, Catherine (editor). 2005. *Hatshepsut: From Queen to Pharaoh*. New York: Metropolitan Museum of Art; New Haven, CT: Yale University Press.

Roth, Ann. 1991. *Egyptian Phyles in the Old Kingdom*. Studies in Ancient Oriental Civilizations no. 47. Chicago: Oriental Institute.

1992. "The PSŠ-KF and the 'Opening of the Mouth' Ceremony: A Ritual of Birth and Rebirth." *Journal of Egyptian Archaeology* 78: 113–47.

1993. "Fingers, Stars, and the 'Opening of the Mouth': The Nature of the *nṯrwj*-Blades." *Journal of Egyptian Archaeology* 79: 57–79.

2005. "Gender Roles in Ancient Egypt." In *A Companion to the Ancient Near East*, edited by Daniel C. Snell, pp. 211–18. Malden, MA: Blackwell.

Russo, Barbara. 2007. "Some Notes on the Funerary Cult in the Early Middle Kingdom: Stela BM EA 1164." *Journal of Egyptian Archaeology* 93: 195–209.

Sadek, Ashraf I. 1979. "Glimpses of Popular Religion in New Kingdom Egypt, 1: Mourning for Amenophis I of Deir el-Medina." *Göttinger Miszellen* 36: 51–6.

1987. *Popular Religion in Ancient Egypt*. Hildesheimer Ägyptologische Beiträge 27. Hildesheim: Gerstenberg Verlag.

El-Saghir, Mohammed. 1991. *Das Statuenversteck im Luxortempel*. Mainz: Philipp von Zabern.

Sauneron, Serge. 1980. *The Priests of Ancient Egypt*. New York: Grove Press.

Scalf, Foy. 2009. "Magical Bricks in the Oriental Institute Museum of the University of Chicago." *Studien zur Altägyptischen Kultur* 38: 275–95.

Schaden, Otto. 2007. "KV 63: An Update; The Final Stages of Clearance." *KMT: A Modern Journal of Egyptology* 18, no. 1: 16–25.

2010. "KV 63: 2010 Season." *KMT: A Modern Journal of Egyptology* 21, no. 2: 45–9.

Schott, Siegfried. 1953. *Das schöne Fest von Wüstentale: Festbräuche einer Totenstadt*. Wiesbaden: Verlag der Akademie der Wissenschaften und der Literatur in Mainz.

1957. *Wall Scenes from the Mortuary Chapel of the Mayor Paser at Medinet Habu*. Studies in Ancient Oriental Civilization no. 30. Chicago: University of Chicago Press.

Seeber, Christine. 1977. "Kornosiris." In *Lexikon der Ägyptologie II*, edited by Wolfgang Helck, pp. 744–6. Wiesbaden: Otto Harrassowitz.

de Sélincourt, Aubrey (editor). 1954. *Herodotus: The Histories*. New York: Penguin Books.

Settgast, Jürgen. 1963. *Untersuchungen zu altägyptischen Bestattungsdarstellungen*. Abhandlungen des Deutschen Archäologischen Instituts Kairo, Ägyptologische Reihe 3. Glückstadt: Verlag J. J. Augustin.

Shaw, Ian (editor). 2000. *The Oxford History of Ancient Egypt*. Oxford: Oxford University Press.

Simpson, William K. 1974. *The Terrace of the Great God at Abydos: The Offering Chapels of Dynasties 12 and 13*. Publications of the Pennsylvania-Yale Expedition to Egypt no. 5. New Haven, CT: Peabody Museum of Natural History of Yale University; Philadelphia: University Museum of the University of Pennsylvania.

(editor). 2003. *The Literature of Ancient Egypt*. New Haven, CT: Yale University Press.

Standage, Tom. 2005. *A History of the World in Six Glasses*. New York: Walker.

Strudwick, Nigel. 2005. *Texts from the Pyramid Age*. Atlanta: Society of Biblical Literature.

Strudwick, Nigel, and Helen Strudwick. 1999. *Thebes in Egypt: A Guide to the Tombs and Temples of Ancient Luxor*. London: British Museum.

Szpakowska, Kasia. 2003. *Behind Closed Eyes: Dreams and Nightmares in Ancient Egypt*. Swansea: Classic Press of Wales.

Taylor, John H. 2001. *Death and the Afterlife in Ancient Egypt*. Chicago: University of Chicago Press.

Teeter, Emily. 1993. "Popular Religion in Ancient Egypt." *KMT: A Modern Journal of Egyptology* 4, no. 2: 28–37.

1997. *The Presentation of Maat: Ritual and Legitimacy in Ancient Egypt*. Studies in Ancient Oriental Civilizations no. 57. Chicago: Oriental Institute Press.

2003. *Ancient Egypt: Treasures from the Collection of the Oriental Institute, University of Chicago*. Chicago: Oriental Institute.

2007. "Temple Cults." In *The Egyptian World*, edited by Toby Wilkinson, pp. 310–24. London: Routledge.

Thompson, Herbert. 1940. "Two Demotic Self-Dedications." *Journal of Egyptian Archaeology* 26: 68–78.

Toivari-Viitala, Jaana. 2001. *Women at Deir el-Medina*. Egyptologische Uitgaven 15. Leiden: Nederlands Instituut voor Het Nabije Oosten.

Tooley, Angela. 1996. "Osiris Bricks." *Journal of Egyptian Archaeology* 82: 167–79.

Traunecker, Claude, Françoise Le Saout, and Olivier Masson. 1981. *La Chapelle d'Achôris à Karnak, II, Texte*. Paris: Éditions A.D.P.F.

van der Horst, P. W. 1982. "The Way of Life of the Egyptian Priests According to Chaeremon." In *Studies in Egyptian Religion Dedicated to Professor Jan Zandee*, edited by M. Heerma van Voss, D. J. Hoens, G. Mussies, D. van der Plas, and H. te Velde, pp. 61–71. Leiden: E. J. Brill.

Vernus, Pascal. 1978. "Littérature et Autobiographie: Les Inscriptions de S₃-Mwt surnommé Kyky." *Revue d' Égyptologie* 30: 115–46.

2003. *Affairs and Scandals in Ancient Egypt*. Ithaca, NY: Cornell University Press.

Walls, Neal (editor). 2005. *Cult Images and Divine Representation in the Ancient Near East*. Atlanta: American Schools of Oriental Research.

Watterson, Barbara. 1998. *The House of Horus at Edfu: Ritual in an Ancient Egyptian Temple*. Stroud (Glouchestershire): Tempus.

Wente, Edward F. 1963. "Two Ramesside Stelas Pertaining to the Cult of Amenophis I." *Journal of Near Eastern Studies* 22: 30–46.

1990. *Letters from Ancient Egypt*. Atlanta: Scholars Press.

Wildung, Dietrich. 1977. *Egyptian Saints: Deification in Pharaonic Egypt*. New York: New York University Press.

Wilfong, T. G. 1995. "Mummy Labels from the Oriental Institute's Excavations at Medinet Habu." *Bulletin of the American Society of Papyrologists* 32: 157–82.

Wilson, John. 1944. "Funeral Services of the Egyptian Old Kingdom." *Journal of Near Eastern Studies* 3: 201–18.

1947. "The Artist of the Egyptian Old Kingdom." *Journal of Near Eastern Studies* 6: 231–49.

Winlock, Herbert. 1941. "Materials Used at the Embalming of King Tut-'ankh-Amun." New York: Metropolitan Museum of Art.

1942. *Excavations at Deir el Bahri, 1911–1931*. New York: Macmillan.

1947. *The Rise and Fall of the Middle Kingdom in Thebes*. New York: Macmillan.

Winlock, Herbert, and Dorothea Arnold. 2010. *Tutankhamun's Funeral*. New York: Metropolitan Museum of Art.

Yamamoto, Kei. 2002. "The Materials of Iykhernofert's Portable Shrine: An Alternative Translation of Berlin 1204, lines 11–12." *Göttinger Miszellen* 191: 101–6.

Žabkar, Louis. 1968. *A Study of the* Ba *Concept in Ancient Egyptian Texts*. Studies in Ancient Oriental Civilizations no. 34. Chicago: University of Chicago Press.

Index

Index